Ride the Rising Wind

Ride the Rising Wind

ONE WOMAN'S JOURNEY ACROSS CANADA

Barbara Kingscote

NEWEST PRESS

Library and Archives Canada Cataloguing in Publication
Kingscote, Barbara Bradbury, 1928–
Ride the rising wind : one woman's journey across Canada / by Barbara Kingscote.

ISBN-13: 978-1-897126-05-9
ISBN-10: 1-897126-05-0

1. Kingscote, Barbara Bradbury, 1928–. 2. Kingscote, Barbara Bradbury, 1928– --Travel--Canada. 3. Canada--Description and travel. 4. Horsemen and horsewomen--Canada--Biography. I. Title.

FC75.K563 2006   971.063'3'092   C2005-907688-7

Board editor: Don Kerr
Cover and interior design: Ruth Linka
Cover images: Frank Bradbury and Barbara Kingscote
Author photo and interior images: Courtesy of the author
Map: Tobyn Manthorpe

Every effort has been made to obtain permissions for photographs. If there is an omission or error the author and publisher would be grateful to be so informed.

 Canada Council Conseil des Arts
for the Arts du Canada

 Canadian Patrimoine
Heritage canadien

 edmonton arts council

NeWest Press acknowledges the support of the Canada Council for the Arts and the Alberta Foundation for the Arts, and the Edmonton Arts Council for our publishing program. We also acknowledge the financial support of the Government of Canada through the Book Publishing Industry Development Program (BPIDP) for our publishing activities.

NeWest Press
201 – 8540 – 109th Street
Edmonton, Alberta, T6G 1E6
(780) 432-9427
www.newestpress.com

NeWest Press is committed to protecting the environment and to the responsible use of natural resources. This book is printed on 100% post-consumer recycled and ancient-forest-friendly paper. For more information, please visit www.oldgrowthfree.com.

1 2 3 4 5 09 08 07 06

PRINTED AND BOUND IN CANADA

For Youth, for Canada,

and for the Biosphere

that accords us Life.

Table of Contents

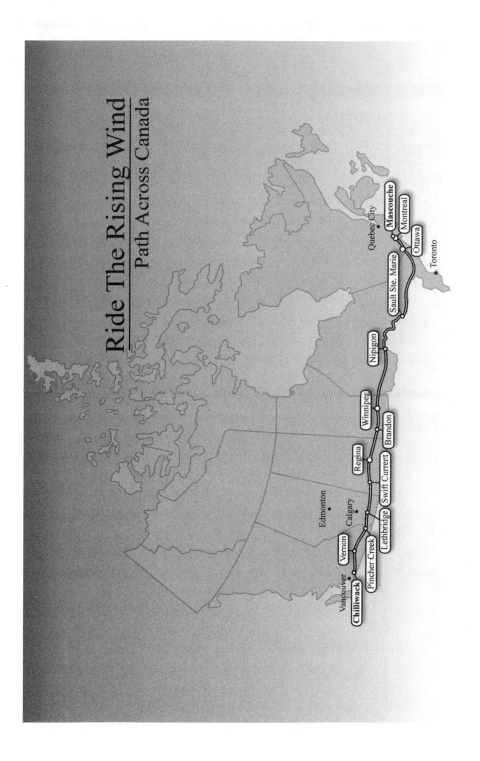

Ride The Rising Wind
Path Across Canada

It's darker now. No moon tonight. Just starlight, but wow, *look at those stars! And there's a kind of glow behind the heights that calms me.*

We're home here, among you enduring mountains. Do I really want to come to the end of you, the end of our special time together?

Can I ever leave you, you familiar forms creating perils and my protection, my solitude and the path beneath my feet? Austere when my eyes are blinded by too much light, you are steadfast for me, there in the starlight.

Now only swamping weariness is real. My horse and I must stop, yet we cannot, for we are committed to go on to the end.

– Introduction –

Jan Loof and I were leaning against the edge of an emptied hayrack. Sunshine played games on his broad, tanned face. We were looking idly across the pasture where the two sons of Zazy, my old travelling mare, were grazing.

Jan looked my way, made me wait while he gathered words. "How did you ever take your first step out?"

His blue eyes held on to me while I studied my feet, not for long. Out from home, I guessed he meant. I looked into my neighbour's honest face. "I didn't know how far it was."

One moment later, we two farmers exploded into laughter that wouldn't stop. The answer was so simply funny, so simply true!

How does anyone know how far it is, to the freedom we've known all along that exists out there, somewhere? Some of us search the whole length of a lifetime, trying dead-end trails. Some give up on the way, stop, take root, and surrender their dream of the freedom to be. Some get rich, and buy things that entangle their feet and defraud their minds.

And some just go, with minimal material means, and keep on going because they can't afford to stop, can't wait for the view from the next hilltop. Bit by bit, what little they started with becomes burdensome. Bit by bit, they let it go, until an impasse comes.

There they must choose: to hold on to that last bit of security, or to trim it off at the risk of retaining only faith in life itself. Some make that final choice, and they find themselves freed to move toward all they can become.

It was a gall on my horse's back that sprang me free of the last of my possessions, free to move toward all that the world held for me, just as I was. . . .

--

On Sunday, May 15, 1949, I rode out from my farm home at Mascouche, Quebec, on a little black mare named Zazy. I was twenty and she was

1

fifteen. We travelled the open road, living wherever we happened to be, with strangers becoming friends, within the rugged warmth of lumber camps, and in welcoming wilderness. This is the story of our sixteen-month journey to the Pacific Ocean, four thousand miles from Mascouche. Along our way, I lost the need for certainty about tomorrow, and found instead the generous heart of my country.

Our journey was completed in August 1950, halfway through the last millennium.

— —

I started out with horse lore gathered and hoarded throughout my childhood. Two men and a small roan horse stitched together my patchwork learning with experience that made it work.

Old Mr. Shaw welcomed my help with the haying when I was only ten years old. His adult son had been kicked out of sevice by Maude the mare. The old farmer needed someone.

I watched the bent little man lift the heavy harness onto his draft team, hitch and drive them. On unbearably hot days, we would rest in the cool stone stable where his boarders stood tied. He would point out their defects and scars, and tell me about unsoundness, injuries, harness galls, and treatments.

I rode a wild assortment of these horses, always bareback, often in bridles mocked up from pieces I found on pegs in the barn. From these unpredictable mounts I got the feel of a horse beneath me. Skill came of necessity through my determination always to bring a borrowed horse safely home.

Cliff Hawkes, always Baker to me, entered my life when my sister Joan got mumps. Baker came to the door as usual with our bread, saw me home from school under quarantine, and persuaded my mother to let me go as his helper. "That way," he said, "she won't get mumps." I was in my glory riding on the horse-drawn wagon.

My job lasted for two years. Baker taught me to hold the reins with respect, conversing with the horse through the bit in its mouth, attuning my driving to the temperament of the animal. I learned how to protect it from weather and flies, to feed, water, and rest it. I watched Baker work his horses over our thirty mile route in all seasons, and bring them back to their stable with heads high and hides dry. Later, as I planned my ride, I knew I could ask thirty miles per day of Zazy. She gave me as many as forty-five.

Wise to life, Cliff Hawkes helped me to deal with my adolescent moods and carry on with the job.

Nell was my equine mentor. She moved with a hitching gait because she had a dropped hip from breaking her ileum when she fell in a well. Nell led a rough-and-ready life like her owners. My buddy Billy let me ride her any time. She went when she felt like going, and balked when she did not. She taught me to compromise.

Billy's parents insisted I use their Universal saddle. It was starved for oil and hard as wood, but I complied until I convinced them that I was in no danger of falling off their horse. After that, Nell and I happily went bareback.

Nell's company gave me self confidence to go among strangers and friends in our town. In quiet, enduring friendship, we travelled through fields of flowers and nodding grasses, and we stood on the riverbank in the biting wind, listening and watching as the ice shoved and the black water of the St. Lawrence broke free.

Nell told me the sad tale of heaves, a slow irreversible asthma. Aging and eating poor hay, had caused her to develop heaves. Billy and I maintained her with medicine in a black bottle and advice from the veterinary column in the *Family Herald*. During the Second World War,

Zazy ready for the road, Mascouche farm. May 1949.

while Billy was in the army and Nell was in my care, she began to bleed from the nose. We had no money to pay for a veterinarian, so I had to call for the help of the SPCA. I heard the shot that ended Nell's life. That day I aged alone.

— —

The ride materialized out of an unforeseen sequence of events. At eighteen years of age I was academically ready to register in veterinary college, yet I needed certification that I could handle livestock competently. Pausing in my search for a summer job, I visited the Dobsons, friends of a friend of mine, on their subsistence farm north of Montreal. Peg and Charlie Dobson invited me to stay and persuaded a local dairy farmer to hire me. Charlie's small black mare named Zazy took me daily to work. Within four months, I had my certification and a home with the Dobsons for two years.

Sharing the vagaries of a small farm enterprise, I found a sense of belonging that would span the chasm that was about to open between us. With mixed feelings, my friends accepted a chance to move with Peg's family to the Pacific coast. Our neophyte farming venture was ended.

What of Zazy's future? Charlie would not sell her and he could not take her. I had the answer: "I will ride her to the coast." Before we left the farm, Charlie gave his mare to me.

Zazy and I travelled unaccompanied and mostly unannounced. For my expenses, I took one hundred dollars, which seemed like a fortune to me. I carried it in a belt pouch with personal items and three maps: Canada east, middle, and west, marked with my proposed route. A camera with a reflex lens hung on my neck. I accepted the loan of a small, unskirted stock saddle, to which I tied war surplus camping gear, an eiderdown mummy bag from my sister Joan, a homemade oat bag, and a .22-calibre rifle, also on loan. I was by choice a bareback rider; I accepted the saddle out of necessity and assumed that my improvised equipment would suffice for long-distance riding. As for the rifle, I had no idea why I would need a gun. Wiser minds prevailed. I took the rifle in its fine leather boot and did my best to stop it from dangling.

Zazy started out wearing rubber-covered iron shoes for grip and resilience.

— —

Zazy was foaled at Beebe in the Eastern Townships of Quebec. She displayed the conformation, strength, courage, and versatility of the Canadian horse, a breed indigenous to Quebec in the French colonial time. I believe she carried as much as fifty percent Canadian genes. Though the breed was almost legendary by the 1940s, I knew it existed because I saw Mr. Gilbert Arnold's purebreds on his breeding farm at Grenville, Quebec.

Like our habitant neighbour's Tit Gar and the early Canadian horses, Zazy was small enough to survive our feed shortage in winter, and big enough to meet every need for horsepower on our subsistence farm. She was our draft mare, our riding mare, our merry companion. She skid the firewood logs in the bush, ploughed and tilled the garden, and took us wherever we needed to go. She loved to spring along over snowy roads, a little black horse with flashing white fetlocks and blaze, making the sleigh fly to the song of the bells across her back. Was that a deep drift ahead? Zazy put on speed to be sure to get through it. Quitting never seemed to cross her mind. On the road, true to her heritage, Zazy never failed me.

At twenty years old, I was physically fit for the road. Walking or cycling, alone or in company, I grew up convinced that I could go anywhere under my own power. That was the code of the Canadian Youth Hosteller. My parents honoured my birthright to choose my path, to be always exploring.

We lived simply, on my father's modest salary from the Canadian Pacific Railway; I was fed, clothed, and educated well. Dad's pass on the railway was my passport to Canada beyond Montreal South. We went east to the sea every summer, and west into Ontario on special occasions. One spring day we went to Ottawa.

Ottawa! Capital of Mom and Dad's adopted country and mine by right of birth. Ottawa, where the times of day and the stars of night were kept under close observation, where coins were minted and money was printed because we had gold in Canada, where rules were made by men in buildings like castles to keep us Canadians right with each other. The bells of the Peace Tower called down to a river and out to all of Canada and to me, three- or four-feet high, listening, rooted, while the music flowed. Ottawa became my own symbol of an expanding universe that perhaps I glimpsed first through the eyes of two brave, inconspicuous immigrants from Birmingham, England.

My parents struggled to accept the mystery of my choosing to spend time building a life with strangers on a derelict farm in habitant Quebec. Why would I want to leave the cozy, secure home that they had built with their own hands and cash in Montreal South? My sister and I were born in that house. It was intended for us to enjoy until we were fully educated and ready for independent living.

Had Dad lost sight of the Quebec boat that he and I watched on summer nights, sailing out of Victoria Harbour, lit up like a birthday cake? Or the icebreaker from Sorel downriver that we welcomed from our freezing-cold viewpoint on the Harbour Bridge above the frozen channel? It was Dad who led my imagination along that line of ice chunks escaping eastward on the dark current toward Mont Joli and the Atlantic Ocean. And then, there were the trains in Windsor Station that enchanted us, each passenger coach bearing in gold letters the name of a special place in Canada. I had to go and see. I happened to land first in Mascouche.

I was too young at nineteen to understand, much less to explain, what had always driven me to reach out beyond home base. I constantly poked at the social conventions that cramped people from civilly expressing themselves, embracing differences, and enjoying a place in the natural world.

Mom and Dad saw that I was happy in the company of animals. True to their mutual resolve, they helped me in every way to follow my own star. Finally it was them who did the footwork that led to the mailing of my completed application for entry into the Ontario Veterinary College. I requested the reply to be mailed to Port Arthur, marked "Please Hold for Pickup," and rode away free of care.

As Zazy and I said goodbye to Charlie, Mom, and Dad on the wiry grass outside the ancient grey farmhouse at Mascouche, I knew I was ready to go. Did Charlie know the gift of belonging that he and Peg had given me? Did my parents realize that it was their nurturing in my childhood that had readied me, first to leave the nest, and now to leave everything I knew as home? All without a backward glance, I was eager to receive the wide world.

PART ONE
Weather Fronts

A weather front is a line of contention between two air masses, expressing their differences at an interface. It is a place of ultimatum voiced by the round earth turning. "I hold you, you cannot leave the system. You must respond to each other and change."

The traveller on the open road must weather the fallout from the clash, and snatch energy from the interface to power her response to the voice of the biosphere: "I hold you, you cannot run away. You must respond to each other and change."

Zazy and I have the road to ourselves as we leave the dead farm. The dark boards on the half-demolished barn by the roadside lean mournfully away from us. The empty face of the abandoned rabbitry looms like a weathered epitaph. I turn toward the springtime. The sun is already high, lifting me to the earthy scent of an infant summer, drenching me with energy. Across the greening fields, the church bell in the 'Little Village' is sending out its message that mass has ended. We are alive and well, and the rest of Canada is calling us in.

Here's Christie's tall white house, all quiet as we pass. And Paquette's oat field. I see that he has already done his seeding. There he is; he's waving from the barnyard. *Shall we stop in?* Zazy asks by the turn of her head. "Not today, Zazy, we have a long, long way to go."

My mare and I have learned to talk together. By gesture, touch, pressure, and tone, we invite, warn, argue, agree, reassure. She uses few "words" to send her precise messages. I am a wordy person, learning from Zazy the universal language of intuition.

Here comes a family of our French Catholic neighbours, wheeling by in their buggy. They nod to me as they pass, escorted by a small cloud of dust. I see another buggy coming, and two more behind at the curve where the road dips. We farmers wave or nod to each other. Their snappy buggy horses trot straight ahead, keeping the high, shiny, black wheels whirling. No doubt the word of our journey has been passed along. Do they question my wisdom as they head home for dinner and an afternoon of visiting on their broad verandas?

Here comes Henri Major's little black Canadian horse, so akin to Zazy. His eyes are bright within his blinkers, his curly mane flies from the crest of his neck, his bold shoulders reach for the road. Of course, it is Tit Gar. *Whee-ee-ee*, he calls to Zazy, his winter stable mate, as he catches sight of her. *Hur-hur-hurr*, returns Zazy, as Tit gar comes closer. Henri's face is one deep smile as he sends me, "Bonjour, bon voyage," from his seat beside his lady. Madam Major looks out happily from beneath the brim of her flowered hat and raises a white-gloved hand. Henri's weathered hands keep contact with his horse, and the trio passes in bold and gentle dignity, home to their farm by the road on which I, too, have lived.

The road ahead is empty now, but I am filled with the goodwill of friends. Zazy brings us to the pavement that crosses our dirt road. We know well the turning westward to the 'Little Village,' called La Plaine on the map, where we used to meet Charlie's train. Eastward the road used to take us to St. Lin, Sir Wilfrid Laurier's hometown, where I went to buy feed.

Zazy clip-clops across the pavement and steps down onto the sand road where I biked once to New Glasgow. It's a pleasant trail with a grassy crest and a track smoothed by cartwheels. I hear a car horn! Way back there, I can see Mom and Dad and Charlie all strung out along the paved road, waving. A final blessing is passing between us, and now we're going our separate ways.

There's the hay barn away across the field to the east, where I loaded bales on the bobsleigh midway through that tough winter before last. We managed, Peg and Charlie and I, with the help of the *habitants*, to keep all the animals fed until the grass came again. Now that story is ancient history, and Zazy and I are on our way to Lachute. I remember how Joan and I biked to the Canadian Youth Hostel there and spent a wonderful day at the Lachute Fall Fair. Zazy and I will have no trouble finding a campsite beyond Lachute tonight.

This saddle with stuff hung all around it is a bore; it feels awkward and floppy, and it separates me from Zazy. Maybe I'll get used to it. This rifle doesn't really want to come; it just won't hang right. But Charlie was worried about my safety and he felt better when I agreed to bring the gun. We do have to carry our home with us, I suppose. I really didn't train in the full kit. Well, we have lots of muscle and we're used to long rides in new places. The only difference today is that we won't be turning back at halftime. I feel as if this day has no bend in the middle, as if my life has been straightened out, like a red carpet rolling out ahead of us. I wonder what Zazy is thinking.

Noontime I guess, because she's asking if we should be turning back as usual. She catches the smell of the nosebag. *Oats! Oats! Where?* she nickers. I buckle on the bag and she reaches in to her feed. Here's the salmon sandwich that Mom tucked into my saddlebag, and Zazy's warm side to lean on while I eat. Now she's watching while I put the rest of her oats with the pile of tack under a tree.

Suddenly, a hellish volley of motorcycles comes roaring out of the trail behind our chokecherry hedge. Zazy rears back and is gone, leaving the last loop of my fine Girl Guide knot to mark my best effort. I abandon my borrowed belongings, grab the bridle, and run after the mare. At the first bend in the road, a giggling crew of little French boys is coming, riding and leading Zazy down their farm lane and back to me in a draft horse bridle.

If horses kept score, Zazy could have disqualified me from the game halfway through the afternoon.

Can't tie knots . . . 0

Loses her balance when speeding truck makes me rear . . . 0

Pulls me over backward as truck speeds away . . . -4

Misses the detour and pits me against whizzing highway traffic . . . -2

Unfurls road map in wind within earshot of those crazy cars . . . -3

I could have tallied up a worse score against myself and slunk spiritually away. This day, however, I caught myself. I would tie a more secure knot next time. I would judge the speed of a truck and wait for it to pass. I would hold Zazy secure against her fears, between my hands, voice, and legs.

This day, I felt as if I had passed through a selective membrane, carried over all the good things from past times and left the shadowy contradictions on the other side. I felt as if I had run all the way along the snow pack between the railway tracks with my dog Rusty until we had come into forever. Rusty had been killed by a car. I was glad Zazy was with me.

*Zazy and me heading out with a full oat bag, past
the old barn on the farm at Mascouche. May 1949.*

Evening came. My image of the Canadian Youth Hostel at Lachute
faded as Zazy paused tentatively, three strides from the top of a maple
lane. The turn of her head toward the farmyard below seemed to say quite
clearly: *This will be a good place to stop, don't you think?* A farmer with a
collie at his side was waving us in.

"Right on, Zazy!" I laid a hand on her neck where equine moms soothe
their babies. We went down and accepted the invitation of Mr. McAdam
and his family. Zazy found feed and a cozy stall in the cow barn, and I
shared the supper table with the extended McAdam family. At night I
slept under a patchwork quilt like those Charlie's mom used to make.

Zazy never plodded; she was always going somewhere. She explored as
she strode, watching everywhere, catching scents on the wind, blowing
her nose now and then like a deer that wants a clearer message. At every
roadside spring she sampled the plants, with my permission.

I couldn't get enough of that second morning. Sunlit snowdrifts inlaid
the hills tracing out poplar colonies mantled with smoky grey catkins.
Meltwater leapt singing over cliffs. Pink and white trilliums danced under
hardwoods, bringing back my joy of gathering flowers with Mom in Tiffin

Woods near my birthplace. The hilly road we walked was stepping over the toes of the Laurentian Mountains. Somewhere among them was a cabin where Joan's friend's father had helped me to know Orion in the moonless sky above our heads.

Calumet was a pretty as my father and my pal Billy had seen it on their bike trip: a village of cottages set in the green lace of uncurling leaves, snuggling beside a waterfall. Dad and Billy had fun meeting the local people. Sadly, I felt distanced from the local people, for they viewed us cautiously as we passed along their street. Maybe cyclists were more usual visitors in 1949. Maybe Billy's fluent French made a difference. Was I an English stranger from a bygone time?

At Montebello, the gatekeeper at the Seigneury Club called a greeting through the wide-open wrought iron gates. His words floated to me and landed gently, like a neighbour's call. I asked about water for Zazy, and the gatekeeper gladly brought her a drink. Here was the warmth I had known with other French Canadians. I was thrilled to find myself standing at the gates of the former feudal estate of Joseph Papineau, the famous leader in the rebellion of 1837 against the English.

In fact, Papineauville was where we found ourselves that second night. The day had been very long, the afternoon hot and dusty. My galls, and the bruises from our fall in the road cut on our first day, mocked the month of daily riding that I had naively called "training." I would need to ride a hundred miles more to match Zazy's fitness. Though I wanted to get her into a stable that night, I was not up to searching endlessly to find one. No farmer was open to my request, and "sais pas" was the nothing that townsfolk on the street would tell me about the youth hostel in my CYH handbook.

Our escort of curious young boys was kindlier. With patience they decoded my French and told me that the hostel was closed, the hotel was just over there, and they knew a dairy farmer who might take Zazy in. A few of the older boys showed me the way, spoke for me to the farmer, and made perfect arrangements. One boy courteously reviewed the way to the hotel, and they left me.

Zazy slept in a stall with all her needs met. I had a beautifully peaceful bedroom in a spruce grove. At daybreak a dewy bovine muzzle was thrust through the branches above my sleeping bag. *Good morning! And who are you?* the black face asked. A dog barked and the head withdrew. I tidied up and followed the herd back to Zazy's stable.

The mare limbered up within half an hour's walk. A skinned hip was the only reminder of the speeding truck that had made her rear and fall in the road cut. I was developing protective calluses. The saddle fitted the mare's back comfortably, and the pack rode squarely and snugly, except at the trot. We simply agreed not to trot.

My sister Joan was expecting us to be in Ottawa on our third night, and that was my goal. She would have taken leave from the laboratory for our visit. As evening brought us into wild marshland far from any sign of dwelling, I knew we were going to be late. I was watching for high land where we could leave the road to sleep until daylight, when car lights appeared behind us.

The lights were as part of the fading twilight. They kept their distance until I saw swamp water to either side. Then slowly they were closing on us. We were being stalked.

I knew we were in danger. I knew the mare would rear on command, and could strike in my defense. I summed up our possibilities. Zazy could neither outrun the car nor exit the road. I would do as I had done when I

Zazy obeying the command to rear, outside the habitant farmhouse at Mascouche. May 1949.

was stalked in Montreal after night classes: keep cool, keep moving, head for lights, and pray. But there were no lights to head for.

Now the car was beside us. Inside were two men. The passenger was trying to start a conversation with me. Politely I played puzzled, kept him talking while I rode steadily and wished I could run. Would Zazy rear and strike to defend me? She would, on cue. It was Peg's rifle that saved us. The man caught sight of it hanging in the boot.

"What's that thing?"

"It's a rifle."

"What for?"

"Oh, I keep it loaded in case anybody bothers us on the road. I'm not a great shot, but it would do a pretty good job at close range." I spaced out my words.

Our visitors put their heads together, murmuring. I was betting on playing too stupid to be trusted with a gun, or too mindless to be worth the risk. I won the bet, they gunned their motor, and in seconds the red tail lights disappeared into the blackness ahead.

Friendly darkness covered our exit up a trail into a haven until morning. By day I reflected on Charlie's foresight of a hazard that had not earlier entered my mind. Why had it not?

In childhood I had no apprehension of anything bad happening to me. Joan was there to fight off the French kids on our way from school over to Grandma's house. Mom and Dad kept gruesome stories out of our hearing. The kidnapping of the Lindberg baby seemed more legendary than actual to me. In fairy tales, someone always saved the day and goodness always prevailed. War and vandalism and theft were deplored, but the plight of victimized children was not thrust before our eyes. I guess this is how I was spared from nameless fears. When danger came, instinct flagged it and reason prevailed.

--

The next day at noon, I rode Zazy across the wooden bridge from Hull, Quebec, into Ottawa, Ontario. The carillon on Parliament Hill rang out, and a stream of cars rattled the loose boards beneath us. Hands, legs, and voice steadied the mare all the way through town. On the main street, she survived the crush of people and cars and a huge streetcar clanging its

A momentary photo op for an eager pony about to leave Ottawa. 20 May 1949.

rod on the track. I managed to obey the traffic lights and smile my thanks to the motorists who gave us the right of way. Finally, Zazy was safe on a farm and I made my way back to Ottawa and found Joan at the National Research Council Laboratories.

Joan welcomed me without complaint and I practiced forgiving myself for being late, while we spent two happy days together. On Monday we filled my saddlebags with clean clothes, food from Mom, plus Joan's freshly baked cookies and noodle soup mix. I mailed home the first of my three Canada maps, along with journal pages, and brought forward the middle map into my belt bag. Then we caught a bus to the farm where Zazy was staying.

Zazy was exuberantly ready to go. Impatient at my final checking, she reared and snapped a cheek piece. Then she casually turned to eating grass while the farmer fixed the bridle with split rivets. I bridled her, we all said a quick round of thanks and goodbyes, and I sprang onto a dancing pony. She settled for a moment while Joan snapped a picture, then I let her go.

We were waving each other onto our separate ways. Different we were, yet so alike in stature and in the way we looked at life. Joan was a lean, fit cyclist, I a hard-boned muscular farmer; Joan wore a neat flowered blouse and green slacks, I a green shirt and Peg's riding pants with leather at the knees; Joan was a chemist and I might be a veterinarian someday.

2

Zazy cantered out of Ottawa on her rubber shoes, following a macadamized road that curved between gardens filled with spring flowers. We were heading west by way of northern Ontario, the bush, the rugged Canadian Shield. I had longed for this, and now I had just plunged into the deep end of the pool. We were actually on our way, taking my confidently chosen route in order to pass overland around the Great Lakes.

Zazy was fresh. Beyond suburbia, she cantered easily along the grassy shoulder of the road. I felt light, like a dandelion seed cruising on air. Spring was playing with colours, gold of breeding finches, green of teetering vireos, yellows and browns of fallen leaves shuffled by a great silver porcupine searching out flowers on a woodland floor. My world was filled with music.

The music changed as we left the fertile bottomlands and came to the meeting ground of two parent bedrocks. Had Shield rocks stood tall at the interface, making a bold statement about the ancient orogeny? This was a tougher land than the capital region, harder to manipulate, more diverse, a place where nature could step up boldly with her brushes and paint the picture.

By nightfall we stood on the gravel apron of the Canadian Shield. I left Zazy in a humble stable and went looking for a bed for myself. I stepped over a tired rail fence onto a wild pasture where plants were guarding the soil they were building among the stones. The air was chilling quickly; dewdrops hung heavy on grass blades. I caught the whisper of welcome from flat-topped cedars and spreading junipers. I zigzagged between them until I felt securely alone, and dived into a cavern of warm air hoarded by the dense juniper canopy around me. I slept cozy all night.

— —

The roads to the north and the west parted company at a small park, a nice spot to eat grass or study a map. I failed to read a storm warning as a man strolled politely over from his car and blew up a casual conversation. Next thing I knew, he had *my* map spread on the hood of *his* car and he was arguing for me to take the southern road. "You'll never make it through the bush with that horse. You'll be back into winter up there. There's no feed to be found. Soon as the heat comes, the flies'll be out to kill you both." He knew! He was a travelling salesman. But how about getting around the Great Lakes?

I held firm until my adviser came to the part about the horse starving. Then, despite my great uncertainty, I yielded to his plan. He showed me how I could go through Carleton Place and across southern Ontario to Georgian Bay. He said a regular steamer would take me from Victoria Harbour or Port McNicoll to Sault St. Marie and thence to the Lakehead. He gave me the telephone number of a shipping agent from whom I could get details.

He left me only partly convinced. The change would make me dependent on commercial transportation. Also, it would deprive me of the north woods. Granted, it would bring me to the prairies in time to earn money to pay my way.

Forty miles later at Carleton Place, I phoned the number I had been given and received confirmation of the steamship service, though without details. I was speaking to someone at a central office who was unsure of the port. I went on toward Georgian Bay, still haunted by ambiguity. Was I drifting far out of my way? Prickly with the irritation, I turned my attack on my camera and packed it away to stop it from dangling.

Beyond Mississippi Lake, we stepped into a land of rock and water, with tall trees guarding the road. A raucous cry from a patch of sky between the guards arrested me. A ragged black bird with handsome crimson crest and white flash in the wings shot across the open space. At last I had seen a pileated woodpecker! Its explosive intrusion spoke to me of the power of the wilderness, and I received its message and felt strong again.

We moved slowly in an overcast afternoon across gravel moraine. Zazy was watching for oases of clover and grass in hollows that caught soil and spring runoff. I was watching for horned larks singing in the sky above their nesting sites, and writing their story to Mom. For miles and miles I saw no sign of human life, but only weathering windblown barns. Oat time put Zazy and me on alert.

Our road was following a railway line with cedar bush falling away to the left and fenced land beyond the right-of-way. Finally Zazy spotted a little-used track leading to a level crossing. We followed, up and over, and onto a farm lane gated a safe distance back to allow a team to halt with a wagon for the gate to be opened. It opened easily to us. I slipped off Zazy's back and we walked toward a distant, grey clapboard house graced with a white porch and green trim.

A friendly brown dog met us by the sleeping peony bed. We were talking together when the porch door opened and an elderly man in coveralls stood looking out at us through the twilight. "Good evening," I said. "I'm passing through and I wonder if you have any hay or oats to sell." A woman joined him and they walked down to the dog and Zazy and me. Quietly we opened our windows to each other.

"Yes, we have horse feed," the man replied. "We farm with a team. There's an extra stall in the barn."

"You are welcome to spend the night here," his wife added. "How far are you going?"

"We're making our way to Vancouver."

"You look like honest travellers. You can go and put your pony to bed. You'll find feed and her stall in the stable."

"Come over to the house when you're ready. You can sleep on the couch in the porch."

The dog showed Zazy and me to the horse stable, and took me back to the house. The man showed me into the kitchen, where his wife had set tea and sandwiches for me. We three sat together. I was fascinated by their story of subsistence farming close to the land and to the sky with its cargo of weather. They were blessed with contentment, and so pleased to hear how Zazy and I had happened to arrive at their door!

At breakfast I met their bachelor son, a big young man, older than me, quiet like his folks, a mainstay to the trio. He ate up and went out to milk the cows and feed the chickens while his mother and father and I said our farewells. No money passed between us; they ignored my mention of it. Zazy was waiting with the brown waggy dog. As I rode down the lane, I looked back to wave, but the couple had already gone about their business.

We came into gentle terrain in sunshine. Zazy drank from an amber stream marked out by marsh marigolds and banked by purple violets, all in their glory. I washed my hair in the stream and emerged numb in skull, feet, and ankles. The flowers seemed to be amused while the sun's warmth reclaimed me. Zazy reserved comment and went on grazing. I tried to wrest my wet artificial kinks from the breeze and put them into an order they would remember after drying. Why ever did I get that perm in Quebec? My hair was born to be straight.

We were hardly back on the road when a reporter from the *Ottawa Citizen* overtook us. He stepped jovially out of his Jeep, camera ready. I thought of my frizzy hair, he seemed unaware of my shame, and I was duly interviewed. I explained my policy of avoiding advance publicity to preserve spontaneity with people, and he went away in high spirits, assured of a scoop. I liked him.

We had more good company along our way that day. A woodchuck stretched tall and whistled from the top of its stone pile, overhung with racemes of scented chokecherry. Horses came to fences to squeal with

What's around the next bend? Zazy carries me riding cross-legged under a waterproof, toward Silver Lake. Near Sharbot Lake, ON. 22 May 1949.

Zazy, kick up, and gallop away. A provincial policeman stopped to visit, and travelling salesmen greeted me and wished us fair weather.

I wished I had never met their counterpart, the man who changed our route. As we moved up onto the Shield rock of the Frontenac Axis, I found myself shivering in sleet, snow, and soaking rain that I was supposed to be avoiding. We turned a sharp curve between rock walls into a blast of icy cold rain driven at our faces. Shuddering, we left the road and waded through wet grass into a ravine to hide from the wind.

Three old cedars stood together, offering us shelter. Inside I was dry enough to check out the birds I had seen and to make diary notes. A red cow was looking in at me, with her calf resting against the curve of her warm flank. A pair of horses came to see Zazy, who was dozing tied to a low branch. I fed a million blackflies before the rain soaked through our roof. But then we were rested from the wind and ready to go.

I discovered, as I fought the grasping wind for my billowing rain cape, that it wasn't being wet, but getting wet, that I had been resisting. Thoroughly soaked, I settled cross-legged and barefoot like a camel rider and began to enjoy the new face that the rain was putting on land and lake. Silver Lake was changing from a flat expanse of wetness into a soft grey infinity. From a misty island a great blue heron flapped along a steady course, stirring up gnats that brought a cloud of swallows swooping and skimming across its flight line. I watched the heron until it melted again into mist.

Zazy wearied at the persistent rain. She regularly reared to protest the motor vehicles swishing past us. She hated cars contending for her road space in rock cuts, and I think her snake face and flying feet alarmed more than one motorist. Luckily her worn rubber shoes still gripped the road.

In the twilight of a forbidding night, I was arrested by a bent figure shrouded in black. She caught me trespassing hopefully among a clutch of dysfunctional shacks. I explained my need for cover and horse feed.

"There's a farm down there," was all she said, and she pointed from under her wrap like a bat. I thanked her, believed her, and found our needs met at the end of the road she had set me on.

Winter had been tough; food supplies were low, yet the England family saw our needs as one with theirs. They shared from what they had left, hay for Zazy and bowls of hot, home-grown food for us people, while my wet clothes and saddle blankets dried beside the wood stove. I slept on a couch, Zazy lay down on her straw bed to rest her legs, and we went away in the morning blessed.

— —

Our story in the *Ottawa Citizen* ran on ahead of us. The Bensons at Kaladar were expecting us; Marg was on the front steps to hail us in. Zazy fell to cropping the lawn the moment the bridle left her head. Mrs. Benson whisked the saddle blankets and my retired jodhpurs into the new washing machine in the kitchen while I changed into jeans. Marg put on the coffee and eats. Mr. Benson and Joe arrived from their service garage next door. Everyone talked at once to the swish-swooshing tune of the washer, and the bits of our lives laughed together and spilled all over the table and drew in the family dog.

Duty called Joe and Mr. Benson back to their brake job on a flat-deck truck. Mrs. Benson hung the laundry to finish drying on the sunny side of the fence. Marg took me to see the stall that her horse Banjo had used.

Marg spoke sadly of parting with Banjo. It was a matter of money. She felt happy again when she fetched his leftover hay and oats for Zazy. She would bag the rest of the oats for us to take. Zazy counted with her left forefoot when she smelled the oats, and for a moment a little glow of fellowship held Marg and Zazy and me.

Marg told me of a good farrier in Lindsay, a day's ride farther on, she said. Next morning she gave Zazy a new pair of rubber front shoes. "I want her to have these," she said from her heart. "I'm sure they will fit her." Gratefully I received them and secured one shoe in each side of the pack.

We three women shared a big hug and the men came from the shop to exchange strong, warm handshakes. No one noticed Zazy's mistake in the crowded parking space. Just as I threw my leg over the saddle, she moved away from an oncoming car, crushing my thigh against the corner of the flat deck. We never missed a beat and left The Bensons in a volley of good wishes.

— —

From that oasis of fellowship, we passed into a solid grey interlude. My inner world greyed to match the weather. Nothing felt right, including my thigh. I wished the bugs would leave us alone. As we slopped along,

I wished the sun would come out and dry us. When it did, out came the bugs. Then there was the sleet to make me appreciate the rain.

I worried about Zazy's feet. The map's version of the distance between Kaladar and Lindsay was more like two or three days, not one. Worrying drove out reasoning. The pack shifted, and I blamed it on the weight of the shoes. The sameness around us made me doubt that we were really moving, and I reran the route change in dark grey. Would it all come out wrong and make us go back to the north route? My vision narrowed to the endless road. I felt caught in a time warp, and then the hamlet of Actinolite appeared in my sights.

Actinolite cast a shadow from the past. I listened in lamplight to the tales of the people whose roof I shared. They would not hear of my camping outside. A wildcat had been heard screaming in the night, and that was an evil portent.

The power of folklore flickered across my reasoning mind as I rode into another day. My thoughts ran back to Baker, my mentor who had helped me to understand horses and people, and to deal with my twelve-year-old self.

During my time with Baker, once in a while something inside made me feel awkward, made me withdraw from action that I enjoyed, like taking the reins, or sharing an afternoon snack. It was as though I had been set back behind a blank wall, and there I was stuck. Baker was never stuck. He would say, simply, "Barb, don't be like that," as gently as if he were asking Sandy to step into a trot. Then he would carry the action forward, and I'd be feeling the wall melt down and I'd be rejoining him.

Baker never changed; he just went on as steady as Sandy's stride through the hours to the end of that day and all the other days. He never gave up on me, never grew impatient. Maybe he knew that I had a fearful need to negate myself lest someone else do it to me. Though he could not alter my feeling, he did what I believe no one else could have done. He led me to see that, no matter how I felt, I did have a choice as to what I would do. And he cheered me on and welcomed me back into the freely flowing stream of life, by his radiant empathy.

I set my sights on Lindsay. Big spiteful cumulus clouds spat hail on the landscape, and the frontal wind froze us wet mortals in its fickle blasts. It challenged me to find a dry surface on which to lay out our belongings and rebalance the load. An abandoned barn with an intact

Upbeat friends after a dark time. Mr. Torpey and Theresa at Indian River, ON. May 1949.

roof served my purpose and gave us a shelter for the night. In the darkness the supernatural stories from Actinolite took on a life of their own, and I found myself listening for the voice of the wildcat.

A wet wind snatched at the waterproofs as I saddled up the next morning. I was owly. I had too many weeping fly bites, too much pain in my crushed thigh. And I was angry with myself for all that had gone wrong. My mood infected Zazy; she shied and shirked, and we were on a downward spiral.

Why were we here, anyway? Because I was stupid, of course! I had made a bad decision; we had come the wrong way. I hadn't much to sing about that whole day, but I was angry enough to intercept the afternoon rerun of self-deprecation, fight off the feeling, and beat the devil to death.

Ready for battle, I rode down from a ridge and spooked a herd of beef cattle. They stood, stared, snorted, wheeled, and dashed away. Their flight line led my eyes to a large red barn with a loft. Our spirits bounced out of the bog as one. Within minutes we were at the Torpeys' farm at Indian River, and our long test in the hinterland was over.

Helping with chores brought my mind out of solitude, and a hot supper sprang me free. My hosts shared my joy. They too had fought the weather to win this prospering home farm. It was time to celebrate! We left the dishes in the sink and went sightseeing.

The children played soccer in the park at the Peterborough Lift Locks while their parents and I ogled at the immensity and power of the lake boat elevator. The massive tank poised on its giant piston dripped water sixty feet above the level of the downstream waterway. Shadowed by the setting sun, this engineering wonder loomed immense.

As darkness fell, the fountains at the City Waterworks began to play in rainbow colours. The children eagerly counted the forms thrown up in their spray. Then we were away to Lakefield to see Rice Lake by starlight. Maureen took her Daddy's hand and we three walked out along the causeway afloat on scintillating water. The velvet darkness and the silence and stars above

Maureen off to school on Zazy.

and below wrapped us in their beauty. Maureen loved it. Six-year-old Teresa was asleep in the car with her mom. Home again, I unrolled my sleeping bag on a cot in the screened porch and drowsed in the music of the night.

Sunshine was softening the bite in the wind as the Torpey children said goodbye to Zazy. The little mare nuzzled the small hands and carefully lipped up the apple pieces they held. Maureen shared the saddle with me as far as the schoolhouse. She waved to her teacher standing at the door and turned to tell me she was going to be a teacher. I said that was a good idea. I swung down and helped her to slide off the horse, and left her running to join her friends, waving as she went.

In a pine grove just short of Peterborough, we were waiting for the noon-hour traffic to pass. Zazy had her face in a clover patch and I was watching pine grosbeaks when a group of American tourists approached me in a bow-wave of gentle friendship. While we stood round sharing the delights of the countryside, Zazy's survival sense of unseen food came into play. She also knew friends when she saw them. Zazy strolled over and turned on her charm. Out came the apples. She counted for them with a front hoof, as cute as a horse can be, and accepted the juicy pieces politely. Next a lady offered her cookies. Zazy timed her thanks perfectly; she crunched the cookie, rolled back her upper lip, extended her head, and burped. We people all went our ways, laughing at her antics.

As we entered Lift Locks Park, a group of schoolgirls materialized in full voice. When the cameras began to click, Zazy began to dance. The more the girls swarmed, the higher she stepped. Her first rear prompted me to send her off at a smart canter through the underpass and out of the park.

A wide, high bridge gave me a bird's-eye view of the city that I could not visit, and the geological whalebacks I would remember: drumlins, dramatically lined up above the water. Held to a walk, Zazy had time to see a monstrous truck approaching. She wheeled to the sidewalk, saw over the railing, and reared back. At that moment a man was passing by. I saw his face pale, felt the mare come down without touching him, heard the opening words of his invective, and sent Zazy off the bridge at a snappy trot in shame.

We escaped up the nearest side road into a green and flowering refuge. Zazy was becoming calm when a gardener popped out from behind a bush, aiming a fizzling hose our way. Zazy sprang into a well-extended controlled trot that lasted until we could safely sail into a relaxing canter.

— —

Thursday was more than half gone. We had thirty-eight miles to cover before noon on Friday to have any hope of getting a shoeing before the weekend. Those shredded rubber shoes had to be replaced. They had lasted all the way from Quebec, but now their metal cores were beginning to impinge on Zazy's soles. We hurried until dark, camped in a fence corner until dawn, and arrived at the farrier's shop in Lindsay by 10:30 AM.

It was mid-afternoon before Zazy and I got away. The farrier had set me up for lunch with a reporter from the *Lindsay Post*, and to that end he had done the trim and stopped short of the shoeing. I grumped in private, but I accepted the woman's invitation and enjoyed her company. The change of pace was a busy kind of fun. And the story was like a pebble in a pond, sending good ripples through the rural community where we found ourselves spending the weekend.

Far short of thirty miles beyond Lindsay, a bee yard in a blooming orchard tempted me to turn down the farm lane. From the bee yard, to the collie that ran to meet me, to the couple that greeted me, this place held out a welcome. Zazy rested, while I flowed naturally into all the action that made the Tiplings' farm an experience of a lifetime.

Zazy resting on the Tiplings' farm at Lindsay, ON. 28 May 1949.

We had just arrived at the Tiplings' house, but already there was Zazy with her muzzle in the lawn! I covered my embarrassment. "Zazy, don't eat the lawn until you're invited."

"She's all right. But you must stay with us. Will you do that? Addie, Barbara and Zazy are staying with us. We'll just find a place for the little mare."

We walked into the shadow of the hovering red barn. Ernie let us into the stable. In that ark of animal havens, a pen just Zazy's size was already bedded with straw. She stepped in through a wooden gate, toured her stall, and found loose leafy hay in her manger.

"Better bring the leather out of the way of the calves." Ernie and I carried the tack to the milk room and stored it under the tool rack.

A cow was watching us, backlit at the half-door near the calf pens. A second cow looked over her shoulder. Ernie opened the door, stepped aside, and greeted the animals: "Come in Tilly, come in Toots." They stepped into their places and slipped knobby heads through the stanchions to reach their hay. Ernie turned the calves loose to suck. "We let the calves do the milking at night," he observed. Replete, the calves began to stray. Ernie led them back to their pen, stripped the udders of their dams, and gave the milk to the pigs. "No wash-up," he smiled, as the pigs slurped up their treat.

We gathered for supper, Addie and Ernie, a teenaged girl named Shirley, and me. Every food item on the table had come from the farm: the platter of roast beef, the wide dish of salad, the bowls of boiled potatoes, cauliflower and peas, the sweaty glass jug of milk, the apple pie and whipped cream. It was like a personal message from the land. Ernie offered our thanks to God, and the dishes were passed from hand to hand

Ernie and Addie Tipling with their farm helpers, Fanny and Topsy. Lindsay, ON. 30 May 1949.

in a chain until it closed at the start. As we ate, we all heard a little of each other's story.

Shirley cleared the table; Addie took me to see her chick hatchery. On the way, she told me: "Shirley is Ernie's niece. She helps me during the week and goes home to Burnt River on the weekend. It's a long way from here, but it gets her away from home and gives her a job where she can learn farming and life skills safely."

Addie walked me through her hatchery operation. Her facilities were entirely adequate without being costly. She supplied as many day-old and started chicks as she could produce, all to local customers. A sign above the shipping table certified her laying flock and chicks to be Pullorum Free. This certified that the laying flock and chicks were free of that major poultry infection. Addie maintained high quality by attention to detail and by strict culling of loser birds. She was professional in her management, and her business prospered to everyone's benefit. I could see how patchwork knowledge such as mine in my early teens could expand into a functional system like Addie's hatchery business.

Ernie toured me round the outbuildings in the last of the daylight. Cattle and sheep sheds, calf pens, and lambing jugs were all vacated, cleaned, and repaired. The animals had gone to the grass farms, and I had come in the interlude between spring and summer work. A modest red tractor stood waiting in an open shed beside a tiller and a hay loader. I knew what haying was like!

"Do you ever get tired?" I asked Ernie.

"Oh, yes. But the neighbours help each other and we all get the work done."

In my days of backyard farming with Billy, I dreamed of such a farm as this, where everything fit together and worked without people hurrying and worrying. We had tried our best on a bit of borrowed land, but we didn't belong there. We had to grow up and move on and find a place to put ourselves.

Ernie and Addie had always lived and farmed around here. They belonged, and they seemed to keep building on practices that worked well. Their farming was balanced on its natural base so that it could evolve indefinitely without wrecking that base. The Torpeys were young, and their farm was evolving in a different era. Yet the values they held were so like those of Ernie and Addie! I hoped those young farmers could hold to their country code and in time enjoy the internal security that the Tiplings knew.

We went for a drive on Saturday. Ernie showed me the land where he and his dad had pulled stumps and broken virgin sod. Ernie got the habit of doing things right the first time because, as he said, there wasn't time to do them twice. Addie showed me the lake where she swam in her girlhood. We admired the beauty of a mosque standing alone in a field, built to the pattern of the Taj Mahal. We had tea with a pioneer couple retired to Oakwood, and heard their news.

Ernie and Addie were actively interested in everything and everybody, connected like a tree with deep and spreading roots. They built for others in the normal course of their own lives. Maybe that was why they could innovate without making neighbours feel outclassed.

On Sunday, Ernie took me to see his grass farms. He parked the Austin in a gravelly field, threw open the trunk, and filled two salt pails from a bag. There was not an animal in sight; he was calling in code to the air as he strolled toward a wooden bunk.

Quietly, cattle appeared, one elderly lone brindle cow, a couple of red white-faces trailing her, wending their way among the hawthorn trees and grassy hummocks. Others came, in social order. Calves tagged along in an untidy bunch. Rowdy colourful steers and heifers came jostling each other, gathering steam as they caught sight of the old cows already at the salt. Ernie talked to them all, and the cattle exhaled the sweet breathe of grazers at peace.

We walked to the car. Ernie said, almost to himself: "Pasture's holding up well with the rains we've been having. Stock is getting plenty to eat."

The sheep at the second grass farm watched the Austin approach. Yes, it was Ernie coming. They knew the car and began to move in a slow wave toward the open barnyard. Inside, they arranged themselves at the low feed bunk under the eave. Ernie showed me the turnip mill and the pile of rutabagas left over from the winter. The animals shuffled and bleated at the bunk as they heard the mill begin to hum.

"I grow a field of turnips for the sheep and let them graze the tops in the fall after the pasture has dried up. Then I dig up the roots and have them for winter feed." Ernie was watching the sheep affectionately as they ate. "They don't need 'em anymore, but they like to have a little treat when I come."

The caretaker tenants of the farmhouse were away that Sunday. Ernie said they were glad to keep an eye on the sheep in exchange for an affordable home in the country.

We drove home knowing Agnes would have dinner ready and waiting. "She wouldn't mind if we stopped by the bee yard as we pass," said Ernie with his childlike smile. "I'd like to show you the bees."

We parked the Austin on the lane and went into the shade of the apple trees. We approached quietly, without protective clothing, and paused at a hive near the edge of the yard. Expertly, Ernie slid out a super and showed me honey being made in the cells. Then he politely slid the tray back into place. We left without alarming a single bee.

Monday came, and Zazy and I had to go. Surely I would find my way back to the Tiplings' farm, and Addie and Ernie believed it. As I rode through Oakwood, a retired farmer in his garden waved and called out: "Have a safe journey!" I realized that I had stumbled into a niche where I could live to the full, a place of simple sufficiency.

3

Where the Beaver River flowed between wooded banks, we stopped for lunch. A red fox with a mouse in its mouth ran behind a rock pile and dived into a vertical burrow. Food was on the mind of everyone. A young robin perched on a root and demanded the worms that its mother pulled from the muddy shore. Gleaming grackles were flying across the water with food in their beaks. Kingfishers in blue and black flashed out from watching posts, plunged for fish, settled back to feed, watch, strike again. An elegant plover in an orange vest probed the far shore. Instantly airborne, it was gone around the bend, leaving its shrill *killdee killdee* hanging on the air.

Goggle-eyed frogs tread water near my seat on a stone, and below a languid brown leech undulated past a dead crayfish. Here, sheltered from the wind by water or bush or stone, life was moving with gentle efficiency. Here too, I found a niche.

Zazy travelled as a happy little horse that afternoon, well rested and fed, comfortably shod with iron behind and Banjo's rubber shoes on the front. We were in the wetlands along the east shore of Lake Simcoe when she told me she needed a drink.

The only choice in sight was an intensive livestock operation built on artificially drained land. I felt like an alien as I wandered around the gloomy yard, looking for someone who would speak to me. Peering into a big dairy barn, I saw endless lines of Holstein cattle. Men were moving among them like robots, and their few words to each other were foreign to me. The men that came near me avoided my eyes. I waited. At last someone understood my gestures and pointed to a pail under a tap near the door. Zazy drank. I felt sorrow and death in the air.

The war was too much with me. Perhaps it was overwhelmingly present to these immigrant workers, these Displaced Persons (DP's). The war had left me with images of human beings running for their lives from the inexorable crushing power of the oncoming tanks in Europe. I guessed the war left them with scars that kept on hurting. Were these silent, withdrawn men still mentally hiding in the woods?

In that whole factory farm, one woman stepped out and celebrated new life with me. She was a wide woman dressed in worn blue overalls, a dark blue plaid shirt with a touch of red, and darkly spattered yellow rubber boots. She happened to come from the nearest piggery as I was leading Zazy from the barn. Our eyes met and a smile lit up her broad face, framed in a babushka. She took my hand and led me into the pig barn and showed me her achievement, a huge pregnant sow in her care. It was a wondrous animal, and she knew without words that I was truly impressed. She glowed as I scratched the old sow's back. Somehow the animal was bringing us past pain and fear into fellowship.

The wetlands were alive with nesting waterfowl, red-winged blackbirds, and frogs, all calling and singing. Swamps boiled out clouds of mosquitoes hungry for blood, daggers at the ready. These were the hosts we were supposed to be avoiding! Where was that salesman now? I pushed back my misgivings, thinking of the wonderful people I had met because I came this way.

We went to higher ground for Zazy to graze and air her back. Deer flies promptly attacked from the shrubbery, lancing our skin to draw their blood meal. Soon a horde of mosquitoes arrived from the swamp. I blanketed Zazy to give her a few more minutes to graze, made a diary entry and checked two birds, then we returned to the road.

— —

Past Gamebridge we stopped at a farm marked: Dan and Bev, Custom Farming. I called at the door of a small barn. Dan came from the alley in front of the cows, and Bev came from an adjoining chicken house with eggs in her apron. We shook hands by the rubbing post of the grey cat. I asked to buy feed, and we were asked to stay.

The horse stable was idle, so Zazy was given a double draft horse stall. A big cobweb hanging above eye level across the left corner delicately announced *Vacancy*. I tied Zazy to the top plank of the manger on that side. A broody hen occupied the feed box on the other side. Dan dumped a generous forkful of hay into the manger and Zazy grabbed at it as it fell. I lifted the load from her back and hung it over the wall of the spare stall. The hen kept an eye on me through her feathery periscope from the depths of her nest.

Bev took me to the straw shed to get bedding for Zazy. I was amazed at my first sight of round bales. They were stacked in a double row to the rafters! Bev and Dan were moving into mechanized farming as fast as their capital could carry them.

While Dan and I each milked a cow, he outlined the strategy he and Bev had adopted for survival and progress. Their first priority was quality of life, for themselves and their twin babies. Dan kept just enough livestock for domestic needs. He had started a few years before with a modest amount of capital, investing in a round baler to simplify his haying and attract custom work from his neighbours. Soon he recovered his cash; he used it to buy another carefully chosen implement, then another. His custom operation conserved capital for his clients and built his business.

In the loft, he showed me a hay conditioner that would speed up the curing and hence the baling, allowing a crop to be stored in its prime. On the way to the house, we stopped to see the multi-furrow plough and discs that were usually in operation far into the night in spring.

This night, there was beef ring work to be done, and Dan managed the ring. To show me how it worked, he took me on his rounds in the pickup. We sped from farm to farm, stopping only to arrange for the slaughter of finished steers. The cattle could be processed as a group at a saving. The whole membership shared the expenses and bought their meat at straight production cost.

We must have made ten calls doing beef ring business, delivering eggs, and collecting sacks. Didn't this man ever tire? "You have to see Lake Simcoe at its best." Dan grinned his challenge. I took it.

The stars were bright and the night was moonless. Down narrow roads we slalomed toward the lake, never slowing until we levelled out on the sandy shore. The lake was black as the sky, twinkling with starlight tickled by the breeze. I could sense the artist's eye in this livewire entrepreneur in the driver's seat. We mused about things that matter to people as we passed slowly by the row of cottages that slept between forest and lake. At the headland, we turned and climbed. A pair of eyes gleamed in the beam of the headlights and a fox shape formed around them. It jumped back and vanished. Minutes later, we were home.

Two farms beside that one lake clashed in my memory, demanding to be recognized, to be stored apart from each other for the sake of peace:

> The one, a physical assault to the natural wetland, a dismal encampment of migrants kept lost in their past for the sake of material gain by an absentee owner and a few hireling managers;
>
> The other, an initiative in appropriate technology taken by two bright young people, working from a grassroots baseline, honouring today while always reaching for tomorrow, owning and developing their venture integrated with the community for the common good.

June arrived under the bluest of blue skies. Our way was crowned with elm trees, alive with orioles flashing black and orange plumage, filled with their rollicking songs. At noon we crossed the causeway at the head of the lake and found letters and food from Mom and Dad at Orillia. There the road left the lakeside lowlands and took us into wooded hills and farmed valleys.

Toward evening, herring gulls flew over and settled to search the freshly ploughed land. I felt the nearness of Georgian Bay; I could hardly wait for the next sunrise. I knocked at the door of a small grey farmhouse and asked the tall man who answered if I could buy oats and camp there. He offered a stall and feed and approved my presence on his land.

In a cedar wood, I built a tiny fire and squatted to have a pot of Joan's noodle soup. After the soup, I drank my canteen dry and snuffed out the fire with damp earth.

Birdsongs faded with the light. Fledglings fidgeted and fluttered, finding their balance in the cedars close around me, settling at last with a *chuck* of satisfaction. Across the fields and down through the branches fell the cry of a gull going to rest. A killdeer called once, and hushed woods carried only the voices of courting frogs and newts into the night.

I broke camp at dawn. Zazy heard me coming and called from the barn. I massaged her while she ate, for we had a boat to catch. I was saddling her when the farmer came to stand and watch. He seemed unreachable, encapsulated. Finally, he delivered a biblical briefing on salvation while

I finished scraping back the manure. A woman came out of the house and stood behind and to the side of her man. Two small children hid in her long, dark skirt and peeked out between the folds. A sad quartet they seemed to me, hanging back in their personal wilderness, trying their best to teach me the way to heaven.

— —

Fresh for the day, we sped to Georgian Bay and came to Victoria Harbour. I expected to see a ship, or at least a port. Instead I saw a fisherman on a small dock. I asked him where the ship docked. His eyes questioned my sanity. "Try Port McNicoll. T'saround the bay." And he returned to his reality, fishing.

We hurried to Port McNicoll. I tied up at the dock and went into the shipping office. "Good day, can I help you?" offered the clerk behind the counter.

"I would like to book a passage for my horse and me on the ship that goes to Sault Ste. Marie," I replied.

The clerk looked puzzled, then he recalled: "Oh yes, that service was run by a different line, sailing out of Victoria Harbour." He phoned the number I had been given, reached a city office, and gave me the bad news. The steamer had been retired long since. The facts fell on me like trees in a hurricane.

Time stood still; so did I. Then I breathed again and let the blame fall where it belonged, on my adviser at the Y in the road out of Ottawa. Aloud, I ranted about his insistence and bemoaned the cost of being caught in winter in the bush or on the prairies, if now we had to backtrack two hundred miles.

The clerk listened patiently while I raved, then suggested the railway as my only recourse. He telephoned the freight agent in town, briefed him, and directed me to him.

The freight agent was as caring as the shipping agent. Evidently I was miles off course, with a water barrier ahead. Together we looked at road maps, railway maps, and freight rate tables. An ugly fact emerged. The expense of a rail trip over the devious route to the Lakehead would be too great for me. My original hundred dollars was already half gone. Zazy waited by a lamppost, unaware of our plight.

There had to be another way; I wasn't turning back! The agent cheered me on. He phoned a shipping company, and a hope brightened into a plan. We could board a pleasure steamer at Owen Sound, just around the bay. There and then I booked passage for Zazy and me on the SS *Manitoulin* to Sault Ste. Marie. The fare gutted my purse, but the trip would land us at "the Soo" where I was told to expect cheap freighter service over Lake Superior to Port Arthur at the head of the lake. We would land right on Highway #1. I checked my map and set off, happily assured.

Place names teased me, tickled my memory. Of course, the connector was the CBC rado program that Mom and I useed to hear on Sunday mornings. Don Ferguson would announce: "News and views from those important parts of Ontario and Quebec that lie outside the cities." He would read from the *Wiarton Echo*, the *Lindsay Post*, the *Beaverton Chronicle*, and all the others. I felt connected.

We crossed the Penetang Peninsula, where I saw at the Martyrs' Shrine a terrible story ultimately about people alienating each other for political purposes. Near Perkinsfield, we were welcomed with gentle courtesy into a French farm family. The father had worked with his grandfather clearing and enriching this land, and the family as a whole was still a vital part of the francophone community on Penetang.

We all sat round the table, parents and four school-age children, and I, a pilgrim from Quebec looking for fellow Canadians. Everybody was talking, minds meeting, the wheel of rapport spinning, our stories emerging, touching, entwining. It was as if our roots were rubbing together and saying: "We have found each other."

The lake was a short mile from the farm, lying in the sunshine, blue to the horizon, warmed by miles of sand. I splurged an hour swimming and washing and laundering. Zazy waded out to my washing rock and amused herself by splashing me with a foreleg. I dried my clothes on the hot sand, and we started to travel along the beach, southward, so I thought.

By error, perhaps due to lack of an internal compass, I had turned north. When the sand became sparse, I began to wonder. When the sun went down in glory behind Christian Island, I knew I had gone wrong. My map said we should not be there.

An Indian man from a lodge saved me from despair. He pointed out the road to a farm that we could reach if we hurried. Certainly the people there would take us in. He showed me on my map a short road back to the place where I had strayed, and his kindly understanding restored my spirit.

Zazy went with a will. She was running on the reserve that any road-wise horse saves for getting home. She seemed to know there was a place for us ahead.

The farm was near Lafontaine and the family was of French pioneer stock like our friends at Perkinsfield. These people spoke little English, and at first they seemed shy to try. When they heard my efforts at French, we put together all our skills and shared a little about our lives, while I ate fresh bread with butter and maple syrup by candlelight. The music of their language was unfamiliar to me, coming from Mascouche, and I was surprised how that hindered my comprehension.

I told them about my drives with Baker up an avenue of hard maples in spring, when each tree had its spile and pail hung on the trunk. And how the woman of the house used to give me a glass of the fresh sap to drink as a tonic, while she and Baker stood at the wagon, selecting her cakes and buns. My hosts seemed to understand my broken French. I was happy to be with them, and I forgave myself for having turned north.

In the morning, I took a deep breath and rode straight back to Balm Beach, then to Wasaga and beyond. We waded in the shallow water and Zazy kept an eye on the wavelets lapping at her legs. We rested at noon under pines, and I had Joan's noodle soup for lunch. At sunset, the cool breeze off the lake reminded me that I had left Charlie's leather jacket on the back of the kitchen door at the Lafontaine house. The coat would nicely fit the boy I met there.

We went inland and found English Canadian farmers all the way to Owen Sound. Mrs. Thompson at Stayner took me to a greenhouse to buy tomato plants, while Mr. Thompson applied his critical horseman's eye to my tack and replaced the frayed straps on my saddlebags with snaps. He also looked ahead to the boat trip and slung a sack of hard grain across my saddle.

The Hartley Lambs of Meaford kept me from camping outdoors to protect me from a wildcat that had the cattle spooked. I took a hot bath there, shared lots of laughter, and sent home to Mom some aeroplanc cactus replicas from the leaf margin of the parent plant. Passing through Meaford, I was asked to sign the town's guest book.

Two miles from Owen Sound, a lady on a farm offered me the use of a vacant stable with a loft, downstairs for Zazy and upstairs for me. My threadbare jodhpurs and good shirt were invited to join the family wash while I walked into town and bought new running shoes, pen, notebook, and film. Finally I scouted out the dock where the SS *Manitoulin* would be tied up later that evening.

Zazy and I easily followed the road and rail line down to the dock. The big white ship was resting against the wharf, waiting to be loaded and boarded to sail at 11 PM. Seeing it actually at anchor, I felt all my uncertainties melt. Car lights could flash, trains could rattle by, forklifts could trundle crates past us, boys on bikes could weave around us and make their silly remarks, and Zazy could go ahead and dance to it all. We were on our way north.

Close to me, Zazy usually danced through her fears. Left alone, she might fight to escape them. I had trouble believing the freight agent when he came out of his office, casually tied the mare to the warehouse door, and said: "She'll be all right there. Will you step into the office with me, please?"

I hoped for the best, but I was not sure that Zazy would be all right. Strange jumbled sounds were echoing behind the door. Around her, strangers plied back and forth on the platform. In my moment of hesitation, I first noticed the tall man in the green and khaki uniform standing near us. "Don't worry," he said. "I'll stay with her."

I believed in this stranger. I left her with him, and I did not worry.

Time passed while I signed papers, and arranged for Zazy's care in the between-decks and the loading of her feed. I stepped from the office into the silence of a deserted roadway. Only the mare remained, with the stranger close by her side. He told me he was Ben; I told him I was Barb. His uniform said to me perhaps he was a Beaver Lumber employee. I did not ask.

"You'll have a long wait," he said. "They won't finish loading until around eleven, and the horse goes on last." I blanketed her against the chilling night air.

Ben's company made time pass quickly. He wanted to know about our travels, and I was happy to share a few touches of our story. He gave me the local news and told me about the lumber mill across the railway tracks that took my attention. He knew its operation from the inside, but he never mentioned himself. I wanted to know about Ben, to hear some of his story, but he kept himself as hidden as the warehouse that was now in shadows.

When Zazy could be left safely, Ben led me up the gangway and gave me a tour of the ship. That too he knew from inside, and he was free to come on board, unlike the general public. He introduced me to officers and crew as we met them, showed me the deck where I would be assigned to a cabin, and took me between-decks, where Zazy would stay.

Everything was ready for her. Her stall was secure between two metal posts and bedded with straw laid on a rubber mat. Her bag of grain lay to the side on a bale of choice hay. When we returned to her, we found that someone had pulled up the blanket and pinned it round her chest to make her snug against the draught between the buildings.

A mobile snack bar stood at the end of the roadway, with its back to the darkness and its face to a circle of yellow light. A small crowd of patrons had gathered there. To me beyond the circle, the snack bar might have been on the moon. The proprietor sent a shy young kid to draw me across the space. He delivered his message: "Joe says there's a cup of coffee for you at the bar." And he was gone like a leaf in the wind.

Ben was grinning. "Bet he did that on a dare. Go on if you like. I'll stay with Zazy."

I braved the light and the crowd and got my coffee while the kid collected his bet. I leaned on the counter, warming my hands on the hot cup, visiting with Joe. The laughter around me felt warm and friendly, like the coffee. I was glad that Joe had pulled me in from the dark.

The passengers were boarding; sailing time was near. Ben helped me to lug my tack on board and left me with the purser. I paid him, left my rifle with him, and followed the steward to my cabin. He set my things on the floor, stepped out, and closed the door.

The cabin seemed very small and hot. I sat on the lower bunk, thinking of the luxury round me, the invisible line separating passengers and officers from crew and longshoremen, and Ben free to be everywhere. I slipped out of the cabin, down the companionway, through the crowd at the gangway, and around the side of the warehouse, and let darkness enfold the little mare and me.

Zazy was cozy in her blanket, but I shivered against her in the damp air. The sky was blue-black velvet with lacy clouds holding a pastel shawl around the moon. We were alone.

"Did you get settled?" A familiar voice reached from the darkness. Ben had waited in spite of the cold. We were as old friends now.

We whiled away a half-hour, moving from the topic of beer licensing in Owen Sound, to Ben's life as truck driver, mill hand, and soldier. Too soon, a deckhand came to say that I should load the mare. I folded her blanket, handed it to Ben, and led her to the gangway.

Zazy paused, spent less than a minute to lower her head and examine the footing, then to test it with one foot. *Okay*, she said, bringing her head up to my shoulder, and we boarded side by side.

No sooner was Zazy tied in her stall than two whistles sounded and the deckhands began hauling in the gangway. Ben grabbed my hand. "Good luck and so long," and he was gone. For one moment, I needed to have said thanks. In the next, I was glad there had been no time for that. It would have trivialized a fellowship that came to stay, deep in the fabric of my life. Perhaps Ben felt as I did.

The passengers were in the dining saloon, having a midnight meal, as I went to my cabin. The ship was still in dock. Zazy was safe in the care of the crew. I felt profoundly uneasy, caught too close to conventional society for the duration of the voyage. I found solitude on the poop deck and settled on my haunches with my back against the bulwark.

Suddenly a great cloud of steam hissed up from water level. The engines began to throb, the straining rudder creaked, the propellers back-watered, and the ship floated free. People on the dock threw frantic farewells to their friends on the deck above me. I stared into the blackness that had swallowed up Ben.

— —

For three days, I rested from my daily duties and celebrated what I saw as the end of my initiation into life on the road. I had had my puppy nose rubbed repeatedly in my mistakes, and I had been picked up and cleaned off by strangers, reinstated among fallible humanity, set back on my feet, and cheered on my way.

Zazy had found her home on the road. She was now inseparably bonded to me, ready to consider any new situation, and aware of her freedom to use her natural discretion in case of danger.

On board ship, I was drawn happily into the full range of action, from the wheelhouse to the dining saloon to the engine room and to the between-decks, where there was music and fun between ports. The captain arranged for Zazy to disembark at least once daily for exercise. At each port of call she savoured the newness, and we had great rides as far as we could go before the warning whistle sounded. At Sault Ste. Marie, I said farewell to good companions and rode up the cobbled ramp to land, feeling roadworthy.

A week later, my choice of route near Ottawa came back to haunt me. I learned that the cargo steamer that plied Lake Superior was an ocean-going vessel with sealed hatches. There was no ventilation. The captain of the ss *Manitoba* could not be persuaded to take Zazy. He was sorry.

Sorry too were the Finnish people and their cow at the edge of town. The cow had been ousted from her stable to make room for Zazy, and the people had put up with me sleeping on their porch floor, and made me welcome at their table.

The helpful personnel at the tourist bureau near the ferry dock and the USA border also were sorry. So were the custodians at the racing stable, who shared in Zazy's care during our grounding in their city.

Among this cheerful company of sorrowers, a newsman from the local paper surfaced. With his help, I tried to exit through "the Soo", Michigan. I proposed to cross the two states bordering Lake Superior and exit the USA at Fort Francis, Ontario, within ten days, as the law required. I knew that Zazy and I could do this, and that our funds were adequate.

We took the ferry to the border crossing point and presented ourselves to an inspector. He checked us out and approved my plan. He was about to sign the travel document when a senior officer rose on his authority and refused us admission. First he declared that I had insufficient money. Then he asserted incorrectly that Zazy needed a US health certificate, obtainable only by my paying to bring a veterinarian three hundred miles to inspect the horse. Finally the first officer gave up, recorded my deportation, gave me a ferry pass, and put me in the care of a kindly official, who escorted me back to Canada.

Disheartened, I dragged myself beside the mare up the ramp and under the arch that said Welcome To Canada. We rested on the bank of the St. Mary's River and watched the water bombers swoop, scoop, and go, swoop, scoop and go, raining river water on some forest fires in that district. I had no idea what to do next, so I waited for whatever might come.

Our reporter friend came. He was not at a loss; he had another idea. Three days later, Zazy and I were at the terminus of the Algoma Central Railway, ready to board a boxcar coupled behind a hissing, steaming locomotive. We were heading for Hearst on Highway #1. The reporter and the railway agent had circumvented the regulations that barred a woman from riding on a freight train and from travelling overnight in a boxcar. They booked us on a day trip, and hooked us into a passenger train.

Everyone was there to see us off, complete with all our belongings, plus fish line and hooks and food for the journey ahead. The engineer blew a tiny burst on the whistle, and Zazy and I moved on a wave of good wishes toward the idling, puffing engine. Trusting in the midst of her fear, she came by my side, and without a backward glance she walked up the resounding ramp and stepped inside the darkness of the boxcar.

Steps followed in order. I tied the mare to the stall rail, swung the supporting timber into place, and secured it. The yardman wired the door tight to within a foot of closure. Zazy whinnied; I went to her and she became calm. The engine bell rang, the engineer took up the slack on the coupling with great care, and our boxcar began to move. Zazy practiced balancing and bracing as, one after another, passenger cars were coupled on behind us. Now the engineer eased the train out of the station.

Our friends in 'The Friendly City' had restored my sense of competence. The very last weather front had passed, leaving me with a wealth of friendship and adventure like magic in its wake.

PART TWO
Bedrock

1

The Canadian Shield means bedrock to Canada. Billions of years old, it floats on the molten mantle of Earth. Pressures below and around the rock have pushed magma into its body, deformed it into cliffs and valleys along faulting lines of weakness, and heaved it into mountain chains. Mile-high ice has ridden over it, grinding the mountains down to rounded nubs that stand naked in our sight, but for a threadbare mantle of pioneer plants reaching down for food and up for sunlight.

Beyond the stronghold domes of bedrock, soil and gravel and water have found their places in the ancient valleys and hollows and slits carved out by the melting ice. Plants in turn have found their niches, and animals have come to share the hospitality of the aging Shield.

For human animals, the Shield can be an evolving, living connector to the ground that we live on, telling us its stories of change and invasion and visitation from space, of colonization, and of reinvasion by rampant human tenants. Our ancient Shield has been constantly rebalancing itself since the beginning of time. It offers to carry stability into our future, if we honour its roots, our roots.

Snow angels are for winter. In summer, when the sun has warmed the rounded bedrock, lie down and surrender to the momentum of stillness. Catch a ride on a neutrino, on its way from space, through you and your rock, down to the beginning of time, and out again into space, infinitely bending, in concert with the conserving curve of the universe.

Through the gap in the freight car doorway, my nose and eyes sucked in messages new to me. Those singing wheels were carrying us away from Lake Superior and into a wilderness of rock and forest and water, the heart of the Canadian Shield. I watched pink gneiss giving place to black rock. I caught the magical taint of train smoke on the breath of the mixed forest. It told me I was moving to a new horizon. It always worked that way on this daughter of a railway man.

At the second stop, the engineer swung down and invited me to ride in the cab for a better view of the Agawa Canyon. At first I shared the fireman's seat. When the view of the canyon was too wonderful to take sitting down, the fireman held my shirttail while I leaned from his door to snap pictures. He pointed out the Prince of Wales Rock, where the train had been stopped to allow the Prince, at his request to touch the rock, the earth, the trees, the face of Canada.

Zazy welcomed me back with her joyous nickering. She was travelling well, eating hay, looking for a treat from Mom's parcel. I leaned back against the hay bale and tried to rest from the excitement. What was I missing? I was back at the crack when the engineer leaned from his window and hailed me. Like a cork, I was out and up front again.

The forest changed to softwoods: spruce, balsam, larch, jack pine, with stands of shining birch among outcrops of rock. We stopped at a mileage marker and set down boxes of provisions for uranium prospectors. Again we stopped, for two men to step off the train at no marker that I could see. Their box was lowered from the baggage car behind us, and before we pulled away, they had shouldered their loads, slid down the embankment, and vanished into the woods. Trails webbed the forest, and soon we were flashing past a pulpwood camp with its oil drums and tarpaper shacks. We slowed to pass a gang of men repairing the roadbed, and threw off a bag of mail for them at the section house.

The day was aging. The fireman showed me how he fed the coal fire and regulated the heat. The engineer showed me how to control a locomotive, though I wasn't ready to share his seat and drive. I did share his sandwiches, because, as he said, "No telling when you'll eat again."

The fireman peeled back the tarp from a cream can, knocked off the lid, tipped water into it, and deftly drank. Then, with a grin, he passed it to me. I put it to my lips, the engine lurched, and the water sailed out over my face and back in the wind to the engineer laughing behind me. I tried again and got it right.

We stopped at a siding an hour out of Hearst. It was time to return to railway protocol; I swung down the iron stairs, landed on the clinkers, and ran back to rejoin Zazy. Those men at the controls had given me a wonderful preview of the Canadian Shield up close.

Evening cast a purplish hue over the forest. We were entering muskeg habitat, where water ruled and decreed that plants should float in a mat with roots immersed, or die. At a glance, it was a lonely vastness. Looking more deeply, I saw a nursery where a mother duck led her string of ducklings in safety, where a beaver family prepared a pond, built a lodge, and swam with little beavers at twilight.

The roadbed was rough; the wheels seemed to be riding on the ties. Within the rocking boxcar, Zazy was balancing easily and nibbling at her hay. A cold draft reached at me from the open door and drove me to curl up in her blanket between the hay and the baggage. There I slept until we landed with a bump at Hearst.

Eleven o'clock was near, and the sky was lighter by far than the rail yards. The conductor looked in to tell me that the engine was going to take the passenger cars to the station and return to spot us onto a siding with a cattle chute. He unwired the door and went away. Released couplings clinked, and the engine puffed a subdued farewell.

Quickly, I packed and saddled up, eyeing the failing light. I expected the engine to return within ten minutes. With haste, we might still get clear of town and find a farm, or at least a place to make camp. A southern Ontario expectation!

We waited. Far away our engine was chugging slowly, as if in protest. Close by I saw lines and lines of tracks, then sheds and shacks bounding railway property. Beyond them the main drag was lined with wooden buildings, chief among them a well-lit hotel. People straggled along the street toward their mecca, voices splintering into the conversation of the shunting yard engines. No engine came our way.

A yardman with a bobbing flashlight arrived to investigate the lone boxcar. He was totally surprised to find us and went away to inquire. I shuddered with the cold, blanketed Zazy over her saddle, and snuggled against her.

Darkness turned to blackness, yet I hoped. Outside sounds subsided to an occasional clatter as the last segment of a freight train was pushed into place and coupled. My hopes fell as each engine went to rest. The rules had been forgotten; we had been forgotten.

Grappling with the prospect of unloading Zazy in the dark and relocating us, I began to hope that no engine would come until morning. Now every stirring locomotive became a threat. Tension added to the chill as rain began to fall. I unsaddled Zazy, reblanketed, bedded, and fed her. I would bed down with her and hope that no one found me. My innocence had been damaged on the dark road to Ottawa. I crept inside my sleeping bag, camouflaged it with hay, and dozed, shivering though wearing every garment I possessed. The abandoned leather jacket came to mind.

Suddenly, someone was coming! I could hear footsteps crunching the cinders. A light glanced along the doorframe and its strong beam explored the interior of the car. It rested a moment on my hay pile. "Hi in there!" I made no sound. Zazy's hooves rustled her bedding. The beam searched again, then the door was sliding shut. The watchman was wiring it against a block, giving us a measure of security. His footsteps on the cinders faded. I was glad he had come and I had a hunch that he knew I was there.

The clutch of night seemed to be holding forever. Dawn released me, and I unwired the door. The rain had passed and a streak of yellow was broadening across the northeastern horizon. I breathed in its promise and my weariness melted.

We were nearly on the road, but not quite. First, Zazy needed water. She had not drunk since the day before we left "the Soo". A boy on early duty did his best to fill her need, but she literally turned up her nose at his water and declined to drink. What could I do? I thanked him and washed my face and hands in the pail.

Next, we needed to find an engine. I went about looking for one, or for someone who could help me to find one. Eventually I met our conductor, who passed swiftly from bewilderment to sympathetic concern. "Have you had coffee yet?" he asked.

"I'd sooner have a locomotive just now, thanks," I said. An instant too late, I caught my echo as a twelve-year-old snip at my asinine worst, braying a lame joke. I had hurt the conductor and isolated myself. It was the twenty-year-old who had to go on without coffee, without fellowship, and without needed advice.

Guessing how long I might have to wait to be spotted to the chute, I hiked into town to report to the Lands and Forests Officer and to mail my diary. When I returned, the boxcar was missing.

Now I had to find Zazy. Was I turned around again? Did anyone see where the horse went? The men on the cinder path did not know. The men on the platform did not say. Then the conductor came along and pointed out a siding. I ran there, just in time to unload Zazy myself. And I did have a chance to say something decent to the conductor who had tried to befriend me.

Within minutes, Zazy stood tied to a fence, our tack and feed lay in a pile on the gravel, and the boxcar and engine went out of our lives. I had in my belt pouch a permit "to enter and travel about, and set out fire for the purpose of cooking and obtaining warmth in the Kapuskasing District." I also had a goal for the day, the Marathon Lumber Company's camp, thirty miles down the road.

We left the rail yard and started down the highway, still in need of water. A Finnish woman at a small farm near town filled that last and most urgent need. She greeted us from her chicken house door and gave a pail of water to Zazy. This time the mare approved; she drank her fill.

Now cheerful confidence took hold of me. We were entering the boreal forest at last and, we were travelling under our own power.

After a few carefree miles, I realized that the pack was shifting. No matter how often I reached around and hitched it up, I could feel the saddle rotating. Girth galls and saddle sores were assured if I failed to act. I rode down into a meadow, reluctantly spread our belongings on the wet ground, and rebalanced the load. Zazy spent her free time blissfully eating grass.

Now the pack felt correct. We climbed to the road, and by cantering we outran the biting flies that had followed us up from the grass. I breezed along, not noticing a small yellow car following us, until the driver came abreast and called out: "Hello! Do you know where you're going?"

"To Vancouver," I replied, as though Vancouver were the next town down the road.

We stopped and the man came out of his coupe. "Have you got lots of fly dope? Those blackflies will drive you and your pony nuts!" Hadn't I heard that before?

I showed him my spent bottle of 6-12 from Joan. He smiled and put a new bottle into my hand. "You'll need to get more when you can," he told me. "There's a hundred and sixty miles of nothing ahead, and three hundred and fifty miles to the Lakehead. I saw you saddling up in Hearst, and I got to thinking: 'Does that kid know what she's heading into?' So I came after you to make sure. Well, good luck!"

Almost before I could say a word, he was gone, disappearing with a wave into his little yellow car. I stood watching it go humming away, straight as a bee, retreating up the dusty road back to Hearst. "Thanks, Bee-Man."

2

Highway #1 cut like a giant ochre knife into the forest, straight to the vanishing point. "A hundred and sixty miles of nothing," the Bee-Man had said. I couldn't buy his prophecy; I was so glad to be here at last, with the boreal forest all around me! His very coming to warn me had drawn the teeth from his warning. I was not alone. And I had not 160 miles to Longlac on my mind, but the manageable twenty-five remaining to Marathon Camp.

We learned mile by mile how to survive in this land governed by the Canadian Shield. The first lesson came as we were cantering on perfect sand-and-gravel footing. Crossing a stretch of filled swamp, I felt the ground yield to a forefoot. With a flying change, Zazy sprang ahead, leaving the road surface dropping away from her hind footfall. Cautiously, I rode back, and looked down a deep, irregular hole punched through the hard-packed surface. Beneath it, black water undermined the road. Zazy decided there and then to travel in future a respectful distance from the shoulder.

Creek water splashing over rocks convinced me to flush out my tainted canteen and recharge it. Thereafter, I regularly drank creek water, and it never made me sick. The chance of human pollution seemed slight in so remote a place, and aeration gave me added confidence to take a small risk.

Zazy smelled out trails that led to good grazing, patches of timothy grass and clover seeded from hay brought in for logging horses. On that first day out of Hearst, we also had a supply of oats and human food, gifts from our Soo friends and Mom.

The Bee-Man had not mentioned the mosquitoes that would mob us after the blackflies went to rest. We found out! I smacked at them, rolled my sleeves down and my collar up, and applied 6-12 wherever they still found a target. As the sun headed down the sky, I watched anxiously for the camp road, hoping for shelter from the flies.

With a pilot like Zazy, I need not have worried. She would smell the camp before we got there, and after dark, her feet would feel the turnoff.

Then I began to wonder, "How does a hobo like me properly enter a lumber camp?" I was in new territory; I had yet to learn about northern hospitality.

Zazy took care of our debut, as she had done a month before in Quebec. A well-beaten trail and the smell of horses was the cue she needed. She strode right up to the front steps of the depot store where a group of men were smoking and talking in the late sunshine. Someone said: "Hi Barbara. Come on in. We read about you in the paper." So our reporter friend in "the Soo" did get his story written in time to catch the press and smooth my way again!

A one-minute conference was held on the steps. The consensus held that I was an expected guest. I was to sleep in an unused bunkhouse, and Zazy was to have a stall in the stable. A freckle-faced boy led her away, and the barn boss and I followed.

We passed between long rows of tarpaper shacks to a big log stable at the back of the camp, a very large camp, I thought. The barn boss chose a single stall and the boy led the mare into it. I removed her tack, slipped on her halter, and tied her to the ring in the manger. The boy fetched hay, and the barn boss poured a draft horse portion of oats into the feed box, setting the giants in the double stalls shifting their great feet on the planks and nickering in hope.

Zazy went first for her grain, but soon she began alternating it with hay in her natural wisdom. She pressed her head to my universal handkerchief as I wiped the dried blood from the blackfly bites inside her ears. She leaned to the caress of the comb, head high, lip upturned, eyes dreamy, while I massaged her skin, powdering the caked dust and sweat. Now I had a greyed mare to restore to shiny black with the brush.

On down her legs, I loosened out each fetlock, checking her pasterns and heels with my hand for any cakes of mud that could break the skin and cause scratches. Zazy tolerated hoof picking only to humour me. I found no stones in her feet and no sign of the thrush in her one black hoof, for which I had carried copper sulphate all the way from home. I left her long tail uncombed until morning, knowing she would soil it lying down. Finally I massaged her legs from hoof-head to elbow and hock. Then I left her.

"If you go knock at the back door of the cookery, you can probably get something to eat," the barn boss suggested. Shy to stretch my welcome, I passed the cookery, then the lake, thinking distantly of my new hook and line. Suddenly, weariness swamped me. I managed to reach the little bunkhouse and crawl into the cot made up for me.

I lay still. Consciousness seemed to be detaching itself from my body and floating above it, deciding whether to stay around or drift away. A question reached me as if from somewhere else: "But who will look after Zazy if you're not here?" Then I struggled to reconnect with my body, prayed for energy to survive, and faded out into timelessness.

A man's voice broke through my stupor. "You ate supper?" He stood silhouetted in the open door. I answered, "No," and he went away.

Was he a dream? I drifted again. He returned, roused me, and from his full arms handed me a paper bag containing two huge bologna sandwiches, cake, and biscuits. Then he set down a jug of milk and a mug on a box beside me. "There, you eat good," he said with great goodwill. "Okay, bring back jug in morning."

I ate, and sank into oblivion. During the night, I sensed vaguely that someone was closing the door. A warm red glow from the oil drum stove was playing on the walls of the shack. When I woke again, the sun was high.

Big dogs and small children were playing along my way to the cookery. A handsome woman wearing a white apron called out from the kitchen door: "Come in and get a cup of coffee." So I stepped into the nucleus of camp life. "Grab one of those cups off—oh, never mind, here's one." She filled it for me. "You can sit down on the bench over there. Would you like some bread?" She went quickly and cut several slices. "Here you are. Help yourself to ham and butter. Don't mind us."

I ate well.

The work went on, and the joshing went on, targeting a shy boy who was peeling potatoes on one side of a washtub. His teammate spiced the story, cheered on from the bread tub by a young man resting now and then with his arms deep in floury dough. Laughter rolled back and forth.

The focus changed as a slim man in a khaki shirt and slacks ambled in. He poured coffee, advised the cook to expect ten new men for dinner, relaxed briefly over his coffee, and was on his feet again.

"Meet Doug," said the cook. He obviously knew of me; we shook hands, he spoke cordially, and I thanked him simply for the welcome. Then he was away, without haste or delay.

I left the cookery, fed and grateful, and went about my business. Half an hour later, Zazy and I were outside the stable, ready for the road. Along came Doug with his camera. From some dark recess, the deadly question pounced on me: "How do I look? English manners, western saddle, improvised tack, no survival skills for the bush?" Doug bypassed all that garbage unaware and went to practical concerns. He handed me a tube of Balmer salve. "Put this on your blackfly bites. You'll need it for the next couple of weeks. I'll have oats sent along the way for Zazy. All the best!" I left with a sense of belonging.

— —

The Nagagami River in its winding canyon cut across the sameness of the forest, creating a rock garden two hundred feet high decked and hung with ferns and flowering plants. My road came to the canyon's edge, followed along the top, and angled down, seeking its way, snaking from ledge to ledge. A current of fresh air swept me out of the torrid stillness of the summer forest into the cool vitality of the river.

Halfway down, a spring in the cliff made a patch of mud on the road, and there a flock of swallowtail butterflies were feeding on fungal sugar. They fluttered up like bits of yellow paper around Zazy's hooves. At a bend, on the sheer edge of the canyon, a tiny chipmunk sat munching a captured butterfly, in counterpoint to the roaring and foaming of the dark water below. We stepped politely past the tiny lyric poet and went down, down, and over the sturdy wooden bridge where the river fretted against boulders unmoved by its force.

I rode up the far wall and left the river, but the Nagagami never left me, its flashing power surging through my memory.

In the midst of the heat, into a clear sky a dark cloud arrived riding on a cold wind, pelting our faces with rain. We dived behind alders for shelter. As we climbed back onto the highway, a band of sunlight was racing toward us. Ahead, the whole southwestern sky was quilted with clouds lit in gold, floating low over the dark spruces. Above all, light played on distant hills, luring me like train smoke.

I stopped on the bridge over the rock-bound Pitopiko River, shading my eyes to see into the forest. Beside the river, log cabins were being built. As we passed the driveway, a jolly Scottish woman came running to meet us under the rustic arch that read: Pitopiko Lodge. She and Zazy were instant friends, and I was quick to follow.

The Mathiesons drew me into the family, and into the party that was underway. It was a celebration of their reunion with an Indian couple that had saved their lives when their car broke down in a winter storm. Local forest rangers were adding a telephone line to the celebration, and their first call reserved a place for Zazy and me for the next night at Pagwa River Forestry Station. Doug and a friend stopped by later, expecting to find us there. I felt comfortingly connected. Doug assured me that the oats would catch up with us the following day. As he was leaving, a couple of fishermen joined the party. Soon after, I retired to my cabin.

The time was eleven o'clock, and I needed to sleep. Outside my window Zazy dozed, sheltered and blanketed against wind and rain. My bed invited me with its gay quilt and fluffy blankets, and I was heading for it when a tap at the door stopped me. "Mrs. Mathieson?" I guessed wrong; it was one of the fishermen who walked in and sat down.

My uninvited guest stayed for an hour, talking about fishing, travel, northern Ontario. I was interested just enough to stay awake, and thankful when his pal called him. He rose to go, wished me good luck, shook hands, and held on. "How about a goodnight kiss?" he suggested quickly. I covered my surprise with a polite refusal.

He insisted. "Just a kiss for good luck."

"I think a handshake's enough. Good night."

I guess I made my point. When his friend called again, he withdrew with a cordial, "Good night." I was glad the door locked on the inside. Was I too proper, or ignorant? Or was I wise? Mother never told me. After the persuasive guy had gone, his simple friendliness remained, and I wondered vaguely what I might be missing.

Rain during the night refreshed the dangerously dry forests and dampened the dusty road. The low hills that had beckoned me were now all about us, with their rocky ridges, leaping streams, forests watchful through the eyes of unseen creatures. Moose left tracks bigger than Zazy's hoofprints on the road. Porcupines shuffled across the highway in broad daylight, in no hurry. A young black bear stepped from the dogwoods, a stone's throw ahead of us. *Oops!* it seemed to say, and made for cover before I could photograph it. In a green meadow where three charred tree skeletons leaned together like teepee poles, brown rabbits were gambolling and feeding on bunch grass. Potash and light were producing a feast of new growth as the forest recovered from fire.

Just before noon, along came a trucker who saved Zazy from having to forage for lunch. He delivered a bag of oats and the following message:

> Barbara:
> So sorry about the oats but our truck broke down at the Nagagami River so couldn't reach you.
> Mr. Proulx said he would carry them.
>
> Good luck. Doug.

We followed a rock-bound stream until its banks bowed aside to make room for a lush meadow by the water's edge. Zazy ate oats from the nosebag and filled out her meal with grass. I saw my chance to bathe and launder. I built a little stone basin in an eddy to save the clothes from floating away, and washed to my heart's content. I hung all but briefs and bra on bushes to dry, and dined on the leftovers from "the Soo".

Hardly anyone shared our road, now that we were well into the timber. There was no local traffic except for an occasional logging truck. Homesteads and cabins were not allowed due to the high fire hazard. Perhaps one car in an hour roared past us at high speed, leaving the taint of burning rubber in the air. Loggers passed us with care. In the heat of the afternoon, Mr. Proulx came by in his truck and relieved Zazy of her burden of oats. He would take the sack ahead to Pagwa River for us.

Just at suppertime, I approached a forest ranger station for the first time in my life. The aroma of pork chops reached out to me, and as I turned into the lane, the scent of freshly cut lumber spoke up. Pagwa River Station was very new! The snow-white beehive containing the weather gauges said so. The paintless, doorless privy commanding a thinly screened view of the highway said so. And now the station was connected by phone with the next human node to the north.

Four rangers were stationed at Pagwa River, among them Andy, the acclaimed cook. Four officers from Nagagami stayed for supper, having smelled the pork chops and decided it was too late to go home and cook. Eight of us pulled chairs, benches, and nail kegs to the table as Andy's powerful frame appeared from the kitchen with a platter in one hand, a bowl in the crook of his arm, and a big granite pot in his huge fist. Bottles of beer popped up and the teapot circulated as if by a power of its own, keeping the tin bowls full. Hilarious tales of first-hand adventures also began to circulate as the beer and the good food did their work, and even reserved Andy was drawn into the jovial drift.

No one fussed over washing dishes. The men from Nagagami crowded into their pickup truck and left. George offered to take me in search of a beaver pond that he had seen up a stream northwest of the cabin. We left the others busy with the radio, moved Zazy from her grazing to the overhead shelter of the future garage, and hiked away.

George was younger than the other rangers, Romanian by culture, passionate about his chosen field of forestry. He spent his winters in study and his summers ground-proofing his learning, and he was passionately eager to share the world that was opening to him. I was there to catch the bouquet!

George read the story of Earth's genesis written in the rocks along our way. The walls of a road cut told us about the cooling period after the fiercest fires in the young planet had subsided. Then, molten silica had crystallized into granite, pink and brown and green with iron salts. A pegmatite dyke like a ladder took us up across the granite face to search out the wine-red garnets nesting among quartz crystals and flakes of black and amber mica. The late sun touched the crystals to light, these last gifts of the roiling fires, carried unformed in a burst of chemicals to crystallize within the hardening granite.

We stood in a quarry where a lake had once formed in a big granite basin, after life arose on Earth. In the tepid water, hordes of tiny animals had lived, died, and settled to the floor of the lake, adding their shells to the ooze that gradually turned into limestone. We found whole shells among the bits of rock around the crusher.

We left the road and pushed through a tangle of tag alder and dogwood to a creek. It was tumbling in full voice down the path worn in the granite by a glacier loaded with stones. The rounded stones, and the elegant seat we found in a mossy stone trough, were signatures left by the glacier in the long winter that ended the life of the lake.

George and I sat in the glacial trough, listening, until the noise of a distant waterfall reminded us of why we had come. Too late we started the climb up the creek; failing light turned us back. It was hard to leave the forest. For just a minute, or maybe five, we sat on a log and found in a single field of the magnifier another page of Earth's story, written by the moss. To George, mosses, ferns, trees, and flowers were named members of a society carrying forward the story of the biosphere. There was a quiet thrill in being immersed in something greater than ourselves.

In the final hour of that long day, we travelled by topographical map through the wilderness that stretched around us for hundreds of square miles. At midnight, I bedded down on a vacated camp cot on the screened porch. I drowsed off into this new yet strangely familiar country, with the spirit of a dogged Irish setter near me. "I got here at last, Rusty. It's just as great as we knew it would be!"

—

Zazy heard me up and washing at the stand behind the cabin. She called and began pawing for her food. I obliged; she thanked me with a muzzle-rub and eagerly took her nosebag. I had just sat down to clean her harness when a bird settled softly on a jack pine branch inches above me. It had a cocky round head and a grey and white suit with not a feather out of place. It studied me from all angles with its beady eyes, then, satisfied, it flew down to the washstand to pass remarks about the men's lathered faces. The back door opened and this scrounger was on the wing to catch the breakfast scraps that Andy threw. The visitor was whiskey jack, the merrymaker who brightens every bush camp.

Zazy and I were ready to leave. George handed me an envelope that I was not to open until I was an hour's ride down the road. We all took pictures of each other by the beehive, and Andy climaxed the event by mounting the little mare and brandishing the .22.

Leaving Pagwa River Station, we were passing out of Cochrane District. The envelope carried the following message:

> From the officers of the Cochrane District.
> To whom it may concern,

We the undersigned wish you to understand that Barbara Bradbury is a swell girl. We have given her assistance in every way we could and if you would do the same it would prove to help her considerably. We remain.

Yours sincerely,

T. Price
G.M. Banks
Andy Gagnon
J. W. L. Johnson
Robert H. Hunter
George Barna

Heat waves rose from the yellow sand under Zazy's hooves in the still afternoon air. Belts of glassy water shimmered on the road in the distance, mirages always backing away from us. The black spruces hung their motionless branches as if mourning for the animals and birds whose sounds had ceased. Only the hordes of blackflies hummed in their endless search for the blood meals that conferred fertility. Their needle-sharp probosces drove us despite the heat, heat that was halting even motorists.

The stillness was ominous. Grey haze hung at the horizon, and from it towered a white thunderhead. Thunder rolled from its feet, shocking Earth. Into the stillness, compressed air fled up the road toward us, herding sand devils ahead of it. It whipped through the drooping shrubs and carried the jack pine boughs into a wild hairy dance. It came, raved its lines, and left the stage deserted.

The sky waited; the forest waited. We two specks as one waited for the next move of the thunderhead. Again wind hit, lashing the treetops, driving a green sheet of water as broad as land and sky over us, drenching the forest from the loftiest spruce to the lowliest herb. Lightning streaked the grey air, and instantly thunder crashed, over and over, until the force was spent and the storm left dazed Earth to lift its head and see its own shining face.

We travelled refreshed. The thirsty road drank up the puddles that the air did not lift off. Stillness returned, heat returned, as if the storm had never been. We wearied with the hours and wanted drink and rest. There was no break in the roadside bush, no access to a campsite. Zazy had eaten the last of the grain at noon; she would need good grazing before nightfall.

Andy had told me to go to his friends' camp at Klotz Lake, and I had been watching for the way in. An unused truck road led us instead to an obsolete gravel pit with a pool in the bottom. We could drink! We could swim until the sweat, the dirt, and the fly bite poison had been washed from us! The sandy beach might spare us the company of the insects, and the cliff hung with roots and vines would hide us while we slept. This might be the best place to stay.

We crossed the beach. As Zazy's muzzle touched the water, a continuous black line receded a foot below the surface. Leeches by the thousands had claimed the lake for their own!

We drank, and I bathed cautiously in the water vacated by the leeches. I took Zazy to graze, but the blackflies mobbed us, crawling into our eyes and ears long before she had eaten her fill. Maybe Andy's idea would be a better choice after all. I thought we were within an hour of the lake. Uncertainties held me back: my lack of means to pay if asked, the riding time to the lake, no alternative if there was no lake before nightfall. Zazy was an invisible target for a fast car on a dark night.

The blackfly attacks abated. Hopefully, I tidied the camp, heeded distant storm warnings, and created a dry cavern under a projecting rock to shelter the kit. Then I noticed Zazy's tail going back into action where she stood tethered, wiped, and blanketed. I heard humming and felt a fiery dart hit my neck. Mosquitoes were closing in by the thousands for a feast.

I could do no more for Zazy. I fled into the smothering heat of my sleeping bag. Sweat carried away the repellent. I hid my head and probosces were driven through the cloth. I wished for daylight to free us to move out.

We were trapped in a huge weather wheel. The western sky was glowering purple shot with dazzling lightning. Crash followed crash, rain pelted. I tented my bed and lay in the deluge, blissfully unbitten. The electrical centre of the storm passed away to the northeast, the rain fell gently, and Zazy and I slept for half an hour. Then the rain passed and the mosquitoes were back.

The next turn of the wheel stopped the storm right over our campsite. I hurried Zazy to the shelter of the cliff lest she be struck by lightning, and there we huddled against the friendly earthen wall while the quarry echoed and glowed in the chaos. The sky teemed water over our world. It ran in a curtain off the roots that overhung our shelter. It filled the cavern I had made for the tack and taught me to put waterproofing over, but never under, my belongings.

I broke camp at dawn in a period of calm. We walked, I shivered, and Zazy grazed her way along the roadside, carrying her bridle hung on the wet saddle. Within a mile, we passed the Klotz Lake road, and two men in a pickup told me Andy's friends wondered what had happened to me. I tried to send back an apology for standing them up.

The sun appeared and set the soaked road steaming. Why did it not chase my dragging stiffness? I defied my lethargy and hurried along; we needed grain. Toward noon, we slid down a gravel embankment into a meadow beside a stream. I laid out the wet gear to dry in the sun, left Zazy free except for a trailing neck rope, stripped and stepped into the water. Then I saw what was wrong with me. My arms and legs were swollen thick and stiff with blackfly poison. The blisters had coalesced into long watery ridges rubbed raw. As I bathed, I could feel the cool water reducing the swelling, freeing my limbs. Afterwards, I applied Doug's Balmer salve. It worked like magic, quelling the fire in the sores. Flies were few in the meadow and Zazy was content; I lay down and slept.

An hour later, I was fit to travel. The kit was dry and we were about to go, when Zazy looked up and neighed to a horse on the bridge. A rider was looking down at us. He called 'hello,' rode down the bank, and told me that he had heard we were out of feed and in some trouble. He had come to take us to Camp 41.

"I'm George." He stepped off his horse. "And this is Ranger."

"I'm Barb and this is Zazy." I cinched up and we rode onto the highway.

Zazy cantered happily beside nimble bay Ranger. We overtook Jim, mounted on big black Star and leading two gaunt greys. Together we settled into a jog that took us to the horse hospital camp of the Longlac Lumber Company.

3

Zazy pranced in anticipation as we turned into Camp 41. She knew rest lay ahead, I believe, by the intuitive power that takes a horse from necessity across desert to fulfillment. My thoughts were jumping between my learning about horse care at ten years of age in Mr. Shaw's boarding stable, to all I might learn from Jim, to veterinary school somewhere beyond the miles ahead of Zazy and me.

We swung down at the open doorway of a stable, wooden and sheathed in black tarpaper. Jim, Star, and the greys passed as one into the shadowy interior, shedding their convoy of biting flies to fall back and disperse in the sunlight. George and Ranger, Zazy and I followed Jim into the refuge.

Jim freed Star to step into his stall near the door, and led the greys into the depth of the stable. Ranger took his place next to Star, and Zazy accepted the freshly cleaned stall beyond a used one in the row. While we cared for the horses, a draft team across the alley watched and wished. Finally Jim offered to show me his cases.

Down the length of the barn ran a double line of sturdy log standing stalls, most of them vacant, a few with the hind end of a horse in view. The horses stood on plank flooring raised above the alley. The draft team had space to drag a manure sled the length of the barn, in through one doorway and out through the other. Light entered at the open doors and through skylights set into the sloping roof.

Jim's busy times were winter and early spring. Most of his current patients had gone to finish healing in the big outdoor corrals. Flesh wounds were the most common injuries, but some horses like the greys were just overworked.

"Come on, I'll show you where to sleep." Jim ended the tour.

We passed his cabin near the meat house and came to a small guest bunkhouse. He left me to explore my shack while he went to tell Alice that I had arrived. She sent back an invitation to come for steak any time.

Alice was older than me. Her sharp face was punctuated by black eyes and surrounded by curly black hair. She drew me with cautious courtesy into conversation over coffee, having assigned Jim to minding the steak. She needed to know where I came from, what brought me to Longlac, and what my future plans were, all in a capsule. Satisfied, she laid on a delicious supper, and we all three shared a bottle of wine.

We ate without much talking, but Alice and I chatted over the dishwashing. "Time to water the horses," Jim announced, and he went to saddle up.

In no time, he surprised me at the door with a bay pony, Nell, to ride. No questions asked, I received the reins, swung up, and rode briskly with Jim through the camp to a hoof-beaten trail. The horses were coming; George had opened the gate. In moments, a hundred wild range horses strung out and flashed past us. Nell sprang into a gallop after them; I sat deep and promised myself that I could stay with her.

The horses fanned out along the lakeshore and began to wade and drink. Nell plunged down the bank and waded in after them. When the water touched my stirrups, I picked up the reins. Nell promptly began to fold down like a laundry rack, and I as promptly kicked her ribs hard with my running-shoe heels. Instantly, she straightened up, pivoted with a great splash, and trotted out of the lake. We cantered up the bank to Jim and George, sitting on their horses, laughing at us.

The wild horses came drifting up in small groups, and the men rode out to control the edges of the herd. Nell and I were to follow the herd and push stragglers. "Nell knows what to do," was Jim's understatement of the evening.

Nell spotted mustangs moving out among the trees and leapt after them like a cat. At her speed, all I could do was let her pick her own way over windfalls and between spiky skinny spruce, while I focused on preserving my kneecaps and eyes. Jim said afterwards that I rode well, and I believed it because he said it and because Nell and I came through our hare-brained ride without a scratch. Did Nell and Zazy exchange thoughts, side by side in their stalls that night?

As I walked home to my bunkhouse, the lake seemed more tranquil, the air more scented, the sky more limitless than ever before. We would be at Camp 41 for another day, because Jim had said, "You might as well stay over tomorrow and rest the pony." Psalms 23 came to mind: *He makes me lie down in green pastures, he leads me to water; he revives my spirit, and for his name's sake he guides me in the right paths.*

I slept and never woke 'til I heard, "Are you okay, kid?" Heat was coming from the stove. I opened my eyes and saw Jim looking down at me with concern. He told me I had slept fourteen hours, and I wondered for a moment if I ought to have been up looking after my horse. His face relaxed and his smile wrapped around me and drew me into the day feeling well, and glad that I had slept that long, healing sleep. "Alice is cooking pancakes," Jim said. "Come on over when you're ready."

While I had been in peaceful oblivion, others in camp had been wide awake. A gaping hole in the screen wall of the meat house, an empty bacon hook, and a huge, muddy paw mark on a window pane of Jim and Alice's shack all said: *Bear!* Word reached Longlac, and before sunset a small army of opportunistic bear hunters arrived with their sons and wives. Armed men sported red shirts and high boots and came jollying each other along. Young sons tried on Dad's mask, or felt around uneasily for one of their own, or just made noise. Women drifted into Alice's hospitality; I stayed outdoors to see what would happen.

Twilight deepened; furtive figures percolated between buildings, flattened on roofs, crouched at corners, straightened against trees. Jim and George and I convened to sit in George's shack, far from the meat house.

By the light of a Coleman gas lamp, George was braiding a sennit to make into a pair of reins. Jim was idling with a strip of leather, a jackknife, and George's good nature. "You know, a piece of this would do just dandy for Star's broken halter." George's Swedish brow straightened at the threat. Jim tried the edge of the knife on the hair of his arm. "Jim, if you cut my strap, I'll cut your ears off!"

"Wonder how the hunt's going. Haven't heard any . . . "Whew! Keep your head down!"

We slid as one to the floor. The rifle spoke again, and silence returned to preside over the tension outside. A mosquito hummed in George's ear. "Damn musketeer!" *Swat!* Jim reached up cautiously and brought the lamp down to join us below window level.

George folded himself onto a very low stool and applied himself to his braiding. Another musketeer found the hole in the screen. George looked up with hand poised to swat, and Jim chose the moment to give the coveted strap another measuring look.

"Jim, if you walue your ears . . . !" Jim chuckled.

George broke into story. He told hilarious tales about driving a mule cart from homestead to homestead, dealing in scrap iron and bones, pigs, spinning wheels, whatever would sell. Jim wandered back through his years as a rancher. Both men had left the prairies for the bush to make a better living. Finally, they had landed on their feet, here at Camp 41, working with horses.

Talk turned with polite reserve to Zazy and to my tack. As westerners the men looked sceptically at my mare's independence. A horse properly broke is subservient at all times to man. Zazy shared the miles with me as a friend, and being free to differ, she was also free to choose wisely. My tack, however, needed constructive criticism.

Lately, after a long day I had noticed small welts under the girth rings and cinches, and tenderness behind her withers, though there was no lump in the pad to account for it. And there were painful pimples on her loins under the dunnage bag. I learned that my narrow cinches were pinching up galls, and that the saddle would always be troublesome because it was skirtless and single rigged, concentrating the load on too small an area of the horse's back. George suggested that a wool blanket folded long would reach behind the saddle and prevent further scalding.

Jim stepped out to say goodnight to the hunters. George and I put coffee to brew on the kerosene stove and loaded a plate with sandwiches. Jim returned.

"Any sign of the bear?"

"Course not! It would take a pretty loco bear to blunder into a bunch of guns like that. Anyway, a bear will rarely come two nights in a row."

The horsemen set to work the following day to refit Zazy and me for the next leg of our journey. They transformed my outfit. The guarded piece of latigo leather now cinched my saddle. Stuffing in the pad was dimpled over the danger spot on Zazy's back. George refolded my blanket and packed the dunnage bag so that it would ride snugly against the cantle. Into the end of the bag he stuffed a jacket and food. I parted painlessly with my water canteen, which, as George said, was of no use to Zazy and therefore of little use to carry. Jim took the clank out of Zazy's footfalls by resetting her front shoes and replacing the hinds with a pair that he had on hand.

Zazy was standing in her stall, tacked up and ready for the road. Jim was leaning against the corner post, looking at me the way he had looked on the morning after I slept so long. "What will you do if you don't find that letter at Nipigon, the one you were telling us about, your letter of acceptance into vet school this fall?"

"I'll go on riding, I guess."

"Where do you suppose you'll get to by winter?"

"Maybe to the coast. I'll have to hurry. I'm guessing a letter will catch up with me and I'll be accepted, and I don't want to miss registration, and I do want to leave the mare with my Quebec friends at Lytton."

"You're a month's ride from Saskatchewan, and it's June now. You'll never cross the dust bowl in July." He spoke like a prophet. He had seen my route on the map.

"Maybe if there's no letter, I'll stay in the bush for a while. I'm happy here."

"I'll need help with the horses once the camps get going after fire season. You can come back here and work for the winter if your plans don't pan out."

"I'll let you know from Nipigon."

So I left Camp 41 with my agenda for the fall of '49 open as the mouth of a feeding cod, while my imagination was spinning to the tune of undreamed options.

— —

I had set out from Hearst in the simple belief that we would survive and reach our goal. A human chain had formed that ensured our well-being to Longlac. At Camp 41 the chain ended. I had no personal connections ahead, and now I knew how people needed each other up here in the bush. I sized up my assets: food for several days, jacket, pack balanced well on my reconditioned saddle, horse shod. Just then I felt the pack slumping. I looked round and saw the cord at the mouth of the dunnage bag dangling. My food was gone! George's gifts were scattered somewhere along ten miles of roadside. My heart sank.

In vain I retraced the last mile or two. I had to deal promptly with the loss. How did it happen? Did I tie the knot, or did George tie it because I asked him to show me his knot? I couldn't remember. Should

I backtrack? How far? There were no mileposts. If I failed to find the goods, I would be wasting time, and if I got all the way back to camp without them, I would be embarrassed, and so would my friends. In the end, I accepted both errors and losses, and went forward toward Nipigon and the Lakehead.

— —

The bridge over the Kenogami River at Longlac showed me the tip of a very long lake. My map showed me a series of these trench-like narrow lakes, all parallel and chained together by rivers draining a huge basin into Lake Superior. Below us a brown carpet of pulpwood seethed gently within the confines of its boom.

The name Kenogami was all that remained of the Native habitation. A row of white houses led my eye around the peninsula to a white church at the tip. Times had changed.

The road tended southwest into stark desolation. The forest had retired almost from view, and tripods set between denuded rocks did their shaky best to support a single telephone wire. Fire had destroyed mile after mile of second-growth, leaving a thin layer of soil rich in potash. Now shrubs and grasses were beginning to lay a green cushion over the earth. All around us, charred tree skeletons stuck out of the mantle like giant black pins. A sharp-tailed grouse fluttered from cover almost under Zazy's hooves, dragging one wing over the gravel in her decoy dance to protect her hidden brood. Her courage moved me; she dared to come so close!

In the heat of the afternoon, we paced out a road with no reference points. A passing motorist said he thought there was a lumber camp near a fork just six miles ahead. That gave me incentive to count the quarterhours. Zazy plodded sleepily and I lost all sense of time and distance.

A whinny sharpened me to the present moment, and Zazy answered the call. A gaunt black horse stood watching us from a ridge of rock. We stood still; it stepped down with painful care and came slowly toward us. Its thin body and sunken eyes matched the mood of the exploited forest behind it. Briefly it trailed us, seeming to be fearful to come closer. Finally it wandered into the bush.

Late in the afternoon, a smokestack appeared at the horizon. Just then a canvas-covered Jeep came up beside us and a field man from the Forest Insect Laboratory at Sault Ste. Marie introduced himself. The real world came back into focus.

The forestry student was doing a budworm survey related to fire prevention as well as timber preservation. I told him how I had toured the laboratory while I was a guest at "the Soo", seeing the wonders of the vivarium, including pupae hanging from threads as fine as spiders' silk. He, in turn, told me what he found and used in the field to estimate the pest population. So he touched the boring miles with the brightness of a completed story.

After the budworm man left us, the smokestack seemed not so far away. In fact, he had told me that it marked the power plant of the Bankfield Mine, located at the junction of the road to Geraldton, only six miles away. Six miles? Where had we been for the last two hours?

On this tiresome day, I worried about the wear of the road on Zazy's feet. The highway was being built from local materials. East of Longlac, the hard-packed glacial sand and gravel were good for us, but now in this rocky mining area, crushed rock made a rough, shifting surface that abraded her soles and tired her legs. I wanted to get her onto turf.

Hours seemed to pass after the Jeep disappeared into the distance, yet the mine chimney backed away from us. Finally it stood with its ramshackle court of tin-roofed sheds and shafts around its feet, watching us depart westward. There had to be a blacksmith somewhere ahead of us. Where was the camp that the motorist mentioned? I never saw more of a camp than a track that led to a few old buildings. After the last thirty miles, they looked good enough for us. Zazy went for the grass.

I was sitting in the smoke of my bug fire, eating cheese, when the budworm man tracked me down. He pitched a screened tent for me, and told me simply to leave it in the morning for him to pick up. He would have pitched another tent for Zazy, but she declined to approach mine, so she had to sleep with the bugs.

The budworm man also brought a fly bar for me to keep. He showed me how to peg it out at the corners, tying the tapes to low branches or sticks to create a rectangular cell screened against insects. The challenge was to get in under the netting without admitting winged company. In case of rain, we found that my army groundsheet would cover the roof perfectly. I watched in grateful wonder as the Jeep bumped its way over the track back to the road to Geraldton.

I slept in peace inside the tent, and as the night air cooled, Zazy came to sleep at the flap, trailing her neck rope. At first light, I rolled my bed including the fly bar, packed and tacked up, pressed my hand into the cold ashes of my campfire, and rode onto the highway.

Geraldton was behind us and Nipigon seemed to be not far away. Across my map, a very long road wandered back toward Ottawa and Montreal, teasing me into thinking that we were almost halfway to Vancouver. To my sorrow, I learned otherwise from a road crew. One jovial sceptic among them announced: "You've twenty-eight hundred miles to go after Nipigon."

A shock wave hit my morale. The distance between Montreal and Vancouver had been casually cited as three thousand miles, and my route on the map had measured closer to thirty-five hundred. Now after all the frustrations and flies and expenses, we seemed to have barely started out. I tried to brace myself for the mileage post I was told to expect, at Nipigon crossroads. Suddenly I needed to hurry to the crossroads.

Zazy was not about to hurry. She did not complain about her aging shoes, but she was listless, increasingly so with every day that passed without grain on her menu. Running from flies had tired her; she lacked the energy even to graze. She needed shelter and feed urgently. Lumber camps were our only hope, and all we were finding were abandoned camps and sawmills. At the end of another tedious day, we tried our luck again.

Half a mile in, our trail opened on a hushed camp. We would trespass in the stable. Zazy was heading that way when a pickup truck came in to view around the corner of a long, windowed building. Camp 63 was not quite abandoned; there was food, shelter, and welcome for us both.

Three people remained in the camp: two Finnish cooks who were delighted to have a visitor to feed, and a Canadian foreman who was spoiling for someone to share his fascination for the history and dynamics of the north woods. Zazy was given first consideration: shelter from flies and good hay. I received all the care of an invited guest, and Camp 63 became an oasis in a time of fatigue, as Camp 41 had been after blackfly attack.

In the dining room, the foreman and I settled on benches across the table from each other, with my map between us on the red-check oilcloth.

I showed him how I had come, and he expanded my line drawn across Canada Section II into a picture story. Taking things I had seen, like the horses hauling logs in the water at Thessalon, where the ss *Manitoulin* passed, the Marathon base camp west of Hearst, the Nagagami River, Longlac with the booms on the water, he wove them all into the story. We saw those long, parallel chains of lakes as highways upstream for the canoes of the voyageurs, hunters, and trappers, highways downstream for furs and now for the logs coming out of the bush to be floated to the big mills at Nipigon and Schreiber and the Lakehead.

I came to understand how the surplus pulpwood accumulating on the lakes meant market glut, hence closed camps and unemployed men. Also, the season created a job cycle. Fire season closed camps every summer. Winter brought new contracts and the log piles grew again beside the forest trails. Toward spring, the piles were hauled to the riverbank on sleds like I had seen near the stable, to wait for break up. The wooden water tank, parked now, would come into use for making skid ways for the final plunge of the logs into the open river. Then they were in the hands of the waterways carrying them to the mills.

The foreman produced a regional map, sketched the waterways I would cross, folded it, and passed it across to me. I would see the system for myself in the days ahead. I folded my new treasure with Canada II into my belt pouch.

Just then the kitchen door swung open, sending a billow of aromas ahead of the smiling Finlanders. They had prepared a sumptuous meal, which they served to the foreman and me with joyful grace, course by course, declining our urging that they sit and eat with us. Rich soup, root vegetables, roasted potatoes with pork and rice were glorified by Finnish delicacies: warm rye bread on a cutting board, green onions grown in the little garden plot beside the cookery, delicate nutty short breads, coffee cleared with egg.

Afterwards, I was offered the luxury of a Finnish steam bath. In my ignorance of its value and of the gift the cooks were offering me, I declined. I did accept the foreman's offer of a boat to use on Blue Lake, just below the stable. Then the foreman went home.

I went down to the lake, untied the little rowboat, and pushed off with one of the homemade oars. Rowing grated on the silence, so I changed the oars for a paddle. Now the boat glided quietly through the narrow neck of a small bay, with a wake of whirligig beetles sculling along.

I put up the paddle, listened into the silence, looked into the stillness. A lone frog twanged his guitar. A thrush played his flute in the woods. Water striders skated between lily pad rafts, and under the water, leeches ploughed winding trails through the greening carpet of algae. The boat glided, baby perch scudded out of its shadow, and pike froze on the mud bottom. Above me in the sunshine, dragonflies hunted like little biplanes doing aerobatics.

Around the bay, behind the fringe of shrubs and alders, the cedars, larches, and spruce stood in a motionless rank, their tips touched with sunset gold. Only a silvery willow standing in the water moved gently, as if in touch with a private breeze. Beside me an aquatic spider was linking five reeds with woven silk. Peace was here.

— —

We left Camp 63 in high spirits, with a whisky bottle protruding from the pack. The foreman had filled it with fly repellent when he came to say goodbye. He anticipated our need, for on that day the number of 'tabanids' attacking the mare tripled by noon. Both horsefly and deer fly populations were moving toward their peak, and we had to learn to live with those hunters if we were to continue daytime travel. We were their prey!

I knew the small tabanids as deer flies. They depended on mobbing us close to vegetation, landing on skin or hide and chewing through to blood. We could avoid the main force of the attack by staying well out in the road and moving smartly along. This tactic, added to the magic of the foreman's repellent, made some of them stop short of the target. If a deer fly did settle, it clung firmly, giving Zazy time to show me where to swat.

Horseflies, the large tabanids, were individualists, less numerous than deer flies but more menacing. They were twice the size, lightning-fast hunters skilled at dodging a sweeping tail or a flying hoof or a swatting hand, indifferent to fly dope, determined to feed on us if they had to chase us half a mile at the gallop. Horses feared them so much that the loggers refused to work horses on sunny days at the height of horsefly season. Zazy would gallop like a crazy horse until she could dive off the road into the shelter of shrubs. We learned to seek deep shade for rest, and at the worst times we hid by day and travelled by night.

Past Beardmore, we climbed an overgrown skidding trail onto a ridge above the Blackwater River boat landing. I chose a campsite in cover of the woods. Shouts of men at work and children at play in the extended daylight, groans of toiling trucks, and the hollow clang of metal barrels being walked on concrete resonated through the trees. I relied on our quietness to preserve our privacy.

I did my best to keep Zazy quiet. I fly-doped her and blanketed her against the mosquitoes, abroad with pre-storm vengeance. Lest she stray and draw attention, I tied her neck rope to a log to limit her foraging. Then I blew the whole plan with a mindless act.

I set up the fly bar over my mummy bag, roofed it with the groundsheet, and crawled inside. Zazy did not see me go, nor could she recognize my new style of sleeping place. I saw her looking for me. I called, adding to her confusion a voice that came from nowhere. Up went her head in an answering whinny. Before I could free myself to step into view, away she ran to find me, dragging the log, burning a hind fetlock with the rope, and whinnying at the top of her lungs. Finally I reached her, freed her leg from the rope, and received her subdued nickering and nudging as a request not to vanish into a mere voice again. Her rope burn was not apparent in the darkness. I salved it in the morning.

We returned to my nest together and before her eyes I crawled inside, holding out a piece of bread to keep her attention as I went. She received the treat and settled to sleep near me, with her rope trailing. Despite our noise, no one disturbed our camp. Rain fell, and I slept dry while Zazy welcomed a bath in the warm showers.

—

We entered a fresh new day in the first pale light of morning. There was grass for Zazy along the road, and one package of noodle soup for me reserved in the pack. The flies were asleep, and the dust of yesterday had been washed clean away from our world. Through a gateway of ancient shale topped by gleaming birches, I looked down hundreds of feet into a valley still in shadow. Conifers on its far wall were catching the glow of sunrise. And beyond them, miles of forest blended its blue-green with the mauve of passing night. This land had to be what we Girl Guides were singing about, by our campfires in Quebec. I had come to the *land of the silver birch*, the *hills of the north*, and I had moved from imagination into reality.

The foreman's map showed me where I was. At Orient Bay the Blackwater touched the southern tip of Lake Nipigon. Log booms lay on the water, waiting for a tug to tow them into the next link of the chain. I studied the map. Nipigon looked close, and Friday was still young. Surely we could reach town by Saturday morning, in time to buy oats and find a blacksmith who would shoe Zazy. Again, I was misjudging the challenge of distance.

The unmarked continuum of highway wore on me. The aging afternoon unsettled me. Zazy was in her fourth day without oats, and the endurance of her feet in those outworn shoes was a matter of time. Toward evening, two men in a truck stopped to ask if we were all right. Our conversation ended my suspense about distance and exploded my plans.

We were yet sixteen miles from Nipigon. There I might find feed of some sort, but no blacksmith. Only with luck would I find one in Port Arthur. I bemoaned the prospect of riding an unshod horse over the next eighty miles to the Lakehead, and the hopeless idea of riding her another four hundred miles to the prairie. The men were sympathetic. They thought together, then they remembered. "There's a fellow we used to work for who keeps a couple of horses in Nipigon. He might be able to help you. You go into town and ask anyone for Jim Martin." They mentioned something about an abandoned camp as they drove away.

The truck was barely out of sight when a drenching cloudburst hit us walking abreast up a clay and gravel hill. Within moments water was pouring in muddy rivulets down the road, into the holes in the sides of my Owen Sound running shoes and out at the heels. Soon the sun shone again, steaming us dry. The sky dumped on us several more times before we came to a side road marked Mileage 56. We turned down the steep, winding hill.

Mileage 56, old, run-down, vacated, earned our lasting affection. On that day late in June, we crossed its corduroy bridge, wet and tired and hungry. The darkness of its log stable hid Zazy from the flies, and the wide stalls gave her space to stand clear of the drips when the rain found holes in the rotting roof. The hay barn, tottering on bales left when the camp was closed, yielded a few edible flakes. I found oat chop in the bottom of a barrel to round out Zazy's supper and feed her in the morning.

Beside Zazy's stall, I found a dry piece of floor where I would lay out my bed on a mattress of hay. Then I went down to the creek, pot and matches and the last packet of noodle soup in hand. I lit a tiny fire and set the soup to boil. There I feasted on my first meal that day and my last in the foreseeable future. I thanked Joan in my heart as I caught up the final noodle and dumped wash water from the pot onto the fire. I buried its ashes in the sand. The creek water bathed me and carried away the cares of the past day and the uncertainties of the next one, along with my aches, itches, and grime. The last rays of the sun dried my skin and whispered, "Goodnight."

Overnight, the wet spare clothing and my bedroll dried in the process of being slept in. I repacked the whole kit at leisure in the sunshine and found two tins of sardines. I ate them both and washed them down when I took Zazy to the creek.

Ahead of the heat of the day, we had wild company: a deer, red and ethereal in a misty creek bed, cottontails feeding at our feet, confident in the care of sentinels, who raised brown ears above the grass and stared at us phenomenal beings. A porcupine grumped, raised its quills, and took the right-of-way.

Lakes named at side roads along the highway echoed a company of people who also walked this way, the pathfinders, surveyors, and engineers who built the road and named the lakes after their women: Helen, Jean, Barbara, Jessie, Polly, Roslyn. We came out of the forest onto the rocky shore of Helen Lake. Inshore, boomed logs waited. Far out on the water, the tugs were at work, mighty midgets towing vast, obedient wedges of pale brown sticks.

Our way lay between the lake and its towering walls. The sun climbed and glanced off the water onto the faces of the rocks. We were melting in an oven and blinded by the glittering glare. Spring water cheered us, and Zazy added comic relief by tilting her head as if to size up the height of the rock.

Near the end of the lake, the land stepped down gently to the shore. A simple, wooden mission church stood above the grassy banks. Musical rhythms flickered among the trees on ledges behind the church, touching into melodies as transient as a breeze. Brown cottage walls appeared through the trees, and dark singers were moving, half screened by leaves.

A mission? A Negro mission, I thought the sign read. Had I really heard singing from the terraces? The singing was gone. The lake was gone. We paced along the sand road, and the trees looked on. Hot, grimy, spent, I tied up my hair in a kerchief to cool my neck. The image of a bridge, a town, and a man named Jim Martin who would rescue Zazy filled my mind.

A crossroad cut off our path. A signpost with three pointers brought me to my senses. To the north, where we stood in our tracks, one white finger told us in black letters and numbers: Montreal 1208 miles. I read Schreiber on the pointer to the east. That was the terminus of the new highway that would connect Sault Ste. Marie with Nipigon and Highway #1. I rode round to read the final truth. The pointer said Vancouver 2800 miles.

No doubt remained. Now I had to straighten up and take the road to the west. We stepped onto the steel bridge over the chasm where water from Helen Lake leapt into the vastness of Lake Superior. I had a bird's-eye-view of our long road ahead, but below I saw the steaming mills along the lakeshore, and the town of Nipigon, and the cottages just off the end of the bridge. "Come on, Zazy; let's go find Jim Martin!"

Two reporters for the *Toronto Star* caught us on film as we stepped off the bridge. I thought how outworn we must have looked, and I scarcely had the energy to provide a story to improve on the picture. I wished them well.

4

"Look for a tall, lean guy down around the landing," a man on the street directed me. "That'll be Jim Martin."

Jim saw us coming and he came to meet us. He asked me simply what we needed. I told him, horseshoes and oats.

Jim took us along the riverbank and up to a grassy common on the flats. He put Zazy in the little stable that his team had occupied and pulled off the remains of her back shoes. We left her shut in the fly-free comfort of the stable, and Jim locked the door to protect our tack. With a touch of sadness, he mentioned the unpredictable characters that lived in the grounded houseboats and shacks between the common and the shore.

Taking my haversacks, Jim led off with a long easy stride up a dirt road, while I hop-skipped to keep up. We crossed a wooden railway bridge, turned up a narrow street, and came within minutes to a white cottage. Jim's wife, Irene, was ready there to welcome us.

Irene smiled up at Jim and he smiled down at her. I suppose he told her my name, but what I remember was the spider-silk connection spun by the smiles that passed between the two. That delicate strand wrapped itself around me too, drawing me to their dinner table as a friend. Beaver, their lanky black-and-tan dog, asked politely for an identifying sniff and welcomed me into his household.

After dinner, Jim and I went uptown carrying the spent horseshoes. Jim knew a welder who had been a farrier. We found him leaning against the open doorway of the shop beside his cottage, enjoying a cigarette in the afternoon sunshine. His eye fell on the remnants of Zazy's rubber shoes.

"Hullo Bernie. This is Barbara and she needs shoes for her horse. Do you think you could do anything with these?" Jim handed over the iron cores.

Bernie studied them. He looked from them to Jim. "Not much left to work with. I might be able to weld a piece on the heels. Closed for the weekend, though. Can't touch 'em 'til Monday." And Bernie butted out and closed the shop. Jim carried the precious bits of iron home.

Irene and Jim Martin, who befriended us at Nipigon in July 1949, and again at their logging camp near Orient Bay in 1950. (Photo was taken in the winter of 1948.)

I went to the post office and found that my mail had inexplicably been forwarded to Fort William. It would take several days to be returned. Lest I impose on the Martins, I decided to camp outside the town and explore the area. My news about the delay did not phase the Martins; they promptly installed me in the 'bunkie' in their backyard.

The Martins usually lived in their camp near Orient Bay. They were staying in town while waiting out a storm that had blown down the sails of their family enterprise. Jim managed his own lumber company, and Irene cooked. Together they had seen days of prosperity when demands for mine timbers, railway ties, and pulpwood were strong and logging contracts were forthcoming. There followed days when Irene's illness held them hostage in town while opportunities passed them by. Now, drought in southern Ontario and Quebec had cut the crop of fruits and vegetables, hitting the demand for paper packing boxes, and the blow rebounded onto the pulp market. I had seen this chain of events in terms of logs on the water, pulpwood in waiting. The Martins made it real in human terms.

The Martins' last contract had been filled at Mileage 56, and it was their horse feed that I used. They dismissed my apology and assured me that trespassing was quite honourable in this country of practical politeness.

Jim and Irene shared their home with Jack, a sixteen-year-old foster son, and their friend Max, who had worked as a mechanic for Jim. Max was trying to avoid the clutches of alcoholism. Life for an addict was easier in camp than in town, but when forestry was shut down, the stability of Irene and Jim and their cottage was a lifesaver, for Max and others.

Living with the Martins meant sharing with neighbours, exciting for me even as an observer. Everyone in the neighbourhood was glad to have Irene and Jim home. Children set up their mock battlefield in the Martins' backyard. When ammunition ran low, the door would fly open and yells of, "Hey Irene, I need summore water!" would cut the air. Frantic warriors would rush to the sink to reload their pistols.

A serious water fight took place on Sunday evening. Just before sunset, the fire alarm sounded. Jim rushed out to join other men following the clanging red engine. The volunteers fought and defeated a fire in a row of homes.

Monday was election day and nothing else! Bernie certainly would not be making horseshoes today. People swarmed around the streets and settled on the Martins' back porch and stairs, lawn and picnic table, bringing their drinks and food with them. Friends leaked into the kitchen, where Irene was busily feeding into the hospitality. Jim was in and out. There were lots of political arguments, and now and then a bit of shoving, but the partying crowd, in their respect for Jim and Irene, never got rowdy.

Excitement grew as the election results began to come over the radio. By the time the winner was obvious, darkness brought on the fireworks. After the last rocket had blasted off, the children began to thin out. Eventually, when enough beer and bullshit had been passed around, Irene shut down the party and the household went to bed.

On Tuesday Jim took the irons back to Bernie. I walked up the main street, past men drunk and adrift, past the Hudson's Bay Store, to the post office. My mail was there, including letters and a care package from home, and the long-awaited verdict from the veterinary college.

Eagerly, I opened the official envelope. My application had been accepted for that very year, and the term would begin on September 26. A dilemma loomed. How could I ride 2800 miles in three months? I went out along the railway tracks to think and pray.

Time, distance, and our state of disrepair conspired against the 1949 entrance date. I could only guess the distance to the nearest saddler and

Zazy at Red Rock, ON, after a rigorous month in the boreal forest. Galls are her main problem under saddle and girth. 5 July 1949.

farrier, and if I found them, I had no money to pay them. Gradually, the next step became clear to me. I would write immediately to the registrar, asking for deferment of my entrance until 1950, and telling him of the job at the horse hospital that would give me money as well as experience. I would write to Jim as I had promised, accepting his offer of a job. Then I would ride on to Port Arthur, allowing time for replies to arrive there. If both were negative, I would be already on my way to the coast. I mailed the letters that day, return address: General Delivery, Port Arthur.

By Wednesday I had itchy feet. Irene lent me sturdy scissors to roach Zazy's mane as Charlie used to do, leaving a neat two-inch feather standing along her crest. I sprayed her for flies and treated the rope burn that began at Beardmore and was reopened at Nipigon by her tether. In the afternoon, Jim picked up the heeled shoes and nailed them on her hind feet. I brought her to the house and saddled for the road, just before supper.

We ate quietly together, friends about to part, for how long none of us could know. Jack and Max were there, and under the table, Beaver was following the action. The Martins accepted no money, not even toward the cost of food. Jim said, "Look us up if you're ever passing this way again."

Zazy carried me up a hilly road toward the backlit escarpment. We slept through a starry night in a grove of saplings well within an overgrown trail. As the sun was lifting the vapours from Nipigon Bay and swirling them around Red Rock, we broke camp.

Access to water became a problem after Nipigon. Miles and miles of muskeg floated on inaccessible water. We left camp without a drink, and by noon we were watching in earnest for a creek with access. Little Squaw Creek volunteered its gravel beach, just big enough for Zazy to stand on. We slid down the embankment onto dubious footing that Zazy was willing to try. It was when she reached forward to drink that the gravel collapsed under her weight. She plunged into the water, carrying me beside her, swam across, and scrambled non-stop up the far bank.

We continued, drenched and thirsty, drying as we went. Ten miles later, we came to a well with a pail at the Black Bay Store. We drank, and I bought rolled oats and cookies to celebrate being alive and almost dry.

Flies were a curse on our daylight hours the whole way to the Lakehead. Two-inch horseflies and equally vicious deer flies attacked us both, driving the mare into frantic flight. Rain and night were equal blessings, and derelict farm buildings hid us in the sunny times as we found cleared land among the forested hills.

At Dorion I turned up a farm lane because the cottage with its porch full of red geraniums shouted, *Welcome!* We stayed there with a Ukrainian couple and their small son. Acre by acre, they were winning arable land from the slash, using gradual methods that saved and rebuilt the soil, where mass methods would have destroyed the fragile cover. They caught my enthusiasm about their frontier farm; they were only too glad to show me all they were doing. The mix of field crops, garden produce, and livestock gave them cash flow without the need to harvest and sell products such as straw that more profitably enriched the land. As in the family farms I had seen in southern Ontario, their industry met most of their needs, not the least of which were peace of mind and pride of accomplishment.

I did notice unthrifty calves with swollen throats in their herd. They added that they also had stillbirths. I recognized the signs, having read in the *Family Herald* veterinary column about iodine deficiency in soils of the Great Lakes Region. It was a joy to us all to know what was wrong and how to fix it by feeding supplementary iodine.

Half a day from the Lakehead, on the wrong side of Sunday to pick up mail, I took time to rest on a ridge where the breeze would fight our battle with the bugs. The view along the cutline drew my eyes to follow the high-tension wires hanging from pylons, high above the land. Suddenly Zazy contorted her body and stood fixed. I stared hard, targeted a green-eyed monster on her flank, then, cautiously—*smack*—sent another tabanid to its death. Zazy relaxed. I looked away again. Yes, there was a farm in the palm of that shallow valley below us.

Down we went. A dusty farmer met us by the house. He was about to leave for Pearl, but he stopped to welcome us. He worked the land; the house was vacant. He invited me to stay over the weekend, camp in the summer kitchen, and use the stable. He also made a significant remark about a small creek where a person might get a trout or two. Even as his truck and its attendant cloud of dust went up the lane, I was digging in the baggage for my hook and line from The Friendly City.

The complexities of outwitting a trout had never entered my head. My idea of fishing was to bait a hook with a worm, drop it into the water on the end of a line, and wait, silent and still. And since fish were shy creatures, hiding might help.

The manure pile behind the barn was full of worms. A green alder branch made a fishing pole, to which I fastened my hook and line. Ready to fish, I left Zazy to follow her heart to food, and hiked across the east hayfield and into the ravine where the creek ran.

It was a modest little creek where I met it, only a stride wide, quietly preoccupied with a deep hole in its bed. I hid behind a water maple, baited the hook, reached out the alder branch, and dropped the line into the hole. A little twitch came back along the line. I flicked it, and a pretty eight-inch speckled trout landed on the bank.

Previously, I had killed only insects. Now I was hungry for meat. I quickly killed the fish with a stick, removed the hook, and covered my catch with a dock leaf. Then I baited and fished again. Soon another trout, then a third, joined the first under the dock leaf. The next two catches were fingerlings; I returned them to the water.

Human voices broke into my hiding place. Foliage hid the speakers and muffled their words at first. Gradually, they rose in protest. I pulled out another large trout. Three people seemed to be complaining to each other, and finally I heard a masculine voice say in disgust, "Come on, let's go. There's no fish in this stream anyway!"

People went pushing through the bushes, a car engine spoke up, quiet returned to the ravine, and a thrush began its evensong. I flicked out my sixth trout, dispatched it, picked up the catch, and climbed the steep bank to the hayfield.

Over the weekend, Zazy grazed by night and hid in the low log stable by day, except when she followed me out to pick strawberries. What nature could not provide for us, the farmer brought back from Pearl. That grocery box enabled me to fry my trout in butter and have bread and vegetables with my meal. I even found canned milk to cover my strawberries and add to my tea. We relaxed in our retreat for two days and let the world speed by, in hot cars along a dusty highway, leaving the twin cities for recreation by the clear granite lakes of the Shield.

I was exploring the woods for plants and birds new to me, when I spotted an inhabited beaver pond. It was formed by a dam the beavers had built upstream from my trout hole. Cautiously I slid down the cliff, dropped my baited hook into the pond, and hid. Ripples began to spread from the flooded alder tangle on the far side. A dark swimmer came gliding in and out among the slender boles, pausing now and then to inspect a potential dam pole. Abruptly it turned out across open water, leading my eye in its wake to just discern its lodge in the dusk.

I watched until the trout began to bite. They brought me out of hiding four times in half an hour, giving me three large fish for a late supper and a small one for breakfast.

— —

Leaving the farm, I was ready for a fast trip to the Lakehead. Two hours on the road killed Zazy's interest. The flies were ever present. The hind shoes were not protecting her feet from the coarse gravel, and she began to go lame. Besides all that, she was living on grass and what grain I could give her in the form of oatmeal. Now a pressure sore began to develop under the saddle, and the combination of dust, sweat, and probably fly bites was beginning to cause girth galls. I did what I could: walked to encourage her, sponged the galls with cold water, washed the girth, and padded it with my big handkerchief, all to no effect.

Punctuation appeared in my gloomy countdown of miles to Port Arthur. The marker at the twenty-mile point also marked an alpine farm on top of a hill. I was drawn in wonderment past the white wooden house, past the domain of a friendly black dog beneath a birch tree, down the footpath toward a small brown stable. Behind it, a human voice rose from a green ravine, hooves rumbled a log bridge, and a boy and horse came climbing up the steep wagon road.

The boy invited us to the house and spoke with his mother in soft German syllables. As she led us back to the stable, a cowbell tinkled from the comforting darkness. In answer, the woman gathered an armful of grass, and we all went inside. Soon Zazy was freed of the tack and eating freshly cut grass with a gold-brown cow and calf. I slipped away to the roadside to flag down the bus to Port Arthur.

A semi-trailer truck pulled over; the driver assumed that I was hitchhiking. He grinned, and a girl leaned across him and another girl to yell through the window above the drone of the diesel engine, "Jump on behind." I jumped, the truck rolled on its way, I grabbed for an anchor hold, and there I stuck, hanging on for dear life to my seat in the centre of the spare tire. That put me between the cab and a mountain of logs swaying along on the trailer. Above the roar of the wind, I heard the screams of the girls as the young man made every curve count for a thrill. Over the bumps I could see them bouncing to the roof, laughing at themselves and at me springing around on my rubber donut seat.

We slowed at the crest of a steep hill and for one mystical moment I absorbed the splendour of the greatest of the Great Lakes, Superior. I felt the wind off the water carrying the scent of boreal forest that carpeted the miles of rolling lowland. Then we were careening down the hill. The logs behind me strained forward against their binding chains, creaking and squeaking as the engine struggled to stay the load. Landscape blurred out through streaming eyes and flying hair. The girls were trying to tie on head kerchiefs in the tearing wind. I hung onto the tire with both hands and managed to be present when the driver looked for me at the bottom of the first hill.

On we went, plummeting up and down and around curves. The bus never overtook us. My ride ended suddenly when the trucker pulled into a side road at the edge of Port Arthur, near the first stand of grain elevators. He was sorry he could not take me into town, riding on the tire.

— —

At the post office, I was surprised to come away empty-handed. I checked at Fort William with the same result. My letters from Nipigon had brought no answers; my journey to the Lakehead had affirmed nothing. I had now to decide whether to continue westward and reach for the prairie, or to try to winter in the north woods with faith in the fact that human kindness and natural resources had already brought us this far. I walked until my mind cleared.

The way ahead would be as tough as that behind us, and twice as far. Zazy would need shoes and rest before starting, and the tack would need to be upgraded. To get that work done at the Lakehead, I would have to find someone to do it, and a job to pay for it and maintain us in town. That was a big order!

Longlac would be a better prospect for all our needs. I would have to assume that the registrar liked the idea as well as I did, and that Jim's offer was genuine. I looked back over the road that had tested us both so fiercely, yet supplied us so generously. I had touched the edge of human fellowship in the north woods that invited me to stay, and a mystery in the solitude that spoke to my soul. I was not ready to leave the boreal forest. We would return into the bush. I knew that, more surely with every mile that I walked and hitchhiked back to the Germans' farm. At evening I said my thanks to the woman and boy at the gate.

Zazy must have known we were onto something good. She ignored her discomforts and took to the road like a horse going home. The insects were negligible. She covered forty miles that night, sustaining an urge within herself to keep going. We rested in familiar campsites, bathed in friendly waters. After Dorion, Wolf River called us off the road to put a comma in our flight. We stepped down into the park couched in the oxbow of the meandering river. Zazy was freed and grazing her fill on the short, hard grass. The day had barely begun, and we were alone. I wandered by the water's edge, slipping from the clutch of urgency into the release of the dark water flowing so inevitably in its course. It held me in its dark arm, secure from the immensity through which I journeyed, present only to the blessing of the water, in union with all of life. On that morning, Wolf River joined the Nagagami to live in my memory.

Protected from insects by an overcast sky and comforted by fresh pavement where before we had endured gravel, we travelled swiftly back to Red Rock. A prosperous Finnish farmer west of the escarpment sold me enough oats for several feedings. While he was bagging the oats, his wife hailed me to come in, dusty as I was, and join her guests for coffee and cake. We were a merry mix of women, delighted to meet, reaching each other through the magic power of eating and drinking together. The afternoon sun flooded the room and touched the flowered china to life, and laid a glow on our tanned faces. These women and their men were part of the Shield country I had come back to share.

I chose to camp in a daisy meadow below the sandstone escarpment, now carmine in the early evening light. While Zazy grazed, I watched a porcupine climbing, shuffling the talus, pulling itself up spindly windfalls across sheer rock faces, gaining a ledge, gathering itself into sleep. We seemed safely secluded—until dusk stole in, rolled up the painted canvas of the escarpment, and heightened my awareness of the highway. Car lights swept the meadow as they slowed at the bend. Dusk drew a scowl over the dilapidated shacks standing on bare rocks across the highway, with their vague signs of habitation. I felt followed.

I packed up and we moved through the road cut to the sloping side of the rock. With darkness surrounding us, I turned Zazy off the empty road. She seemed to see with her feet. Accepting her head, she climbed with the confidence of a goat until we were on a high ledge screened by saplings. I tied her among them, laid my bed between rounded rocks still warm from the day, and slept in peace.

Dawn slipped chilly fingers inside my sleeping bag. Zazy nickered and I gave her a nosebag filled with oats, to our mutual joy. While she ate, I climbed to the top of the sheltering rocks and looked down on rainbow mists drifting along the watercourses. Soon I was shivering in those mists along Helen Lake. Morning matured into a hot, windless day and we fled before the flies into the welcome of Mileage 56.

With a clear conscience now, I fed Zazy well on hay and on oats augmented with chop. I looked around the buildings for any leftover human food, but all I found was a tin of custard powder. I took it to the stable, parting the cobweb curtains into the feed room. There I tried to sift some oat flour out of the chop through my fly net. Down at the creek, I mixed the product with custard powder and a chunk of butter I had managed to keep from the Pearl farm. I added water and cooked the mess. It smelled good but the texture nauseated me, so I fed it to the fish that I had tried in vain to catch an hour before.

Flies mobbed us in the afternoon as we bathed and drank. I hung laundry to dry and we took refuge again in the stable. Zazy fed and I slept until evening sounds roused me to be on the road again. We were going back to Longlac.

Fifty-five miles seemed not too far now. Clouds masked the sun, inhibiting the horseflies from biting, so we omitted a midday rest and pressed on through a humid afternoon. Plodding and bedraggled, we caught the attention of a motorist speeding by. He stopped, raised his tall person out of his sports car, and advised me in a kindly tone: "You two look as if you'd had it. Better go into Camp 51. It's down the road beside the bridge. Give this to the cook." He scribbled a little note, handed it to me, folded himself back into his car, and drove away.

PART THREE
Camp 51

1

Connie,
Put the bearer up in the cookery and tell Myles to look after the pony.
Tom Tansley

Zazy and I continued eastward, following our shadows, until we came to the bridge. From its unlovely iron railings, we looked down at a sluggish river sliding around the boulders in its bed as it thirsted in the July heat. Just beyond the bridge, a side road ran back and lost itself in the forest. I rode around the locked chain gate, took faith in Tom Tansley's advice, and left the highway behind.

Near the foot of the road, a sawmill whined and hummed at the will of sweating bronzed men. Zazy shied at the noise and hurried past. The road led us on and on, until it dipped at last into a gully full of ferns and climbed to overlook a T-shaped nest of buildings and trails set above the river. We had arrived at Camp 51.

The cookery watched us from the far end of the camp road, like a dot on an exclamation mark. At our approach, the screen door flew open and Connie stepped out. It had to be Connie, her smile said so, and her snowy apron agreed. I told her our names as she was glancing at the note I delivered from her boss.

Connie said, "This is Myles; he'll look after Zazy." Myles had been hanging back, with his peaked cap pulled down almost to his beer nose. As Connie named him, a boyish half-grin slipped around his mouth, and when I handed him the reins, he grew taller and smiled. I lifted off the saddlebags and Myles led Zazy away to the stable.

Connie led me promptly down the length of the dining room and left me in a small room with a cot. "Supper's on for the men; we'll eat after them," she said as she drew the door closed. I listened to her quick steps as she set out the bowls of food.

"Okay?" she called softly.

"Ready!" A man spoke out from the kitchen.

The screen door squeaked open and banged shut, the music of the iron triangle rang out, bunkhouse doors on the hill outside my window swung open, and men began streaming down the path. The dining room resounded with the thud of heavy boots, then all fell quiet, except for the muted clatter of cutlery interwoven with muffled messages. There followed the rhythmic *clomp* of refilled bowls landing on the table. Soon I heard the tread of boots again on the floorboards. Within ten minutes, the screen door banged behind the last lone lumberjack.

The men seemed barely to have left when Connie called me out for supper. Already she had removed the signs that thirty men had just eaten from that table. It stretched its polished linoleum face the length of the room, featuring tidy islands of condiments at handy intervals along the white expanse. Andy the cook appeared, fastidiously dressed in white, to greet me with his gold-plated smile. He sat with his back to the window, and I settled opposite to him. Connie hurried in with two steaming dishes, dispensed them, tossed me a smile, and sat a noticeable distance from Andy. We all helped ourselves to the food. Connie ate sparingly, even restlessly, like a person whose work was far from finished.

We were into stewed fruit and pudding when another man trod the platform outside the door. Without looking up, Connie announced, tongue in cheek, "Here comes The Late Mr. Korolek." A ruggedly handsome blond Ukrainian joined us, stopped at an unused setting on Andy's side, lifted himself with obvious care over the bench, and sank to his seat. "Well, how are you tonight, Nick?" Connie inquired.

"Oh, not too bad." Obviously there was more to come. "My back's not too good. Can't take the shaking on the bulldozer anymore. I've got an awful bad tooth, too." Nick lifted back an unruly curl and began eating. Talk moved around to horses, and he showed me a wallet picture of the horse he left behind on the Saskatchewan prairie.

Nick ate heartily, then we all finished with tea and Connie had a smoke. Andy rose and retired to his room. Connie cheerfully refused my help. She whisked away the food and dishes, mirthfully warbling in half-voice, "There's a gold mine in my mouth, far away-y-y-y," and sent me off to see Zazy.

Nick came with me, along the sand road that ran the length of the camp above high-water mark. He pointed out the bunkhouse road up to the right, the scaler's shack, the office, the garage, the machine shop, and the blacksmith shop. Yes, there was a blacksmith in Camp 51!

We entered the best stable I had seen in all my travels in the north. It was built for the comfort of the beautifully muscled draft teams that stood paired on either side of the wide alley. Myles' workhorse, Andy, had a single stall almost at the end of the barn. At the very end, dwarfed by the black Percheron, stood Zazy, leisurely sorting through her hay.

Nick waited while I groomed the mare, then we all three went to the river. The air was cooling pleasantly, birds were coming out to sing, and sunset colours poured through the trees on the far bank. This camp was taking me to heart. Zazy drank, I stabled her, Nick went to attend to his truck, and I returned to the cookery by the back door.

"Come on in," called Connie. "The boys caught some whitefish at the falls. There's plenty if you'd like to try some." I joined the small gathering in the kitchen.

Matt was in his element, tending the fish as they sputtered and sizzled their way to golden brownness in the big iron pan. He mumbled happy things in Italian as he transferred them one by one to the heated platter and refilled the pan from the heap of fillets on the cutting board. None of us presumed to offer help to Matt. He was an artist at work. Andy, of course, sat aside waiting to be served. As soon as the platter was well covered, Matt invited us all in his lovely Italian English to begin to share the feast.

Andy had been surprised by my appetite at supper. Now he was taken aback to see me eating my share of the fish. He expressed his concern for my health privately to Connie, and privately she and I laughed over his incomprehension of real hunger.

I went to bed refuelled and refreshed for the trip next day to Camp 41. There had been no confirmation from Jim about a job; I had to hope that he meant what he had said.

At breakfast Connie told me that Andy was about to leave for three weeks' holiday. She said she would cook, and she would be happy to have me stay and 'cookie' for her. This day suddenly seemed like the wrong one for going to Longlac. Here was a job as well as a blacksmith. Why court uncertainty? When Tom Tansley drove into camp at coffee time, he hired me, effective whenever Andy chose to leave.

Without delay, Frank the blacksmith removed Zazy's shoes and trimmed her feet. Myles reserved the stall next to Andy for her and turned her loose to roam in the daytime. Zazy soon found the way to the cookery window, where Connie learned her nicker and handed out oatmeal cookies in reply.

Connie told me about the company I would be working for. Tom had inherited it from his father, who founded it. Old Mr. Tansley established a high standard for the care of his horses, as well as a tradition of fairness to his employees, and Tom carried on both traditions. Connie said Tom was now the manager and co-owner with his brother-in-law, Mr. Sinclair. Sinc was a rare visitor to the cookery; he was the busy brain and hands behind all the technical operations of the outfit.

Andy remained another week. During that time I learned all I could about being a 'cookie'. It entailed stoking the wood stoves, preparing vegetables, laying tables, waiting on tables and washing dishes, sweeping and scrubbing floors, helping to lift sides of beef and pork from the hooks in the meat house, cutting meat, supplying the coffee table at midday and evening, and generally supporting the cook. Connie tutored me without pressure.

Twilight curtained off camp from forest and drew friend closer to friend. Paul the bullcook started the gasoline generator, and lights came on in the buildings. Men grouped in the dining room for coffee, strolled outdoors, retired few by few up the short flights of wooden stairs into the bunkhouses. There each man's possessions made a tiny home base for him. On the first night after I decided to stay a while, I had to struggle with the fact that I had left the open road; this camp was now my home, this little room my private base.

"Come and have some fudge with us," Connie called to me from the circle of friends having evening coffee in the kitchen. Restless, I chose the solitude of my room. Sounds from a struggling battery radio penetrated the wall. The wind moaned in the eaves. Lights from the bunkhouses shone in at my window, and beyond them at the edge of the clearing, lanky, curly-headed poplars swayed to and fro against a leaden sky. I needed to go out and blend into the gloomy twilight, to shelter in the lee of a boulder when the rain was released, to be held safe by Earth. But nearby were people who would ask why, and I would not be able to make them understand.

After a blissful week of riding a barefoot mare free of tack, helping Connie casually as she invited help, and hanging out in the coolness of a rock-walled pool near the foot of the falls, I returned to the cookery one afternoon to find that my holiday was over. Andy had left, and Connie supplied me with the details. He had tried to coax her away with him, and she had kept out of reach while reminding him of their differences.

Camp 51, my bathtub near the falls on Blackwater River. July 1949.

"Oh, I could remodel you," was his answer to her line.

"Sure, just like an old car!" ended the discussion.

Andy left alone, and Connie relaxed and took up her new duties efficiently. I did my best to cookie for her. She and I were two women alone in a camp of thirty men. I kept in mind for future reference the evasive techniques I had seen Connie use as she had worked under Andy's regime, during my first week of vital revelations!

Waiting on tables was my biggest challenge. At first Connie chose to allow me to avoid it, to leave it to her. Then came a moment of overload when she angrily snatched away the option. Her adrenaline rush hit me squarely in the hesitation, and I was launched into the dining room on my own wave of fury.

Doing the job proved to be easier than avoiding it. The men helped me by leaning aside to let me to reach past them to set down bowls and to receive empties from their hands. Soon I was worrying less about offending someone, and insisting on taking responsibility for all my duties.

Going barefoot in the dining room was an innocent mistake. Shoes, by my practical standards, were worn if needed and if my only pair had not disintegrated. I had no reason for wearing shoes anywhere in camp. The problem arose when the men seated at the table could not hear me coming. Without warning, my arm would appear between two loggers intent on their food, and decorum would startle and take flight on some choice expletives. Never realizing that someone was trying to tell me something, I cheerfully declined an advance in pay to buy shoes.

The rumour reached the cookery that the men were considering taking up a collection for me. I got the message, thanked Connie for allowing me an afternoon off work, and rode away to Geraldton with Nick in his two-ton truck.

Connie had done her homework; she had set up my shopping trip to coincide with Nick's dental appointment. Absorbed in conversation, I ignored the blurred-out roadside that I had seen at Zazy's speed as a frontier for pioneer plants and a banquet table for small mammals and birds. On the main street of town, Nick and I parted company and went our respective ways. We reconnected in an hour or so, I tolerating new shoes, he tolerating an aching jaw in place of his aching tooth. He bore his misery with only an occasional groan and spit-stop.

I wondered why we were taking the old road marked Closed just before we came to the highway. I supposed it was still connected to the new road farther on. Then Nick posed the question, "How about you learn to drive the truck? This is a good place to begin."

I declined, he insisted, I protested, he ignored my confessed lack of experience; I rose to the challenge and changed seats with him. After a few jolts that extended Nick's jaw ache to his head, I put the truck into motion. I liked the feeling of several tons of metal under my direction.

"That's fine!" He clapped an encouraging arm around my shoulder, and left it there. "Now let's put her in second."

I was content to stay in first. Nick held firm. "You just step on the clutch and take your foot off the gas." I must have stepped on both pedals. The engine roared a complaint. I let out both clutch and accelerator, and the truck lurched and came to a violent halt.

I offered Nick his seat. Nick dismissed my apology and urged me to try again. This time I got it right. We were gathering speed in second gear. Nick moved closer, ready for an emergency, I supposed. "How's the tooth?" I was keeping my vision trained on a spot just beyond the weathered red hood.

"Not too bad." He hitched himself over to assist the steering with his free hand. Cars on the highway sounded suspiciously close. Presuming we were about to merge, I drove blithely on, eye on bonnet tip. Suddenly Nick kicked my foot off the accelerator and tramped on the brake. We jolted to a standstill. I looked where he had looked a moment before. In front of the wheels, the pavement ended in a jagged drop-off. We changed seats in full agreement, and he drove home.

"How did it go?" Connie was visibly ready for an amusing reply.

"Great!" I glowed. "Nick let me drive his truck." Connie grinned, and waited. "And see my new shoes?" Connie liked my choice, and went back to her soup pot, still smiling.

Mom's parcel of female clothes came in the mail the following day. Now I could dress in a skirt. Mom and Dad would send my winter clothes and skis later, when my address was assured.

Nick did not give up. He moved the school to the bush road upriver from camp. Skippy, my adopted terrier, came with us, riding in the truck or barking alongside. Despite the distractions of Skippy and my barefoot sensitivity to the pedals, I was progressing well.

Sadly, the venture came to a dismal end. I was to back around a slight bend on a grade. Somehow I missed the turn and landed the rear axle firmly on a stump. Speechless, Nick reached an axe from under the seat and laboriously chopped away the stump. He drove home.

Our evenings together did not stop with the driving lessons. We walked, or drove and parked, and talked about life in camp as well as the life we each had left behind. Nick gave me insight into the morals and thought patterns of the men in the bunkhouses, for my sake and theirs. I gave him in return the fun of picking berries with a pal. The bush blueberries were like enough to the Saskatoon berries of Nick's prairie boyhood to give him real joy. Next morning, Connie would be warbling: "I found my thrill-l-l, on blueberry hill-l-l . . . " while she turned our pails of berries into pies.

A month later, the scene changed; Nick stopped picking me up. I could never imagine the reason, and neither he nor Connie would talk to me about the change. They talked to each other, excluding me, and I added the feeling of total rejection to my sense of loss. Zazy and Skippy were always my friends, always ready with a fellowship I could believe in.

—⁀—

Three weeks passed after Andy left on holiday, and he did not return. Nick said Andy would never return. Was it time for me to go on to Longlac or to ride west? Connie urged me to stay for the winter. I was uncertain what the mail might bring, so I waited at Camp 51, keeping my options open. Maybe a letter would come from Jim Prowse at Longlac, confirming his offer of a winter job at the horse hospital camp.

In mid-August two letters came in the same mail. One was postmarked Longlac, curtly written in a feminine hand. It stated: "Stay away, kid! Go home and ask your father for advice!" That was Alice Prowse marking her territory. I was staggered by her assault and the impact it made on my hope to work with horses. I recovered, laughed over it with Connie, and wrote off Longlac.

The second letter was from the registrar at the veterinary college. He heartily agreed to defer my entry into OVC until the fall of 1950. Money up front was a good idea, he thought. Also, I might have female company in the Class of '55, compared to none in the Class of '54.

I decided to stay at Camp 51, assuming that present arrangements for Zazy would continue. No changes were mentioned in the office, so I signed the contract. Connie and I put music on the turntable and twirled around the kitchen in celebration.

2

The final terms of my winter employment were a seven-day week at $4.75 per day and a fee of $0.75 per day for Zazy's board. I understood that both Zazy and I were settled at Camp 51 until spring.

Two weeks after I signed onto the permanent staff, the management changed its usually dependable mind. Zazy had to go. She was accused of causing fighting among the geldings, as evidenced by the skin flap on a Belgian's rump that Frank the blacksmith was seen sewing down. She would cost the company far more than seventy-five cents per day to feed. Also, her stall might be needed when the winter contracts came in. All this news was made the duty of the foreman, Neil Arthur, to convey to me.

Neil was a tall, lean, prairie farmer at heart, unfailingly kind to people and animals. Though he could not explain why I had not been told sooner, he allowed me time to find another place for Zazy.

It happened that a German farmer from Wild Goose Lake came to ask Myles to help him with a farrowing sow. The farmer offered to put Zazy out with his horses to graze in the bush until winter. The pasture was twenty miles away, wild and unfenced. A vision of the gaunt black horse near Geraldton calling to Zazy held up a hand of warning, but I had no other option than to accept the farmer's offer.

Nick volunteered to truck the mare, and Connie gave me free time to go with him on Sunday morning. We loaded Zazy into the high-walled box, picked up the farmer at his lakeside camp, and drove by a devious route to the pasture. From among some ruined shacks, three raw-boned horses came to look at the disturbance. Zazy greeted them as she walked down the ramp.

"She'll probably stay with the others," the farmer said. "She'll be safe here until the snow flies." I had my doubts.

I led Zazy to good grazing and hurried back to the truck. She followed me. I gave her grain in a ruined stable and we drove away.

The pressure of work carried me through the day, then I went with Skippy to the falls and we sat together, listening to the fluting of the hermit thrush. I worked through the first few hours of the next morning without spirit, knowing winter would mean that Zazy had to be moved to another place. Then a strange thing happened at coffee time.

Mr. Kelly the clerk, thin and pale as usual, sauntered into the cookery, filled his mug, found the jelly doughnuts, and targeted Connie with his current bit of sardonic humour, also as usual. Between bites he dropped the unexpected word, that he had nearly run into a black horse wandering on the highway in the small hours. It had to be Zazy!

Alarm bells were ringing in my brain, but dinner had to be prepared. I was giving the soup a final stir when the screen door banged and the fire warden walked in. He spilled his news to Connie, but I eavesdropped.

Then he turned to me. "Sure your horse came back. Myles said she trotted in and went straight to her stall."

Connie set me free to race to the stable. There Zazy stood, slightly footsore, but as Myles said, "As happy as a dog in a meat house."

The sawmill crew talked about how she swung in off the highway and trotted gaily past the mill, head and tail high. Guided by who knows what force, she had found her way back to me over twenty miles in twenty-four hours.

Her exploit amused the men and roused some kindly humour in Tom Tansley, but the verdict did not change. Tom would ask his sister in Port Arthur if she would keep the mare for her use. I tried to ignore the cloud that hung over our future.

Life with Skippy and Zazy was free-flowing fun. Zazy found trails in her daily wandering and showed them to me at night. It was around this time that Nick and Connie began to grow distant from me. Confused, I leaned on the love of the animals, spontaneous, requiring no promises. Somewhere among these cloudy days, my twenty-first birthday passed, unnoticed even by myself until cards came from home.

Suddenly, a snarl about me from a rough minority in the bunkhouses reconnected Connie, Nick, and me. My critics insinuated that I was weird, complained that I was incompetent, and agitated to have me fired. Most of the crew were unimpressed. Connie would have none of the political seduction. She knew the basic complaint: I was occupying the niche of a more cooperative female. Nick stood by me.

Paul the bullcook and Harry, his helper, had difficulty accepting me as a normal person, yet their work around the cookery brought us into amiable contact all day long. My rapport with Zazy puzzled them. My affinity for the forest by night as well as in daylight puzzled them. And why did I carry back stones and bits of plants? For two middle-aged White Russian immigrants carrying the vestiges of Old World traditions, I was a needling contradiction. I was innocuous, disinclined to bite, thankful for the fire they lit in the dining room, the water they pumped into the barrels, the light powered by the generator they started at night. And I respected Paul's authority about camp rules.

To Paul I was an enigma. He wanted me gone. Connie knew the consequence of such deep mistrust, and she dulled the point of the hidden knife by sharing the bench in front of the kitchen stoves with Paul and listening with a straight face to the old man's gossip in Russian. Later she told me his stories in hilarious English, and we laughed them off.

Harry walked mind and body in lockstep behind Paul. He worried about me on cue from Paul, but when Paul was away, Harry was free to be his naturally trusting self. He used to step into the empty dining room before mid-morning coffee time and call cheerfully: "Where's the shweet-mama?" Connie's answer might come back from the pastry board near the kitchen window. Harry would stop by the coffee table to fill his mug, and call again: "And where's the 'nother shweet-mama?" My greeting might come from the storage room, where I sat peeling potatoes. And I could smile, because I knew that Harry's simplicity was melting the wall between his master, himself, and me.

Harry could not stop the momentum of scandal, as the stories grew wilder. I, supposedly a woman, was seen running for pleasure, barefoot, and disappearing into the woods. One rainy afternoon, Paul saw me shrouded in a rain cape, sorting through gravel by the roadside. Joe the scaler, out measuring the butts on a pile of logs, happened to see me too. Joe called to me, and we talked about this perfect weather for spotting fossils. Paul did not ask; he remained a stranger to fossils.

Connie's lightheartedness dismantled my fear of complete alienation. She knew I needed the familiar ambience of animal company and wilderness to balance my strangely new social life in a bush camp. "I don't want to see you back 'til five o'clock!" she would say, brandishing the broom.

Skippy ran along the riverbank when I chose to wade in the water in the heat of early August. At the little island below the falls, he could gain the pebble beach with one brave plunge. There, we nestled in the arm of a tired old cedar that leaned over the water. Soon the dainty water thrushes would arrive to look us over, timid ones to peek, bold ones to edge closer and scold. They shared that margin of water and land with a company of purple finches, carmine gems busy finding seeds dropped from overhanging shrubs.

Zazy took me overland, where the three-toed woodpeckers stepped from the pages of my bird book onto real trees. Ravens made themselves known to me, sending their croaking calls across the desolate clear-cut. Solemn black figures, they perched like spirits on top of lone leaning spruces that clung to life through scorched roots held by the tangle of raspberry canes.

One chilly dawn, when Paul was away, I rose at 4 AM to light the fire in the dining room. What I saw from the kitchen window melted my grouch. In the pink mists that lay over the river's weedy shallows, a moose family, bull, cow, and calf, were feeding. Casually, they thrust their heads under water and drew up long, dripping masses of plants. They stayed until the smoke from the fire rose above the cookery in the still air. Then, unhurried, they moved as one, splashing across the river in easy strides, swaying through the alder screen into the fingers of the forest.

Connie and I had a close encounter with nature without ever leaving the cookery. First, we heard weird moaning in the night. We called it our Indian spirit. It ceased, only to recur in chorus, a swelling chorus wailing by night and day. At mealtime it raised nasty comments from the men. We began to suspect substance rather than spirits.

One evening I happened to drop my pen through a crack in the floor. Connie's friend Roy obligingly ripped up a board to retrieve it. Around the lamplight shining down through the hole, feline faces began to gather like moths. Our Indian spirits were queens in heat, toms in combat, and kittens in the making. We dropped food down and saw clawing paws seize it instantly. The uncounted population probably had sprung from a few cats abandoned by the former tenants of Camp 51.

At noontime the next day, Connie vanished from her station behind the dish-up table. I skimmed around the end of the counter and stopped in my tracks. There on the floor she knelt, silent and still. I peered over her shoulder. Connie was dangling a sliver of bologna over a crack while furry paws reached through for the prize. In no time the cats learned to beg, their green and amber eyes and clawed paws applied to the widest cracks where meat was handled above their dark home. Myles' pig pail went wanting, and the cats prospered.

Diversity struck. A skunk became involved with the cats and fired off its essence at pie-making time, and again at dinnertime. Cigar John, the union man, removed his cigar and voiced his complaint to the management. He asserted that the dogs were to blame, and he argued successfully to have them removed. Neil took Skippy to his home in Jellicoe. An orphan puppy that someone had abandoned simply disappeared. Only Myles' black Lab, Rover, stayed. Myles had been barn boss for old Mr. Tansley. Myles had only to threaten to leave if the dog went, and Rover's place in Camp 51 was assured.

For all of Myles' job security, he nearly fell afoul of the cook one Saturday morning. He had painfully accepted Little Paul's duties for a week, and for four days he had managed to keep some wood in the woodbox, some water in the barrels by the sink. On Friday, he failed to pump water. Then came Saturday!

The dipper scraped bottom in the third and last barrel as I prepared to wash the breakfast dishes. The water in the pots on the stove was low. Floor scrubbing had to follow dishwashing promptly, if the floor was to be dry before the men came in for lunch. Connie and I grew tense. Minutes passed. We listened for the bang of the back door. Half an hour passed. I diced vegetables for soup. Connie went on an errand to the office and returned with sad news. Myles was trying frantically to pull the pump on its wheelbarrow out of the river. A quarter of an hour later, two sheepish individuals arrived to give an account. Rover kept his tail between his legs and let his master do the talking from under the cover of his cap.

Frank and Mr. Kelly rescued the pump and delivered it to Myles, who gratefully wheeled it down the ramp by the meat house and onto the platform over the well. He attached the hose and carried it through the back door into the first barrel. Now, to start the pump!

To Myles, that pump was like a balky horse. He approached it

Starting the pump: Connie brandishing the priming bottle, Myles and Rover the dog cheering as the motor kicked in. August 1949.

masterfully, wound the cord around the starter and pulled. The engine replied with a sputter, and sat silent. Myles tried again and again. Defeated, he bleated, "Connelly!" She always knew how to get things done.

Connie stepped onto the catwalk and looked the problem over. Priming was all that was needed. She opened the little duct, delicately poured in gas from a green bottle, closed the duct and recapped the bottle. Then, with a flick of the wrist, she awoke the pump. Connie brandished the green bottle, Myles snatched off his battered cap and waved it high, Rover barked, and the engine settled down to a purr. The lifeblood of the cookery's Saturday morning activities was flowing!

Myles drained the tall enamel teapot into his special mug and sat down on the bench in front of the stove, with his back against the wood box. Connie was at her pastry table. The barrels were across the room. Water rose to the brim of the first barrel, and filled the second in tandem, while ridiculous tales of adventure came spinning out of the old man's memory. The stories grew wilder and wilder. Myles chuckled, glancing slyly at Connie. Artfully she led him on, smiling at some tale yet untold. Lost in fanciful romances with his playmates, Stovepipe and Step-and-a-Half, he mused over the toecaps of his dusty black boots, cocked up independently before him. Connie's radar ears caught a sound behind her. Came her scream, "Hey! Your barrel's running over!"

Myles sprang up. "Oh chee, I ain't got no remember at all!" He swept the flowing hose out of the overflowing barrel, up the hall and out through the open door. Too late we saw the supply truck parked outside. A spurt of water caught Neil squarely in the knees as he came around the corner with an armload of groceries. Myles dashed to the well at a bumpy run and choked the pump into silence.

Myles had a mischievous 'remember' for things that were not quite true. He started rumours about Matt one Sunday morning.

Matt had been exuding his usual goodwill as he prepared to treat us, one and all, to his native Italian spaghetti. He tested and fully approved the aromatic sauce simmering on the stove. His black eyes shone as he drained the tangle of swollen noodles. Then the barn boss sauntered in and began idling out his gossip.

Matt flushed silently. Myles should have trimmed out the details of misdemeanours with somebody's wife. Our half-concealed amusement drew on the old quidnunc. The price of a plate-glass window and court costs were mentioned. Myles revelled; Matt fizzled! Finally his temper boiled hotter than his sauce, and Myles knew he had gone too far. Connie snuffed out the last of his courage with a murmured, "Watch out, Myles. He's pretty handy with a knife."

Myles drew his cap down a little farther, set his cup on the coffee table, and headed for the front door, with Rover at his heels. The long black tail cleared the passage a split second before the screen door banged behind the pair.

3

Drought held up a withered hand of warning over the bush. In Camp 51, Louis la France imposed a ban on forestry, double-checked the fire-fighting equipment, and kept watch. Our world was tinder dry.

Alcohol followed idleness into the bunkhouses. Old scars were opened, deep longings were mourned, and reason took a holiday. Little Paul came by taxi from town and sought out Connie with a pair of unpleasantly lusty eyes. As they met, he drew a flask of whisky from within his white shirt, and set off events that altered cookery life for days.

Characters changed, established order disintegrated. I went from wide-eyed wonder to disgust to fear and loneliness. On the second night, Connie was out, God knew where. Her danger was my danger, for we were friends. The quietness of the cookery after the last man left was ominous. I went outside and walked to the stable under a generous moon. Zazy heard me and called. I rested on her strong back as we followed our favourite trails into the healing solitude of the forest.

Soon I was on my own feet, weathering the changes, getting my day's work done, and stretching to help Connie keep meals on schedule. Night was my time to rest with Zazy.

Fire season lasted until the fall rains began. By then most of the loggers had drifted away and the cookery had settled into a slow pace. The woods were stirring with autumn fever, and I had time to become a part of that healthy process of change. Warblers and grackles and waxwings were congregating and preparing to take to the flyways. The crowns of the silver birches around the lake threw a gold halo on the water. Always on the lake trail I saw sharp-tailed grouse, for the broods were now safely grown. I hummed to announce myself, and the birds did not flush. Hunters came into camp asking if I saw grouse, but I never could remember where.

I followed a moose trail through laurels along the river until it led me onto higher ground. I felt there was something ahead for me. A flash of colour stilled me, screened by thin young spruce. I sank and lay still under the eyes of an alerted bird standing on open ground. The bird relaxed; I wormed closer. It faced me, and the brilliant black bars on the chest and the scarlet cheeks said, *Hudsonian spruce grouse*. In ritual solemnity, it danced back and forth across the floodlit stage, echoing springtime. I barely breathed as the dance went on. When the lowering sun reminded me of supper duties, I stalked away as carefully as I had come, content to know that the dance continued.

Fall rains brought fungi to fruit on the forest floor. In the dampness, flat lichens expanded on rocks and curly forms on rotting stumps wore scarlet frills. Rains washed the dust off the limestone outcrops, showing their fossil lampshells and crinoid lily stems. What were fossils doing on the Shield? There was no one to ask. There had to have been a sea!

Joe the scaler caught me pounding limestone with a hammer in the hollow of a granite boulder. "Are you cracking butternuts?" he called on his way over to see for himself. His brown eyes were dancing.

"No, I'm crushing limestone for Connie's cactus plants. Mom sent them to live on the windowsill above Connie's baking table and cheer her in the winter."

Fall rains taught me a lesson in deep-fat frying. A volley of raindrops had chased me into the shelter of the hallway, where I stopped to drip and heard Connie swearing vehemently in the kitchen. She was standing at the stove under the skylight, turning doughnuts in the fat vat with her long, pointed stick. A raindrop fell, and out of the vat jumped half a dozen grease devils to ignite and dance on top of the stove. It was not the first drop that had landed. If a burning bead were to jump back into the fat, cook and cookery could burn.

Connie was aware of the risk to herself, but she also valued the dough that had fully risen; it had to be cooked or wasted. She would continue frying.

I seized my apron off its hook, wrapped it round my shorts, and teamed up. Gingerly she proceeded. I sugared each batch as it came out of the vat. Soon the floured boards bearing the limp white discs were emptied, and other boards were loaded with crisp golden doughnuts. Connie gauged the interval between the drips and moved the vat safely off the heat.

Relaxing over coffee and hot doughnuts, we evolved a new rule: Check the sky when sweet dough is rising. Fair weather means doughnuts; a rain cloud calls for cinnamon wheels, baked in the oven.

Crises never cost Connie or me pounds. She topped two hundred, and

I outgrew my frog pants. Tom seized the chance to tease. "You're nearly two axe handles across, Connie. Better take up riding on Barbara's horse."

Along came an exceptional Saturday afternoon. The perogies lay row by row on floured boards, ready well ahead of time for boiling. Bacon and onion were already chopped. Danny, a veteran logger, had just returned from a prospecting trip. Connie and Roy, Pat, Nick, and Danny were all in a jovial mood, ready to try anything now that the brandy bottle was empty. Sunshine mellowed the tangy autumn air. This felt like the day for Connie and Zazy to go for a ride.

I brought the mare to the back door of the cookery. Danny began to worry about the safety of this woman, who was his perennial friend through his alcoholic bouts. Roy and his buddy Pat were all for the adventure. So was Connie. We helped her to mount Zazy, she took up the reins, and they were away up the road toward the old camp. We watched from the meat house.

Zazy plodded evenly up the hill until they reached the side trail to the Office, as Harry called the toilet. Connie was uncertain. Zazy took the initiative and headed along the Office trail. Beyond it she paused where the path dropped steeply to the river. *Shall I go on?* she asked. Connie pulled a rein that conveyed a definite *no!* Zazy turned back.

As they came toward the cookery, Zazy's gait was verging on a jog and Connie was calling something about brakes. They passed the meat house and seemed to be heading for the stable when Danny and I intercepted them. Roy and Pat helped Connie down and we all laughed.

Nick now stepped into the fun. Zazy allowed him to mount, but when he tried to stand on the saddle, she moved off and he dismounted ingloriously. She and Nick harboured a small grudge after that event, until they settled their account one day near the machine shop.

I had stopped after a ride to chat outside the shop, and Nick was there. He took the halter shank from me, jumped onto Zazy's back, and kicked her in the flanks. She began to rear, but he spun her round. Nonplussed, she spun tighter and faster, then with a lightning lifting twist, she dumped her rider. Calmly she carried me away from the embarrassment and up the trail to the lake.

Maybe gossip about Zazy reached Mr. Tansley's sister in Port Arthur, for she decided against boarding the mare. When he brought the news, he said that she could stay in camp. Connie cut loose the moment that the door closed behind him. She left off making holobtsi, snatched me away from their iron pot, and led me into a wild victory dance.

— —

Connie broadened my vision of humankind. She saw beneath the mask and usually found goodness there. I had to learn to take less seriously the gap between mask and character. Barago shook up my mindset about how people should look and act. Here he came, stalking up the dining room to his place fourth from the top, swarthy, toothless, unshaven. He wasn't nice to look at; he was scary. He got my attention, scowling under heavy black eyebrows, rumbling displeasure at a hard potato or an empty soup bowl. I couldn't ignore him, so I had to deal with myself. As for Barago, he went right on being himself. He taught me how to laugh at things.

One unbelievable night, I sat sandwiched between Nick and Barago in the truck, rolling home under the bright, cold stars long past midnight. In the back of my mind, I was thanking a deity trimmed to fit my prejudice for taking care of poor little me, and enjoying the adventure at the same time.

Nick had meant only to deliver a load of firewood in Geraldton and call on a friend. Barago had meant only to pick up a bottle at the bootlegger's and spend an hour with Annie. I had thought I would shop. The timing went wrong. After the shops closed, I walked around town, found the parked truck, and waited in it until Nick woke me up. Nick hounded out Barago and eventually we were on our way home. Barago was awash with beer and unloading out of the window now and then. His nausea passed, his spirits soared, and his rough Slavic voice rose in the strains of "Springtime in the Rockies." So he regaled us until Nick hushed him up as we wheeled into camp.

Three and a half hours later, I opened unwilling eyes on a Sunday. I did not expect the wake-up bell to reach Barago, but I was wrong. "Baraka Baraka!" came a drunken shout as he trailed in among the early risers. Any place at the table would do on Sunday. He swung his long legs over the bench in front of a platter of fried eggs. A long arm went for the eggs, a sly look went Connie's way, and he tipped the lot onto his plate and handed wide-eyed me the empty platter. Connie reloaded it and whispered to me to make sure that it started its journey a safe distance from Barago. He was chuckling softly. As he left the room, he turned and called out: "Thank you."

That very Sunday, I had an unexpected chance to reflect on the meaning of things. Nick offered to take me to Beardmore to attend a church service. It was up to me to find a way home in time to prepare for supper at 5:30 PM.

I found a friendly church, where a dog was welcome to lie under the pew of an elderly lady, where prayers came to life and life was completed by the observed presence of God. The service ended and the people dispersed.

I checked my watch, divided five hours into thirty-five miles, adjusted my clothes for running, and set off at an easy trot. Miles slipped by even though the heat of the day was rising. I waved to a truckload of campers at a spring, and soon they overtook me and picked me up. Sitting with three fellows and a jumble of equipment in the shade of a canoe, I bounced along as far as the camp road.

Now there was time to spare. I strolled around the pretty orange and black snake sunning itself in the dust near the gate. I reflected on the crazy contradictions and the wonderful surprises that made up this life into which I seemed to have fallen by chance. Even at the worst of times, I would not have been elsewhere that year. Though ill will often seemed to run alongside goodwill, I might catch myself or anyone else on either side, when I was being honest about things.

A healing, freeing presence kept me hopeful when others drank and fought in despair. Little Paul noticed it and somehow said so. Harry was simply able to enter into the peace I knew. Mom and Dad, Peg and Charlie, and my reverend cousin John shared in their letters the roots of my own faith. So did the wilderness, where I sang the hymns of my childhood and gathered in the meaning that life in Camp 51 was adding to my song.

— —

The first day of September was marked by a frost that froze the water in the hose. Before the month was out, turnips froze in the meat house and snow whitened the ground.

Cold and warm fronts tugged the seasons back and forth. One day I lay sheltering under a windfall, watching cold rain drenching the world. The next day I was drowsing on a bed of warm moss while a grouse a few yards away stood on a poplar log to reach winter buds. One night Zazy and I dreamed on a hilltop while rosy clouds lay in level ridges at the western edge of a turquoise sky, and a young orange moon plunged into the twilight. Within a week we were going silently into the light of a half moon convoyed by white clouds in the southern sky. The trail turned. Suddenly, lightning stabbed out from the black drape that hung in the northwest, while the northern sky still glowed behind hesitant green curtains. Swiftly, scowling clouds moved across the moon and swept round to hide the aurora. In inky blackness, Zazy felt our way back to the river, across the floating causeway, and up the trail to the stable.

A violent storm ended our Indian summer. Zazy and I went out after hours to join in its abandon. Rain pelted us, gales blew over us, and we glowed within. Every few seconds the crash of a falling tree rose above the noise of the wind. A rotten poplar cracked and fell right behind us. We moved on cautiously. A gust sent a birch sprawling across the road in front of us. As one we turned, jumped the poplar trunk, and cantered home.

Storm damage occasioned repairs that put Little Paul into a poisonous humour. He didn't sing as he cut our wood. He raved at Connie and me for using too much wood and for causing the skylight to break. To add to our misery, another stray puppy adopted by the woman in the trappers' cabin left proof of its visit in the dining room. Paul was the one who found it, and he laid the blame on us.

Paul's storm ran its course like the storm that broke the skylight. Harry allowed an extra stride or two between himself and his boss, and the men in the bunkhouses ignored Paul's troubles. Cigar John, the union man, was on good terms with Connie at the time, so Paul did not have a hearing ear in which to foment another cloudburst. The weather settled to be clear and cold. In two days everything was repaired and tidied. Connie paid a visit to Frances in her cabin and asked her to keep her dog at home. Connie also took time to chat with Paul and Harry, helping our lives to find a new balance point. Harry was visibly relieved when peace was restored.

My peace of mind had to weather one more storm. Mr. Tansley asked me how long I intended to keep the horse in camp. He spoke of a riding academy in Port Arthur, where he thought she could be used for her board. I was floored by his reversal. It hung like a broken law.

Again, Nick came to my rescue. He said he would take Zazy and me along with Cigar John in his truck to Port Arthur and help me to find a boarding stable for the mare. On a Saturday morning, we loaded her and set out along a white highway. Snowbirds rose up and scattered before us in the wind like bits of paper. Cold gusts found cracks in the cab of the truck, and I pitied Zazy standing in an open box in those icy blasts for several hours.

Within one hour, Mr. Tansley drove up and stopped us on the road. He said that plans had changed and Zazy could go back to stay at camp. He told Nick to leave the mare at Camp 63 for the weekend and pick her up on his way back. Nick pulled into Camp 63 and I unloaded Zazy and stayed with her. As soon as the truck was out of sight, I jumped on her back and rode her along the snow pad beside the road back to Camp 51. I wanted to believe Tom Tansley, but I decided that just in case he forgot again, Zazy and I would leave together.

Nick brought a new saddle pad from the Lakehead. During the next week, he put an evening's skilled work on my tack, fitting the pad to the saddle, adding lacing to better secure the pack, and overhauling the kit so that I was ready to face winter on the road if the need arose.

4

Snow banked the cookery, sealing off draughts. Snow filtered in at the eaves, piled up and peered down from the joists. Snow masked the skin of ice on the river, deleting the profile of the floating bridge. Snow spun from flying hooves as the band of resting horses, with Zazy in the lead, went rollicking up the bunkhouse road.

On one raw November morning, the thermometer was registering −34.5°C. The rhythmic ring of Paul's splitting axe carried snatches of his song into the cookery. An icy blast swept up the dining room as the storm door was pulled open. "Everybody works but father," a jolly voice sang out, and the doors slammed shut. "Twenty years a butcher, and never cut a gut!" the voice announced to thin air. Old Joe the scaler was sending his comedy act ahead of him to seed a jovial mood. It worked again; Connie and I came around from the kitchen ready to laugh at anything, and joined Joe near the barrel stove.

It was then that we sensed a cloud rolling in.

Joe got round to telling us that he was about to be replaced by a younger, supposedly hardier, man. We'd miss his wisdom as well as his humour. I had never faced this point in another person's life before, and I feared lest Joe be institutionalized, stored away to live on his memories.

Now crashed in. Joe fell silent. Paul stopped singing. Silence lay on the last ring of his axe. Paul yelled: "Horse in the river!" He ran to fetch Neil and Myles, I snatched up a sweater and ran, too. I could see a dark horse, that lone wolf of the blue roan team, floundering in an ice-ringed pool. I got closer. He was helpless, over his depth, growing torpid in the intense cold. I ran out along the whitened causeway.

Neil and Paul followed; Myles came with rope, axe, and whip. He beat the horse to keep him struggling while the foreman tied the rope in a bowline round his neck. Then we four pulled while the horse plunged toward the bridge. One-two-heave—*splash!* Paul stepped into the river. Neil grabbed his arm and pulled him out.

"Chee! Dat water she's-a-cold!" Paul made for the bunkhouse at a bumpy run, with his clothes freezing stiff around him.

Gus the Smiling Swede doing chores with a horse. Bunkhouses, office, fuel and generator in background. Camp 51, winter 1950.

The horse in the water was almost too tired to try. Neil changed the bowline to a slip knot, and he and I pulled as hard as we could toward an island under the causeway. Myles chopped ice in front of the horse and beat him from behind. Now the choking animal plunged for his life and gained the length of his body toward land. We slacked, he breathed, Myles chopped, and then we pulled and beat again. At last his forefeet found solid ground. One more pull, a shout from Myles, and a mighty equine effort brought him scrambling onto the causeway, sending Neil and me waist-deep into snow.

Myles left with the horse while Neil and I were standing in sunshine, brushing snow off our bodies. The blue roan in the stable shook off the water and shivered until he warmed himself. Then Myles let him out to find his playmates. Paul thawed out his clothes. The glow of the present moment claimed the morning. We all went back to work.

— —

A contract for railway ties salvaged the fortune of the company. Like many others, it had been stalled by the surplus of pulpwood afloat on the lakes. Now new men arrived in camp and old acquaintances reappeared.

Irish Danny returned, looking thinner than ever. His face was lined and his square shoulders seemed to sag a little more. Danny spent a few days in agony, recovering from gastric ulcers brought on by alcohol. He was as kind-hearted as ever, blaming no one but himself for his misery. Through most of the winter, Danny stayed in camp, and his health improved. He seemed content with the company of his bunkhouse mates at night, an occasional chat with Connie and me, and most days the company of his horse and the birds who shared his lunch. "Them whiskey jacks takes it away as fast as you can give it to 'em. Don't give the chickadees a chance to get near." As he spoke, he was stowing a heavy knucklebone into his lunch bag. "But they won't lug that in a hurry!"

Len was another winter perennial, a stable compound of honour and immorality. Our paths first crossed on a Saturday, when he rattled up to the cookery with his half-Native wife and six children in an old army truck. That truck ran as proof of Len's skill as an auto mechanic. The visitors trooped into the cookery and invited themselves to supper. Len was a firm believer in wine, and on that one point the whole family agreed. Len brought the bottle, Connie accepted a glass to be sociable, but I declined with thanks. My only taste of alcohol had been at age three, when Mom used to give me a tablespoon of brandy in hot water and honey in the night to ease my leg pains.

Len took offence at my refusal. He needled me. "Jesus Christ drank wine, didn't he? Why shouldn't we?" His wife scowled. Her man was setting me up for a fight. I held my peace and continued setting the tables beyond the turbulent family. Connie was in and out of their conversation only to be polite, knowing that we had to be ready to serve a meal to twenty men within half an hour. As the wine supply ran low, argument rolled back and forth between Len and his wife about anything and nothing. Len poked out a question as I passed, "If you wanted a man, wouldn't you be glad to get a guy like me?"

With tactless candour, I returned, "No, I wouldn't," and walked on, longing for comic wit like Connie's to turn such a point.

Feelings cascaded. The woman darkened and abruptly left the dining room. Len overtook her on the back porch. Angry words reached our ears, then the sickening sound of blows and the cries of the woman in fury and pain.

Matt had been busy in the kitchen all the while, making spaghetti. Now he found himself embroiled in an old dispute. Tension mounted. Len attacked Matt. Roy saw serious consequences of a free-for-all in the kitchen between a hysterical woman, a jealous man drunk beyond reason, and a fiery Italian. Roy intervened and found himself between two fires.

Matt had not been drinking; he restrained himself. Connie ushered out the children and appealed successfully to their mother to leave. Soon the whole gang was packed into the truck and gone. As the dust settled, we took our bearings. Somehow, supper was ready on time. Connie rang the bell, the crew came in, and the brawl was history.

During weekdays, Len lived at camp, stayed sober, and was quite a different man. The company depended on him to keep the big Mack trucks operating, carrying logs from the bush to the mill. Connie and I leaned on Len one night when all was not well in the cookery.

It was two o'clock in the morning. Roy and his friend Pat, directly against Connie's rules, had established themselves in the dining room with a case of beer that they meant to drink before they left. Connie was scrupulously firm about male visitors leaving the cookery before Lights Out, but when these two men defied her and opened their first bottles, we could do nothing but go to our rooms.

We neither hoped nor intended to sleep; we knew that no good could come of this drunk. Beer always made Roy argumentative and shortened his Irish temper. And Roy had been a prizefighter. Alcohol was a direct threat to Pat's life, the aftermath of wartime head injuries. The long-standing fellowship between the two men had been undermined recently by Pat's promotion ahead of Roy at the sawmill.

Connie and I waited in our rooms for disaster to strike. To whom might we go for help? The bosses were twenty or thirty miles away, at home with their families. Even the clerk lived off site, in a cabin near the mill. We had no telephone. That night, the cookery seemed more isolated than ever. I started at the crack of a beam in the cold. I listened to the silence. A wolf howled beyond the camp. Low voices reached me, then the clink of a bottle cap against metal. The voices rose, and we caught the drift of an argument, kindled in disparagement of other people, fed on disputes about work at the mill, flaring in Roy's jealousy of Pat's new position.

A lull came in the voices; we listened. A beer case crashed to the floor; we sprang to our feet. Connie's door opened a second before mine, and we began picking our way in the dark among the benches and tables toward the centre of the room. The pot-bellied stove glowed feebly. We could just distinguish Roy leaning over the still form of Pat on the floor, and repeating, "He jumped me; I didn't hit him."

Pat groaned. Insensible, he flailed out wildly with his arms and feet. Roy looked unpredictable. Connie's voice shook. "Don't hit him, Roy. Please, don't hit him." And she tried to pull Roy off the man under him. Pat convulsed, knocking her aside. Sensing our helplessness, Connie ran out through the snow in her bare feet, up to the bunkhouses for help. Len was the person who came.

Roy was quickly sobering up. He put the strength of his neat, trained body into saving his friend from injury during his seizures. Gradually they ceased, and Len and Roy helped Pat to a bench. He sat, speechless, limp, and gasping. When he was sufficiently recovered, they carried him up to his bunkhouse and put him to bed.

-- --

Connie generally kept her sorrows to herself, but on that night of turmoil, we sat together while she unravelled the strands in the lovely, tough tapestry of her life.

Connie the child loved her Ukrainian mother and survived under the belittling power of her stepfather. Connie the teenager escaped the Brandon of her childhood to work in a restaurant kitchen in Winnipeg. Connie the woman became a respected cook in lumber camps: competent, wise, kindly. Yet the woman within her travelled alone, until she met Mickey in a camp. They simply belonged together, and Connie was fulfilled.

Too soon, Mickey fell ill with a fatal bacterial infection. Connie watched him as he died. Broken at heart, she needed a strong friend. It was Tom Tansley who gathered her up and brought her to work at Camp 51. A decade later, he did the same for road-spent me.

Connie's candour helped me to recognize her recurring sorrow, and her enduring strength to accept me with all my warts.

On the morning after the fight, Connie and I were making bread. She was prickly, not singing as she usually did. She growled at me for shaking in the flour too quickly. I was surprised and fell silent. She began whistling. I finished adding the flour, and moved to stoke the fires. She straightened up from the tub, pulling the kneaded dough from her fingers and stretching her back. Into the space between us, she said, "I sing when I'm sad and whistle when I'm mad." She was informing my silence. I began to see how she coped with both her past and with me.

Connie also whistled when I dropped out of a nicely kindled argument. Maybe I took her too seriously and spoiled her fun. Or was I on a nasty little power trip? Shades of my withdrawals from Baker in my early teens warned me, and made me think. I played the trick less and less often.

— —

The cutting crew increased as winter moved on. The contract had to be filled before spring. Faster and faster we were swept from one meal to the next, from one meat-cutting session to another, until all our haste could not fit our work into a day. Inevitably a second cookie had to be added to the staff. So it happened that Mike darkened our door.

Mike arrived on the bus from the Lakehead, smartly dressed and carrying a large suitcase. Connie introduced him to me. He took my hand, bowed, and smiled suavely. We drank coffee together and went on with the preparation of supper. He immediately assigned himself the leading role.

Mike had me fooled. Connie knew him of old. She wished there could have been a different choice, and she hoped Mike had changed. He appointed himself to wait on table in my place, and to refill the serving dishes, bypassing Connie at the dish-up table. He had worked here before; he knew everything. Within two days Connie saw her need to take a firmer grip on the reins of management, and I had to share the pull of the bit.

Mike was a talker; he took the boredom out of the kitchen. He had a smattering of knowledge in arts and sciences, and strong opinions about Canadian lack of *cultoor*. This quality, as defined in a mixture of Ukrainian and Croatian to Connie, spelled out sex from A to Z in Connie's humorous rendition to me. *Cultoor* was Mike's hobby, and he spent the duration of his time in Camp 51 trying to interest me in it. Instead he led me to explore at a safe distance the bizarre purposes of his warped mind.

Mike invited me to a movie in Geraldton. I accepted. Connie briefed me for my date. Mike and I travelled with a carload of friends, chauffeured by Ben the sawyer. The movie was innocuous; the show in the beer parlour where we rejoined our company was far more exciting. Camp tales about Saturday nights leapt to life and ran riot in the dusty files of my memory.

Mike joined in a round of beer. I sipped ginger ale, self-consciously

Geraldton, ON. Parked cars mark the hot spot in town,
site of my immersion course in pub biology.

at first. In no time I became a fascinated onlooker, content to let the conversation detour around me. The room was neither as shabby nor as crowded as I imagined it would be. In fact, it was clean and bright, with people sitting at round tables, talking quietly as they drank their beer.

The waiter brought another round. My soft drink was lasting well. Four young women settled at a table near ours. After the waiter had filled their orders, they looked us over to their satisfaction and returned into their own circle.

Across the room, on a stairway, a seductively clothed woman stood looking out. A minute later, she was gone. A man left his table and went up the stairs. Near our table, the women were becoming less contained. Two were refilling their glasses and one was tipping the bottle to her lips. Ribald jokes began jumping between tables.

The night aged. Ben suggested that we all empty our glasses. Connie and Little Paul were in conversation. Roy was imbibing and gazing into space. Mike's thin lips were slightly more curled than usual, his black eyes more darting. Through the smoke above our heads, I could see the prostitute with the phoney face taking another client.

Midnight was near. Ben tried again to get his passengers on the road.

Connie was ready to go, Paul was satisfied, and I was out of ginger ale. Roy insisted on one more round, because Mike had joined the party late.

The four women were deteriorating rapidly now. One was dishevelled and tearful; two were arguing in high-pitched voices, one was flirting with a drunken man. Somewhere across the room, a chair fell over. Tension quelled the noise. Ben put on his coat with an air of ultimatum. As he picked his way among the disarrayed tables to the door, we followed and plunged into the bitter cold on a billow of beery air.

Mike and I shared the front seat with Ben. Mike's hands seemed to be on a private tour, and I was the territory. Ben noticed and saved the situation by following my lead into a rapid-fire conversation about anything remote from sex. Between us we kept Mike from his goal until all the miles to camp were behind us.

— —

Winter freed Zazy and me to travel new terrain. Ice paved the lakes; snow cushioned the stony roads. One mild Sunday afternoon, a raven joined us as we galloped up the old camp road. It flew with its mouth open, just a few feet above my shoulder, turning its head to look at me, showing me the silvered margins of its black wings as they caught the long rays of the sun.

Mike asked if he might accompany me on my next trip. I was planning to go across the ice to see the creek that fed the lake. Reluctantly, I agreed to take Mike along, and the date was set for the following Sunday.

Mike had his own agenda. The questions he had been discussing in the bunkhouse about my resistance to his charms had reached Connie's ears. On the morning of our Sunday date, he boasted to Connie in Croatian that he would solve the mystery of my gender before we returned. Connie relayed his intentions to me in English with a twinkle in her eye. So it happened that Mike, Zazy, and I went walking up the bunkhouse road three abreast, with Zazy in the middle. Mike suggested we leave her behind because the weather looked blustery. I assured him that Zazy and I went together in any weather.

Mike ignored my advice to dress for intense cold. The weather did bluster; the wind drove fine snow toothed with ice crystals at us. Mike tried in vain to hold down a fedora that was making a poor union with his upturned collar. Deep drifts across the trail to the lake made me size up aloud Mike's low shoes, silk socks, and loose trouser cuffs. I suggested we turn back.

"That's okay, we go on," he said emphatically.

I ploughed in, following a fresh moose track; Zazy followed. Mike tried to object, but the wind blew away his words; he followed. The air felt warmer in the shelter of the bush. Mike suggested we sit down and talk, and he began pushing past Zazy. I was not about to sit down in an unfrozen bog with the temperature at −28°C. Zazy simply mistrusted the ground, and she decided abruptly to leave for the lake ice. I nearly bowled Mike over as I skid past him, travelling on the end of her halter shank.

Mike was now quite ready to head for camp. I dropped the topic of moose, and Mike promptly popped the word 'kissing' into the gap. I baited him with the topic of chastity. With Zazy between us, he had two choices, speech or silence. I kindly refused his offer to demonstrate the kissing he was unable to find words to explain. Zazy kept her place, all the way home.

Mike told Connie that he had enjoyed the hike. Predictably, he left supper in our hands, and retired with a large cup of hot coffee and mustard plasters on his heels. Our outing subdued him for several days.

As Mike's obsession drove him, I became skilled in evasive tactics I had learned from Connie during Andy's tenure. Peeling potatoes in the dimly lit stockroom was the greatest challenge, but I met it.

The approach of Christmas heightened Mike's melancholy. A glass of Connie's wine was enough to close the jaws of despair against the cooling flow of reason. "Barbara, come sit down, talk to me," he pleaded. I sat in the vacant dining room with him and listened to the sob story that Connie had grown tired of hearing: European women by the dozen sought him for his *cultoor*, yet he was unappreciated in Canada; his very birthright was denied. I shuddered. Now I too was rejecting him.

Mike's sob story ended with: "Better I kill myself." I took him seriously, groped through his history as a war survivor and a DP (Displaced Person) for something that might lend value to his life. My quest was hopeless; his self-pity had devalued all his blessings. He rose, walked unsteadily to the rack where the carving knives hung, looked them over. He drew out a long, pointed triangular blade, tested the edge and took up the sharpening steel. Seeing me about to leave, he came slowly up before me.

"I kill myself!" He spoke into my face, drawing the knife slowly over the steel very close to *my* throat. I stood petrified, trying to look unconcerned.

Connie glanced out from the kitchen. Roy was there, a trained boxer, now sober, rational, humane, and unafraid of confrontation. Connie called out: "Come and have a drink with us, Mike." Mike took his suicide–homicide equipment and joined Connie and Roy. His morose mood stuck on him. Suddenly he stood clear, grasped his shirt away from his chest, and slashed. "Oh," cried Connie almost under her breath. I looked, but no blood appeared. Mike had just spoiled a good shirt, and relieved his inner tension.

Roy calmly took away the knife, while Connie and I tiptoed around to the knife rack and hid the remaining blades. The men were talking quietly. We seized the chance to shut ourselves in my room and steady our nerves. Mike missed us and came looking. He tried our doors, called to us, pounded on my door. "Barbara, I want talk wit you. Is Connie there?" Neither of us moved. He pounded, the feeble hook strained, and the door bent. We leaned full force against it from inside. "I know you're in there. You hate me because I'm DP." He grabbed at our feet under the door. We jumped back, still leaning.

Roy called him off and somehow calmed him. We heard Mike go away and shut himself in his room. Connie silently unhooked the door and went to her own room. Roy joined her. I was scared silly, sitting alone. Mike was drunk and I had hurt his pride; I had failed him. He would brood until he saw another way to get at me. I was afraid to wait for the next wave. Maybe he was psychotic.

I eased open the door. The dining room was empty. I moved quickly and silently between the benches and the wall. A moment later, I was out at the door and running through the tingling cold night. Unchallenged, I melted into the darkness of the stable and huddled in the warmth of Zazy's broad chest. Perhaps I would stay there until morning. I shivered in my light dress and pressed closer to the mare. I waited. My bones told me the meaning of the white rime around the window frames. Through the ice-coated panes, the yard light sent a diffuse glow. I wished the generator would stop, to make the stable darker. Shod hooves rang hollow on the planks, and quietness returned.

My heart raced. Someone was fumbling the latch. The door creaked open. "Barbara." It was Mike's voice! I kept silent. He called again, commandingly. The length of the stable separated us. I remembered that he was afraid to walk behind the horses. Would the liquor make him brave? He was fumbling round the door, perhaps looking for the light switch. I prayed he would not find it, and he did not. The door closed and he was gone. Would he ask Myles about the light switch?

The generator stopped and darkness prevailed. The temperature was dropping. Zazy shifted her weight and nuzzled my shoulder. Profound quiet had come over the camp. Now, through the frosted window, a glint of light flashed on the ice crystals. Was it the moon? No, it was bobbing. I heard the crunch of feet on dry snow. Somebody was coming with a lighted lantern. Mike was not to be outdone. The latch rattled and the door opened. "Barbara," a voice called out, "Barbara." The voice spoke into the shadows beyond the circle of light. It was Roy's voice.

The cookery was warm, because Harry had thought of our comfort and stoked up the fire last thing before going to turn off the lights. Connie was reading a murder mystery in her room. Mike had not been heard for some time. Connie was far from sleep, and my mind was racing.

"Let's get some of these decorations up, Barbarichka." Connie was setting out a little pile of cardboard boxes and a couple of paper bags. By the light of gas lamps, we unpacked the ornaments, cut and twisted crepe paper into streamers and pinned them at the corners of the room, draped tinsel and hung balls across the windows, until we felt quite festive. Finally we fetched out the cutlery from under a sack of beans in the stockroom. After that night, whenever we suspected that Mike was drinking, we hid the knives.

—

Harry was the first man to see the cookery decorated. The light from his swinging lantern danced off the balls and tinsel as he came walking down the dining room to light the stoves. Harry was aglow with happiness, and his smiles were the best medicine for all that lay on our hearts after our wild night. The next men to walk in were our DP buddies, Big Steve, Frank, and Vinko. The dining room's Christmas dress touched off the wonderful smiles of these tall, lean loggers, who were always full of thanks.

Connie was cheered by our friends, but sick at heart. She had seen too many Christmases at camp. Mike roused himself sullenly into half-speed. He had tapped the generous supply of wine in the bunkhouses, and he was showing what we could expect from others of the crew.

Before supper, the communists like Little Paul and the Canadian veterans like Big Red clashed on the subject of Canadian government and the Commonwealth. Paul was criticizing everything Canadian, and Big Red had heard enough. He ended Paul's sermon by grabbing him by the ankles and dunking him in the water barrel. Paul swallowed his pride; it burned inside him into a raging hatred.

At supper, Little Paul was silent and Big Red was offensively noisy. Whisky in the bunkhouse spirited away the remainder of Red's common sense. Paul lay down on his bed, and with a few pointed insults he baited Red. The big man moved nearer and nearer, until he came within striking range. As he bent over Paul, he caught a smashing blow from a bottle across his forehead. Bloody and furious, Red could have killed Paul on the spot. Roy managed to talk him down, then he and Nick got him outdoors and down and into the cookery. Gory, tousled, deflated, he sat quietly while Connie cleaned him up and patched his gash, then Nick took him to Beardmore to enforce the peace.

At Christmastime, no worship was shared. Nothing happened to reconnect weary people with their lost faith, but not everyone made a drunk of the holiday. Big Steve and Frank and Vinko worked as usual until Christmas Eve, adding to their piles of logs beside the bush road. Their earnings were not to prosper the bootlegger and the beer parlour, but to bank for a future in the Canada they believed in. They were content to drink a glass of wine or two with Connie on Christmas Day, share the rest of the bottle in the bunkhouse, rest a day and eat turkey and trimmings, and return to work refreshed.

I missed Christmas Day at camp, and Connie told me later how it all turned out. On the day before the eve of the holiday, she sprang a surprise gift on me, a train ticket to Montreal. She packed me off with Neil to Jellicoe, and he put me on a train to arrive by December 24. The family was there at the gate at Windsor Station to welcome me. The interlude with Mom and Dad, Joan, and terrier Daisy was sheer joy, like meeting on a mountaintop. It did not unravel the Canada trip at all, and yet as I left the folks at the train three days later, I found myself in tears.

Paulooshka, Little Paul in fond or festive mood, hailed the New Year 1950 by beating on the triangle at midnight.

— —

Mike spent his final weeks at Camp 51 trying by clever lies to destroy friendships. His behaviour became erratic. One day he was icily silent. The next, he was saying he was beginning to love me. That was my cue to lug our potato tub out of the dark, secluded stockroom into the bright, populated kitchen.

Mike's campaign was unnerving. Connie escaped by reading pocket novels far into the night. I rode along the highway, sometimes wishing never to go back. Strangely, when my urge to leave was most intense, Zazy clearly showed it too, for she would resist turning back. But we had to return, because Connie had said that my leaving was not the answer, and I believed her.

I stood with Zazy on the bridge, looking for the river. Its flow was all but hidden under the winter-locked boulders in its course. Just so, the deep flow of affection between Connie and me was all but hidden by the shroud of discord laid on us by Mike.

The storm broke. Once too often, Mike threatened to quit and went on strike. He strolled out of his room at breakfast time and watched Connie and me rushing through three people's work. She greeted him affably just to ease the tension, and he returned an insult, followed by an ultimatum: Fire me or lose his valuable services. He was surprised to hear that he was free to leave. He poisoned the atmosphere until the bus for Port Arthur took him away the following morning. The air cleared like a snow cover swept by a chinook.

Connie and I sped merrily along, keeping pace with the routine and doing the baking at night. We worked by Coleman lamplight to the music of Strauss, Wagner, and Offenbach played on Connie's turntable. Some of the men who had shared our trials with Mike now came to help us, making lunches, cleaning, washing dishes for fifty men. Floor washing fell off the list when the temperature dropped so low that water froze to the planks before we could mop them. After we had fully recovered from Mike, Connie gave Tom Tansley the nod and he hired Helen, a young Ukrainian woman, to cookie with me. Helen melded well with the team.

5

In the dead of winter, wolves came close to the camp to eat garbage. Zazy refused to brave them, so I left her in the stable and skied by the lights in the sky. I wanted with a passion to see wolves. Their songs drew me, their tracks teased me, their unseen presence informed me, especially in a long valley with a young forest on its floor.

Now in the moonlight I was making for that valley. Herringboning up shining white hills, breaking through the lips of drifts to skim down into blue shadows, up and down across the scintillating land I moved, while Orion the hunter journeyed across the sky with his brilliant dog star Sirius. Above the valley I watched and listened. Below, I waited on a beaten moose trail. Not a wolf came in sight, yet I felt intensely watched. The wolves won the game again, but I travelled that night on planet Earth with my head in the universe.

Camp 51 Kitchen Crew (l. to r.) Barbara Bradbury, Connie Evans, Neil Arthur (behind) Helen Zamrykut. March 1950.

Winter claimed all of March. A storm blocked the roads in northern Ontario and shut us down. Fifty-one lunches were devoured as a mid-morning snack and the whole crew turned out for dinner. The next day the blizzard had passed, but intense cold and deep snow kept the men from work. By the following day, news came that Sinc had bulldozed the bush road. In haste, we made lunches for the men, and soon the long procession of horses, bobsleighs, men, and trucks began to move up the bunkhouse road.

That same day in the afternoon, I rode Zazy up to the work site to see how the deep snow affected the operation, especially the cutters and their horses. There was Vinko, working away cheerfully with his frosted, red roan horse, both of them in snow up to their knees. Myles kept the Tansley horses well fit for their demanding work.

Myles had a singularly cheerful greeting for Zazy and me as we returned to the stable. Even under the peak of his woolly winter cap, he could not hide his happy anticipation.

The next morning, Zazy and Andy and the others received their feed from Frenchie the deaf Frenchman. Gus the smiling Swede helped with the chores. In the cookery we missed Myles at his usual place at the top end of the table. Second helpings of eggs were going the rounds when he staggered in, excusing himself loudly, to everyone's amusement. Connie knew Old Myles was on a bender.

All winter Myles had been sober, but once started on the booze, only a drought could stop him. He was worse by afternoon. Tom and Neil happened to come in and find him explaining to

Barago with skidding horse, blanketed during rest. March 1950.

Connie how vital he was to the functioning of the company. "I got lotsa money," he boasted. "I got eight tousan' dollars an' a bottle o' wine."

The tall lumberman winked at the lean prairie farmer and the two men

The jammer loading logs onto the Mack truck. Zazy watching the work. March 1950.

Vinko and Barago and their skidding horse cutting pulpwood at Camp 51. March 1950.

helped themselves to coffee. They settled on a bench with Myles between them, backs against the table edge, long legs sliding out to let the heels find the crack between the planks that fit. Tom and Neil had taken on the old man, bargaining to borrow his eight thousand dollars, when I left on the foreman's snowshoes.

The snow on the barrens had drifted firm during the recent storm. Under the March sun, I shed jacket, sweater, and mitts, pocketed or tied them around my waist, and rolled up my shirtsleeves. My bliss blinked out right between two cute little treetops standing a foot high. Down I plunged and came to rest in a white-walled cave. I knew just how Alice felt. The saplings had held hands during the storm and kept out the drifting snow, forming a pocket. The air down there was cold.

First I dressed again for winter. Then I reached up and tested the snow pack around the hole. It broke back. The trees would not support me. I freed my feet and set my snowshoes on the surface as a base. The first shoe sank a foot under my weight, shortening the distance I had to lift myself. From it I could gain the second shoe set on solid snow. One heave, and I was in sunshine again, wise to cute little treetops.

Myles had disappeared from camp when I returned. If he slept that night in the bunkhouse, he may have noticed a difference in his bed. Neil had seized his chance to change the flannelette sheets, pillowcase, even the nine grimy blankets that Myles had used for years.

Tom knew the probable course of Myles' bender. He arranged with Frenchie to care for the horses until the barn boss was back on the job. Within the next twenty-four hours, Myles drank dry his alcohol supply, and twelve hours later he walked unsteadily into the cookery and sheepishly told Connie how thirsty he was. She rationed out one small glass of whisky to him. For another day, we kept our eye on the tall bottles of liquid extracts in view on a high shelf, while Myles recovered his balance.

Later that week Myles was sitting by the stove, shivering at the thought of driving a horse all twelve miles to Camp 51A. Vinko's red roan had to go to the subcamp that cut mine timbers, and a bigger horse had to be brought back. I thought: "Does he really not want to go? I'd love to go, but not on a sleigh. I'll just ask quietly, so he can refuse quietly and there won't be any waves." I waited for an opening. "Mr. Myles, I'll be glad to ride the horse to 51A for you Sunday morning, if that time's okay with you." Amazingly, Myles agreed, and he stopped shivering.

I was on the road before sunrise, with Zazy's Pelham bridle and saddle blanket on the horse. He cheerfully settled into a snappy trot that made the snow squeak, ate up the miles, and kept us both warm. Behind us the sun was sending its rays to rest against the spruces and draw long shadows on the ground. I could see a fuzzy coat of frost crystals forming over us, whitening us from head to foot. Inside my roomy leather shoes and woollen socks, my feet were warm, and the rime on the outside told me that the moisture was escaping properly.

The sun climbed. We slowed to a walk. No car shared our road. Now I was watching for the turnoff to the camp. At a bend above a shallow valley, the scent of wood smoke reached me, conjuring thoughts of breakfast. The horse offered to trot again. The scent grew stronger. Now I could see a thin, blue-grey taper rising straight out of the forest. Matt's chimney was sending a welcome message. Minutes later my mount was eating hay in the stable, and I was sitting not too close to the stove in Matt's bachelor shack, pulling frozen socks out of frozen shoes. Matt was aglow, putting on fresh coffee, pulling the spaghetti pot from the back of the stove, tilting the frying pan with its sputtering cargo of eggs, all the while asking about our journey and the latest news of camp, and

Frenchie and Myles with the horses Ricky and Andy. Camp 51, late winter 1950.

telling me about his solitary life tending the 51A horses.

"There's Rocky." Matt motioned through the window at a lanky black horse capering with a dozen others in the clearing between the stable and the spring. Rocky was to carry me back to camp. "Pull up your chair now, Barbara Mia," said Matt with fatherly affection, rubbing his hands together for joy. We both ate heartily; I realized Matt had been waiting for me.

We went outside to catch Rocky out of the bunch. They all took one look and galloped for the bush, pausing a moment at the spring, merrily defying us to take them. Matt went up and sent them back toward the yard. Down they came, manes, tails, and heels flying, with Rocky in the lead, bucking and kicking. I still don't know what made him stop by the stable and let me take hold of his halter.

"How's he to ride, Matt?"

"I t'ink he's okay, Barbara. I don't know of anybody that's rode 'im."

Rocky accepted the bridle after I let out the cheek pieces several inches. He tolerated a rather narrow bit. Matt said he would spare me the burden of Rocky's collar by sending it along with the blanket with Neil in the morning. I set a hand at the base of Rocky's neck and sprang the sixteen-two hands onto his back. He accepted me in less than a minute. Then I took up the reins and he showed no concern. I nudged his body ever so gently with my thighs, and we set off for Camp 51.

The curb bit was a novelty to Rocky, I suppose, for it held his attention while the first car passed us. He was ready to dance when the second car came, so we took to the deep snow. We travelled there until he settled into a good trot, then travelled on the shoulder and enjoyed the rest of the trip. His long legs covered the twelve miles in less than two hours, and I was back in my dress and apron in time for dinner.

Spring stepped in that very night. It decked the meat house with icicles and willed away the waves of snow that leaned against the cookery windows. Zazy walked on bare ground on the old camp road that had been impassable only two days before. By the end of the week, I saw moss on the knolls. Yet the line of teams and sleighs, teamsters and cutters crossed the river ice and added daily to the piles of logs being massed near the shore. We could see the morning exodus from the window above the sink, and from Connie's baking window we caught sight of the other teams going up the bunkhouse road, leaving and returning in daylight now that Earth was tipping us toward summer. Orion had almost set by evening, and one night in his winter place, the aurora borealis flooded the sky with pale green light overlaid with rippling rainbow curtains.

I counted the days until Zazy and I would be on the road. "When do you think you'll be leaving?" Neil would inquire with a twinkle in his grey-blue eyes, glancing at the big flakes of snow falling past the dining room windows. "Myles says you and he should go with a covered wagon and a rocking chair, a couple of hens, and you in the back telling fortunes."

Just a week after the thaw, a blizzard began piling snow again. This time the bulldozer was at the subcamp, so we were properly snowed in. About noon on the second day, an Ontario Hydro plough opened a way for Sinc to bring the bulldozer back to Camp 51. He soon had a trail broken through the drifts so that the sixty men could return to work

Communications with the outside world gradually were restored. A letter from Mom told about spring flowers blooming in the garden in Montreal South. Easter was on the way.

On the first night in April, a big white moon was looking into my window. Its soft light showed me the edge of the clearing, where my old friends, those two long, lean, now leafless poplars, were bowing to each other. Harry the bullcook brought a load of liquor from town that night, so there was singing in the bunkhouses.

The Easter moon laid a path of light above the dark camp, on its way through our night. Maybe men moved in their sleep as renewal was beamed to their ancient marine molecules. Would change survive the light of day?

Connie freed me from camp routine to share in the Eucharist of Easter morning. She took on the whole workload despite a severely cut finger, and sent me in Earl's taxi to Geraldton. Earl left me at the Anglican Church.

The nave of the church was graced with flags and filled with people. Caught up in fellowship, we shared the story of Easter, the prayers, the praise, and the Holy Communion. We sang Mom's favourite Easter hymns. The sacrament connected me to Mom and Dad, to Connie who had freed me to be there, and to the power to grow. After the service, the congregation burst into the glorious disorder of Easter greetings. Smiles, open hands, open arms all moved the meaning of the moonlight into the light of day.

The sun was melting the icicles on the church roof as I stood watching for Earl's taxi. Snow banks were starting to leak water from their feet. The gentle air touched off memories and planted newness here, everywhere, now! Earl picked me up and we started for camp. He drove slowly and we talked about his life around Geraldton and Port Arthur, and mine as I journeyed. The afternoon was mellow, too nice to waste hurrying back. Earl pulled over and we listened to each other saying nothing for a few minutes, then Earl gradually gathered me close to him and kissed me, wonderfully long. Then he simply set me back, started his taxi, and without another word, he took me the rest of the way back to camp. I said no more; I was savouring a strange feeling, as if I were moving into a new dimension.

6

On Easter Sunday night, I started to pack. On Monday morning, winter took control of human affairs. Blowing snow and intense cold shut down logging operations, and all but thirty-five of the men left camp. Then dysentery broke out. The crew blamed the cookies for leaving soap on the dishes, until the doctor came and diagnosed viral gastroenteritis.

I became ill after supper on the night that the camp closed. I walked across the ice bridge and up a logging trail and lay down in the snow, hoping the cold would chase the nausea. It failed utterly, and I dragged myself home to bed. Tom Tansley looked into my smelly room a day later and offered to call in the doctor. I was afraid of the doctor; I had heard he was a drug pusher. He came the next day and gave me pills to stop the dehydration. The illness lasted a whole week, relieved me of fifteen pounds, and left me weak but even more restless to be gone.

There was an element of personal disgust in my wishing to be gone. While I was too weak to walk, I had to use jerry cans in my room in lieu of the Office. Cold controlled the odour, but the final disposal was my dilemma, too embarrassing to mention even to Connie. I chose a place where I was sure no one went, and where I thought the river flooded in spring, and secretly rid myself of the shameful cans. A few days later, Little Paul was cursing me roundly in Russian. I had chosen the wrong place. I wanted to leave their rotten camp that moment, forever. I was crushed with shame for days.

There was also a sunny side to my misery. During my illness, a young Yugoslavian DP named Franc was retired from the mill with an injured foot and sent to cookie in my place. He volunteered to exercise Zazy, and when I saw him ride, I welcomed his offer. Zazy took kindly to him from their first meeting.

Franc told me about his father's horses at home before the military took their pick, and about his being placed as a DP on an elite horse farm in the Laurentian Mountains of Quebec because of his history. He had made the most of his chance to ride hunters and to learn dressage. Zazy responded to his finesse and shaped up beautifully.

Together we walked, Franc and I in company with Zazy. We talked about war, and horses, and the agony of having them confiscated. We tossed around the problems of New Canadians. We looked frankly at the perplexities of cookery life that I had faced as a girl with a sheltered childhood. We ventured into our dreams for the future.

April unfolded until Orion and his dog set with the sun. Winter had ended in the sky. Franc and I were standing in the stable doorway, looking at the stars, when we heard a crash followed by rumbling. We

Franc Potocnik, my flame, riding Zazy. April 1950.

hurried to the riverbank. In the moonlight we saw black water outlining blue, slow-moving cakes of ice. One pile of logs had broken loose. During the night, another pile went. Winter was ending on the river. The rising water took only a few days to clear the ice and carry the logs out of sight. On the sixteenth day of April, herring gulls returned in full voice to hover above the garbage sled and perch along the roof ridge of the trapper's cabin, shrilling their news of spring.

Winter lingered in the woods until the last, and out on the slash between the knolls, patches of snow carried me one more time on skis to the edge of my favourite valley. Its rock wall seemed conscious of itself, aware of each pregnant ledge bearded with dripping icicles, each weathered stone face wet with shining melt water. I could still see snowshoe tracks entering the valley, where the prospectors in a mid-winter gold rush had come to probe the cliffs. The tracks looked huge, expanded and embossed on the sinking snow.

I skied along the top until the valley ran into snowy forest. Feathers scattered under a tree marked a death and a feast. I tackled the hill to the flat floor with caution, only to be carried away by my skis under a branch, round a tree, over a mogul into a tangle of skis and shrubs almost at the bottom.

Where did you fall from? asked the first whiskey jack on the scene. It was perched on a twig three feet from me, cocking its head to favour one eye and then the other. Down through the branches came others of its kin. Chickadees flitted close to see, and went away whispering. I straightened my skis, bribed the jays with cookie crumbs to accompany me, and slid to the bottom. The sky had changed to yellow-grey when I came into a pure stand of baby larches. Moving among the delicate trees, I was at one with the magical silence of the young forest and the fine snow sifting down in the wind.

— —

Dominic Ichikawa came to reign as second cook at Camp 51. Under his regime, silence had no place. "Ey-yi-yi-yii!" came his crescendo squeal. Connie jumped and turned pale, expecting to see Dominic scalded full length. Nothing, nothing at all had happened. No, just Dominic!

Dominic now cooked the first course in a meal, Connie was in charge, and she did the baking and general management. Helen and I worked along with them. Our Asian livewire with his flashing black eyes kept the emotional ferment bubbling.

One morning we women were peacefully at work in the kitchen. Rhythmic banging of a meat cleaver in the hall was keeping us informed that Dominic was busy cutting pork chops. The cleaver fell silent, then, a blood-chilling yell pierced our peace. A split second later, Mumsy the cat shot from the end of the hall, hair and tail electrified, running for her life with Dominic after her, cleaver in hand.

How he hated cats, especially cats on the meat table! Mumsy spent the rest of the day hiding out under Helen's bed. Helen defended her cat in her spiciest mix of Ukrainian, English, and body language. Dominic scorned her. These two opposites lived at violent odds. Dominic found a renewable target in Helen's rigid ways and arbitrary values. Helen set moral limits around herself as a guard fence that kept her mostly protected, always at risk.

Helen had the misfortune to room next door to Dominic. One evening she caught sight of his face peering under her door. Helen's outrage blasted up like a thunderhead, powered by her enemy's fiendish laughter. She would have quit her job if Connie had not instantly squelched Dominic.

I presented a less predictable target to this wiry little pest. His joy was to stalk me when I was setting the table and grab at me. Usually I jumped clear; sometimes he got me. Once or twice I fired a fistful of cutlery at his head. One afternoon I won the game purely by chance. He came sneaking up behind me as I stood at a side table, icing a cake. On the spur of the moment, I whirled on him with my shining spatula. He bolted down the dining room screaming and fled out through the door, sure that I was after him with a butcher knife.

Connie moved through camp chaos in dynamic balance. Her intuitive genius, her wit, and her generosity freed her to rise above challenge, to forgive, and to love with wisdom. Connie had outlived her fears but not her great capacity to love.

Dominic changed the tenor of life, but spring changed it more. The snow softened, rushing the company to complete its contract before the bush roads broke. Already the horses were punching through the crust, and often the men were caught out in rain. More and tougher lumberjacks were hired to speed the winter work to a finish. They scowled and cursed about the food, and on pouring wet days, they passed their time throwing knives at the bunkhouse stove pipes.

The days lengthened. Sun and rain conspired to melt the remaining snow. On the twenty-third of April, I carried my skis up the bunkhouse road to its junction with the lakeshore trail. There in the shade of the trees, the snow held me up for one last look at the frozen lake. Yielding ice sent a sharp crack racing across the expanse that Zazy and I had crossed a month before. In the twilight, the hooting of an owl came floating like a phantom voice through the forest. A small moth fluttered on blue wings. The next day, I found the lovely pink arbutus trailing its blossoms across a rock.

Connie and I were prowling around the idea of our parting. "I'd like to give Zazy a nice new blanket," Connie decided out loud. "Where can you get a horse blanket?"

Nick had a catalogue from Birts' Saddlery in Winnipeg. Connie borrowed it and found a whole page of blankets advertised, with prices given for the various fabrics and instructions for measuring a horse. I was dazzled by the scope of this wondrous catalogue. Connie went to her sewing machine for a measuring tape, and I raced out to fetch Zazy. She was duly measured, and the order was sent in the mail that afternoon.

Soon after, Little Paul and Harry stopped by the baking table where Connie and I were rolling out cookies. Paul spoke. "You going away soon, we want give you present. What you like to have?" Joy rose like the song of a hidden bird.

I said I would think about their kind offer and choose something. Connie helped them to understand what I meant. "Maybe you like nice dress?" Paul tendered, and we all thought about that. Then the men left.

Connie was happy; she had been the flux among us all. When she was ill, Paul and Harry had shared my concern and the extra work. Paul had forgiven my error in protocol when I hung my underwear in view on the clothesline. Harry had sat with Connie and me, simply enjoying a story, or a piece of cake, or the cookery in Christmas dress. When he was sad, he talked in Ukrainian to Connie, looking at me as if I too understood. And so I did, in a way. Paul, in the quiet after a nasty storm among personnel in camp, had found words to ask me where to find peace. We were no longer strangers to each other.

"You know what I'd love to have, Connie?" She paused over the folding of a cabbage roll. "A new bridle. It would be a very special keepsake from Harry and Paul." Connie finished the last roll and set it on its bed of pork rind in the iron pot. Out came Birts' Catalogue. There was a picture of a fine English russet-leather bridle with double reins, just what I wanted. Connie talked over my choice with Paul the next day. He was visibly disappointed that I did not prefer a dress, but he did approve my choice. Another order was mailed to Winnipeg.

— —

Franc and I went out to celebrate spring at the old camp. We found the ruined shacks on an island created by the rising river. The backwater froze our bare feet, and the warm grass thawed them. We sat with our backs against a sun-baked wall, listening to the splash of the river and the whispers of moisture moving in sod.

We launched someone's beached canoe, tethered it long to a tree on the bank, and worked it out to midstream with a pole. When the flood hit us broadside, Franc hastily advised me that he could not swim. We cautiously hauled ourselves to shore and left the canoe well above high-water mark. Then, shoes in hand, we flung a dare at each other and dashed back through the knee-deep water to the road, leaving the old shingled buildings to their dreams.

At dishes the next morning, I looked down to the shallows where I had seen the moose family. I called Connie. Quite close to the bank, three canoes glided, disturbing the water scarcely more than the long shadows that they cast. It was as though a hand below were carrying them forward, bidden by mystical paddles. Subtly as dawn, the flotilla vanished in silence around the nearest bend.

Connie said the canoes carried Native families from Macdiarmid, returning for their annual muskrat trapping around the old camp. They would pitch tents and stay while high water favoured their fur harvest. It was their spare canoe that Franc and I had borrowed. I wondered if they came only for fur. Did they leave their lakeside village because the wilderness called them, now that spring had come? Would they have understood what was so hard for Connie and Franc to grasp, that the highway was clear of snow and the grass was sprouting green and I had to be on my way?

Zazy knew. She was reluctant to turn back on the night when we tried out her new shoes. Until she joined me on the road, she had been a homing horse like most of her kin. Now we were one in our urge to see new ground. We were leaving practical security. I was shelving temporarily my future with Franc, and surely I would come back to love him again. Now I couldn't stay, while the prairies and mountains and ocean were still strangers that I needed to meet and know and live with.

Franc and I sat above the lake, watching the water shimmering through the lace of uncurling birch leaves. He had brought a blanket; I had the feeling that I was overlooking its meaning. We talked of the day when my veterinary training would be finished, of hiking in the mountains of Yugoslavia and ranching in Canada. I saw life with Franc in my future. I saw endless possibilities for us, as fixed yet as free as the flags on a kite's tail. Did he need a surer sign?

The morning of May 15, 1950, dawned opalescent grey, pulsating with promise. On the back porch of the cookery, the familiar haversacks stood linked together to serve again as saddlebags. On top of them lay a fine woollen polo cloth blanket, Connie's gift to Zazy. Against them leaned my sleeping bag, rolled in the old khaki rain cape/groundsheet. Hesitantly, I decided to send home my fly bar, thinking we would be out of the bush before fly season and onto the prairie with nothing to hold up a fly bar.

Cardboard boxes contained the clothing that Mom had sent through the previous year, packed around souvenirs of camp: a pillowcase embroidered for me by Helen, an apron made by Connie on her new sewing machine, fossils and rocks, grouse feathers from the lakeside trail, red-capped lichens, a weasel skin prepared by Nick, complete with claws. I added the fly bar, and set the boxes with the skis back against the wall for Neil to pick up.

Neil would ship my belongings from Jellicoe Station. Frank would forward the rifle to Peg and Charlie at Lytton, as I expected to have no further need of it.

I brought Zazy from the stable, with her saddle resting on the quilted pad laced into place by Nick. She wore the handsome bridle and reins given to us by Paul and Harry. I treasured their gift and they shared my happiness over it. Their smiles melted away the shadow of chagrin they had felt when I did not choose a dress.

While I packed the load, Zazy counted with a hoof to keep oatmeal cookies coming out of Connie's pocket. Then we all, Harry and Paul, Helen, Dominic, Connie, and I, simply said goodbye, for how could we say things like "just for now" without falling apart? I mounted, Connie stepped from the porch to give Zazy "one last keess on the noze because she is bewdeeful," Zazy lifted her lip, burped her thanks, turned and carried me along the stem of the T that is the camp road.

Camp 51 was quiet. The men were at work, except for Mr. Myles, who waved from the bunkhouse doorway, and Franc, who met us at the stable and walked with us to the highway.

At the mill, the jack ladder was catching up logs from the river and presenting them to the saw. Friends waved. We passed the posts that held the heavy chain during fire season. I slid off the mare, and Franc and I shared a hug and a kiss to remember. He gave me a leg up, and Zazy walked toward the iron bridge over the Sturgeon River. Franc headed home to camp.

Zazy and I paused on the bridge. Upstream the river came surging out of the woods, running high with meltwater, churning flotsam. Downstream it foamed over boulders and drove its load of stones against them, grinding and chipping.

I thought how caddis worms in some quiet pool at the edge of the flood might someday gather the tiny shiny flakes of granite and olivine, and glue them into splendid tubes to encase their soft bodies. I imagined them humping their camouflaged tubes across the sandy floor of the pool.

— —

Camp 51 had changed me; I was not the same person that rode east across this bridge in my skin ten months before. Some awkward corners had been knocked off my perception. I thought of the friends who had helped me past the boulders obstructing my living at ease with people from day to day. Nick, Roy, Matt, Harry, and Paul, near the end of my time Franc, and always Connie—they had brought me round several sharp rocks with the chips flying. Trust grew among us, so that our friendship seemed to be as a caddis worm case, built for change to fit creatures born to grow and emerge and fly.

Blackwater River and the iron bridge
at Camp 51 road. May 1950.

Camp 51 had changed me. I arrived with a respect for people. I left with a passion for them. Franc was part of that changing. He was ready for us to share the air to the full; I needed to finish my first flight alone. I left Franc, hoping that the bits chipped off our differences might build toward a beautiful future for us together.

PART FOUR
Faring Forward

1

Fare forward, you who think that you are voyaging;
You are not those who saw the harbour receding, or those who
*   will disembark.*
Here between the hither and the farther shore while time is
*   withdrawn,*
Consider the future and the past with an equal mind.

Not fare well,
But fare forward, voyagers.

T.S. Eliot, "The Dry Salvages", *Four Quartets,*

Zazy carried me off the Sturgeon River Bridge onto Highway #1.

"Hello! You're on the move again!" The familiar voice of the Canada Bread salesman reached through the window of his panel truck as it glided to a stop. He was happy to hear how well we had wintered. He wished me good luck until our paths crossed again, and drove away. What a wide world, this meeting place at large, alive with fellow travellers!

A taxi stopped beside us and Earl stepped out. My first flame, Earl was the one whose warmth had split the tough case on the jack pine seed and awakened my sense of womanhood. Our hands found each other's, any words would do, and we hugged into life a memory to keep. In the next moment, Earl was gone, on with his day. And on went mine, while our times together replayed for me in rainbow colours: coffee in the cookery, a taxi ride with Connie, Roy, and Helen over a white road under a jet-black sky, and my ride home at Easter, when Earl pulled over and gave me my first kiss.

Other friends shared the highway: a crew repairing springtime damage, Mounties who were expecting us and who would keep in touch and make note of us to the next patrol, a long-distance trucker who waved in passing. We stopped in Jellicoe at the invitation of Mrs. Neil Arthur, to have tea and let Zazy enjoy the sprouting lawn grass. Foreman Neil had already brought my boxes and skis to the railway station.

Sinc came along in the afternoon and rescued Zazy from the burden of the miles. He grinned his familiar grin, spoke his usual few words, loaded the kit into his pickup truck, and took it ahead to Beardmore. Zazy took heart and we arrived before dark, having come thirty-five miles. The Sinclairs and Tansleys were out on the street to welcome us into their homes.

We rose early, ready to travel. I wanted to take giant steps to new ground beyond the Lakehead. Hide would toughen, legs would strengthen, and endurance would grow as we tackled the miles. Next Nipigon, then Pearl, then one night at the home of Franc's mother in Port Arthur, then we'd be launched into all of Canada to the west.

An afternoon deluge swamped my preview, and a stormy sky continued to dissolve my boldly envisioned horizon as we slopped along side by side in the mud. Through my stupor, *wham!* A shod hoof slammed into my right buttock. I exploded! "What did you go and do that for?" Zazy was standing across the road, looking surprised at me. I burst out laughing.

Rapidly my mind spread out the likely sequence of events that had happened in a moment. Zazy had shied from something I never saw. I grabbed for a rein and missed. With her lateral vision she mistook me for her attacker, swung round and kicked like lightning. I turned as fast, catching the kick in the rear instead of in hip or abdomen. Her honest error was easy to forgive.

We were drying nicely in the sunshine that broke through the clouds as we passed Macdiarmid, home of the muskrat trappers that had graced the river at Camp 51 in early spring. At Orient Bay, a magnificent spray of shining water fell over the edge of the escarpment. We had reached the head of Lake Nipigon. We crossed the neck of land that held the lakes named after the women of the road builders, and I expectantly headed again for Nipigon.

A cloudburst caught us climbing a steep grade and soaked us, head to foot. I squished along in shoes full of water. Zazy plodded beside me with water streaming from her drooped ears and bedraggled mane. "Same hill, same weather, wrong year!" I mused aloud. As if on cue, the Mileage 56 sign came into view. Gladly we parked in its threadbare stable for the night.

The hail that pelted the roof the next morning held us to our shelter. My feeling that we were not alone heightened my urge to stay hidden. I watered Zazy before dawn, carried grass to her in her stall to go with oat chop from the old barrel, and returned to the wet bed that the heat from my body was drying.

We were watering at the creek before leaving in the afternoon when an aged man stepped out of a shack on the bank above us. He stood looking at us in surprise. I walked up and explained how we came there. He was a friend of Jim and Irene Martin, and he told me that we had passed their camp only a few miles back up the road.

I had to see Jim and Irene again! One hour's ride took us back to their road. Jim and Irene were camped with Jack, Max, and, naturally, Beaver, behind the great rock that creates Orient Bay's bridal falls. What a welcome we found!

Zazy was made comfortable with Jim's team in the stable, and I joined the family circle in the kitchen. They told me they were cutting stall timbers on contract, with Max now a sober mainstay in the enterprise. I told them about our time at Camp 51. Behind our happy talk, out the windows the sunset wrote poetry on a small lake.

— —

Zazy gained enthusiasm as she hardened to her work. The road surface improved and we moved quickly toward Port Arthur. At the junction of the roads to Nipigon and Schreiber, men at the maintenance depot of the Department of Highways hailed us. They fed us and happily showed us their pet yearling moose, Abdul. His mother had been killed on the highway when he was a calf, and the men had raised him. He was free to wander, but he came on call to meet us. Zazy may have been the first horse he had seen. He kept his distance, and stared after us when we left.

We passed through Nipigon and around the Red Rock escarpment and stopped overnight with two ladies, sisters from the Orkney Islands, in their cottage by the road. The younger was the widow of an engineer who had supervised the building of many miles of the road behind us. At teatime, we sat round a wide, opened album with the light from a Tyndall table lamp brightening black-and-white photographs on flat black pages. Caught in a bubble of mutual discovery, we let our memories run off leash back through time and space to those warmly familiar sites: a construction crew at some difficult bend in the road, a hilltop with a view to the Blackwater River, a tent camp with an open fire beside a lake. We would hurry through our story to meet each other on the spot and celebrate.

On the road again, I stopped to admire a bed of pansies early in bloom. The elderly gentleman who was tending them brought a pail down the stone steps from his garden to the spring at the roadside. His brown face was wrinkled and wreathed in white hair. He held the pail for Zazy, speaking tenderly to my little black horse.

We passed Wolf River, with its arm full of driftwood. At Dorion I could see the geraniums showing green through the porch windows at the Finnish farm where we had stayed. We passed the generous trout stream running through the farm at Pearl. At Blend Creek, a Danish family invited me to camp with them. They were easygoing, gracious hosts, and their four children were thrilled by our journey. Just before we left, each child rode Zazy in full gear.

At the outskirts of Port Arthur, a motor coach tooted under its breath and stopped behind us. To my joyful surprise, Franc stepped off the bus to greet us, while our old friend the driver smiled and waited. Franc reboarded, calling to me to hurry into town, and the driver called "Good luck!" as he drew the door shut.

Within an hour we reached the stable that Franc had earlier found for Zazy. I arranged for her care, shouldered the pack, and headed for Mrs. Potocnik's house. It was easy to find, a small blue-grey cottage with a wide veranda. I rang the bell and waited, travel-worn and loaded with baggage, content to have arrived. A small, elderly woman answered my ring and stood looking through the door, hesitant, seeming confused at my appearance. Finally she opened to me, and we found ourselves happy to meet but struggling for a common language.

Franc came soon and rescued us. All his relatives and friends from camp followed, and we had a grand reunion. Somehow we all found seating at the table, and more amazingly, bedding places in that small house. Close without crowding, we spent a happy weekend.

I slept in a big bed with Frank the blacksmith, Frances, his wife, and Alvin, their little boy. Frances rose early, and Franc came and popped into her vacated spot beside me. I popped out like a piece of toast, and Frank and Alvin seemed not to notice the change in bedfellows. Leaving the bed to the three males, I went to visit Zazy. I had a journey to complete; I was not ready to start on another one with Franc.

Back at the house, I rejoined the family for a day of visiting threaded through almost continuous meals of tasty food created in finest Yugoslavian tradition. Franc left without ceremony on Sunday night with the other people from camp. I went to the stable the next morning feeling loved and happily unclaimed.

The horse dealer had fed and watered Zazy. Unasked, he evaluated her at sixty dollars. I smiled, paid her board, tacked up, and rode out along the cobblestone street.

2

Zazy and I left the Lakehead through the dirty skirts that trailed around Port Arthur's west side. Patchy small industry and grubby houses squatted on land snatched from a natural wilderness community without a second thought, to favour a human community to which the land was assumed to belong. This sordid process declared itself with neither dignity nor shame, for miles into our morning. Motorists marked the perimeter zone by ignoring the posted change in speed limits. To me at our speed, it was an obsolete battleground where the battered corpse of wilderness lay unburied, for everyone to see and no one to mourn.

I was glad when we reached land shared by vigorous forest and full-time farmers. Kakabeka Falls threw spray in my face and filled me with a great healthful joy. Zazy stood a rein's length back from the brink, preferring to trust her own judgment. Beyond the falls, trees were gradually reclaiming land from failed farms. Small patches of weedy pasture offered Zazy sparse grazing, and whole oats were not to be found. For the next hundred miles, she depended on a few wayside stores selling porridge oats.

Untimely winter had held us in Camp 51, while too well I knew that fly season would sweep in with the lengthening days. Now as the sun penetrated the overcast sky, the blackflies launched their first attack. It was hard for me to think of anything but flies, and the fly bar gone with the boxes. Twelve days' journey, three hundred and fifty miles, separated us from the prairie. I felt compelled to outrun the peaks of the insect populations; the success of the ride hung on our winning the race.

Roadside parks blessed us not only with spring water, but also with grass between picnic tables, shade from sun-dependent biting flies, and shelter from view in the woods. At Firesteel Park, I also fell in with risky company.

Darkness was an hour away and no one was in sight when we entered the park. I unburdened Zazy, left her free to graze, ate bread and cheese, and scouted for a campsite. The sanitary facilities caught my attention— they smelled so pleasantly of new lumber! Convention promptly gave place to our practical needs in this time of stormy weather. I proceeded to lug the equipment to the small building denoted Ladies.

Zazy came too. "Go back and eat grass," I said firmly. Zazy stayed. I took her back to the grass, picked up the rest of the tack, and came staggering to the shelter, just as she arrived. I quit arguing, dumped my gear in the lavatory, grabbed out pencil and diary, and went and sat with the mare at the grazing ground until the light began to fail.

Back at the Ladies, Zazy ate her oatmeal while I arranged my bed on the floor between the wall and the double seat, with the rest of the tack at the foot. Zazy gave her nosebag a gentle swing to let me know that she was ready to have it removed. I obliged, and she was content. She slumped one hind leg, lowered her head, and slept. I stepped in through the doorway and wiggled into my mummy bag.

I dreamed that Connie's fluffy cat was crawling on me. "Go away, Mike," I mumbled. Half awake, I slid a hand under a furry abdomen and lifted an animal off my face. It rustled, and I was wide awake! My bedfellow was a porcupine. The visitor bristled in alarm and stumbled through my baggage, trying to find its way to the door. I waited, not even breathing, knowing the blinding consequence if it brushed my face, now that its quills were erect. Only when its silhouette appeared in the doorway did I exhale.

Confused, the porcupine climbed the doorframe and hung at eye level, a ball of quills with a well-armed mobile tail, waiting for its enemy to go away. I covered my face with an arm and wriggled outside. Rather than waiting for that slow thinker to feel safe enough to leave, I took Zazy to graze in the picnic area. She strayed to the grass at the roadside. I tied her to the leg of the table under which I had chosen to doze. Wrenching and scraping sounds woke me just as I was about to be run over by the table. I gave up on sleeping, found the Ladies vacated, pulled out the tack, and saddled up. We paused only for a drink and a splash at the Firesteel River before we left the park.

With Zazy travelling on oatmeal and both of us watching for grass, we came to English River. Near the bridge, a big cottage with a wide, screened porch suggested tourism. "Do they have a store? Do they sell oats?" I wondered. Zazy, with slackened girth and bridle hung from the pommel, put her muzzle to the grass while I started across the lawn. A man and woman came down the steps to meet me. They lived by the river and accommodated fishermen in summer. They had no supplies to sell, but they invited me in for tea and a sandwich while Zazy grazed and we shared each other's stories.

An old logging trail deep in good grass called us off the road that night. At last the rain had stopped, and we saw a beautiful sunset. I made my bed under a fallen spruce. As hordes of insects took over night duty from the daytime contingent, I swabbed Zazy as liberally as I dared with fly spray given to us by campers. Earlier in the day, I had nearly discarded it when it popped its cork, soaked my clothes, and threatened the last of my cheese. Now, I gloated as the flies came up against an invisible barrier around Zazy's head. I blanketed her body, left her free, and crawled under the windfall while she watched me go. In the night, I saw her by moonlight, standing asleep with her head pushed through an opening between the branches of my shelter and her muzzle as close to me as she could put it.

Dewy morning air brought out the scent of chokecherry blossoms and carried the clear song of a rose-breasted grosbeak. We passed from evergreen woods into birch and poplar stands between pastures and fields. Here, roadside springs were neatly cribbed and graced with stone steps that Zazy trod as well as a person. At Ignace, I was able to buy oatmeal.

Such comforts never lasted long. In the heat of the day, the road was passing through muskeg, treacherous footing for a thirsty horse. As the sun dried the air, we looked in vain for accessible water. Boys in a truck handed us apples, and a Coca-Cola truck driver gave me two bottles of pop, yet we needed water. A small lake came in view, sparkling blue.

We pushed through shrubs growing in firm sod, until the lake with its fringe of sand beach was before us. I expected Zazy to head for the water. Not so. Where the sod stopped, Zazy stopped. I dismounted. She seemed to say: "I won't take you there, but I'll walk beside you." I stepped onto the sand, and she took a short stride forward. Instantly the sand grabbed her forelegs and began to suck her down. In the same moment she lunged backward, rearing on those powerful quarters, lifting herself and me free and swinging us back onto solid ground. Shocked, saddened by my folly, I turned away from the tempting water. We retreated through the shrubs.

As Zazy pushed her way to the road, reality took over my brain. Fear set in. A Canada bird sprang me free from my terror. Its song from the tip of a wizened tree made me look up. Flowering laurel brushed my sandy legs, bringing me back to earth. We were alive, and Zazy had saved my life and her own.

Late in the afternoon, we came to Borup's Corners. There was a little country store with water at a well and food for us both. We rested that night with a kindly German couple outside Dinorwic.

I wanted Zazy to rest and feed in the peace of a stable again the following night. Finding the right farm was always as much an act of intuition as of reason. Beyond Dryden there were few options, mostly because it was Sunday evening and farm folks were not home. Finally, fighting my gut feeling, I went to the door of a vaguely forbidding farmhouse. There was no dog to guide my choice by its welcome or surliness.

A courteous young man answered my knock. He heard what I needed and led the way to the stable, which Zazy had found for herself. He gave her a stall, apologized for having no hay, but supplied her with oats and a straw bed. I hung her bridle and saddle with kit attached, over a low partition. I could be road-ready in one minute, according to the rule that had formed in my head early in our journey.

I asked, "Is it okay if I sleep in the hay barn in the field?"

"Sure," was all he said, and I took my bedroll from the pack. It was then that I noticed a younger man hanging behind him. He added, "My brother can take you back there."

"I can find it okay, don't bother, I can find it." But the younger man insisted on taking hold of my sleeping bag.

We set out side by side. Within me, yellow warning lights were flashing, changing to red as we approached the bank barn looming in the light of a moon just past full. "Thanks for the help." I grabbed away my bedroll as we stood at the door. "Good night!"

He hung there, sallow-faced, hedging like a small boy. "I'll come in with you. It's lonesome back here."

"I'm used to being alone. Good night!"

He grabbed at my free arm; I dodged. "Won't you let me have just—" and he pulled at my bedroll. I interrupted him sharply. He kept wheedling. I tucked my bedroll more firmly under my arm and marched away from the barn. He followed a stride behind. I felt at risk and turned so that he had to come up alongside. He began to sniffle. "None of the girls will let me fuck them. My father is dead and I don't have money to take out girls. My brother bullies me. They laugh at me, him and his wife."

We were walking at a good clip by then, and I was feeling sorrier by the minute for this spineless and pitifully isolated youth. I was also feeling greatly relieved that I had kept the upper hand without ugliness. "I'm going to the motel. Thanks for your company." I terminated our walk.

"You won't take the horse away, will you?" I lied that I wouldn't, then I strode across a grain field toward lights at the edge of Dryden. He stood in the moonlight, his weird eyes trying to follow me. I put darkness between him and me, hid behind a rock pile, watched the door close and the porch light blink out. Then I stalked back into the stable. Zazy remained quiet. I slipped on her bridle, threw all the tack on her back in one sweep, cinched up, backed out. Shadows grabbed for me, but we were gone. I was on her back, trotting across the yard. The screen door squeaked open. "You're taking her away." Bitter tears found voice, humiliation was his sure fate, and I could not save him. I hardened myself.

"How much do I owe you?"

"Nothing."

I was gone at the canter, sad, scared, riding to the beat of my heart. *The Lord shall preserve you from all evil.* The promise poured calmness through the mesh of my racing thoughts. I slept at Joe's Place beside the highway for a token charge, and Zazy slept safely in a quiet corner behind the motel.

— —

Zazy needed shoeing before we began the several hundred miles to the prairie. I found an Austrian farrier in town who would do the job for the cash I had plus the sum I carried in a cheque from Camp 51. My father had told me when I was young that a cheque was safer than cash to carry on a trip. I was too young to catch the difference between a personal and a certified or traveller's cheque.

I left Zazy with the farrier while I went to the bank. Maybe he read the handwriting on the wall. The teller at the bank refused to cash the cheque. I raced back to the shop to halt the shoeing at a point where I could pay with my cash. The farrier had merely removed the hind shoes. I explained my financial straits; he adjusted his leather beanie above a fringe of black hair and bent again to his work. Between spitting, he hummed a Strauss tune, as if in conversation with the familiar disorder in this quaint locus of his homeland.

Zazy left the shop fitted with new hind shoes and wearing the old front shoes reset. I left the shop with eighty-eight cents, two postage stamps, and a useless cheque. We went to the telegraph office.

I needed to have a wire sent home asking for cash from my savings to be sent to Kenora. The agent told me that not even by night rate could he send the message for eighty-eight cents. I sacrificed the silver dollar that Dad had given me when Queen Elizabeth II was crowned, added twenty-one cents from my cash, and launched the telegram. One of the postage stamps carried the endorsed cheque back to Connie for certification. The other carried an explanation of my wire to my parents.

"Don't worry about food for tomorrow," Jesus had advised his travelling buddies before he sent them on a journey that was to occupy the rest of their lives. "Just take what you need for today." Not a bad idea for me at that moment in my journey. I had sixty-seven cents in my pouch, and ninety miles to travel to Kenora. Why worry? Today I was not very hungry, and I noticed that Zazy was making the most of the flourishing roadside grass.

Beyond Oxdrift village, the first pulse of summer was bringing customers to a roadside ice cream stand. Zazy shied as an old car teeming with youths wheeled in. The price of a cone tried hard to tug itself from my sixty-seven cents, but the whole sum was earmarked for oats. The crowd soon overtook us, shouting and laughing and handing out a dripping strawberry ice cream cone. "Thought you might like one too!" said the shaggy kid beside me. With a rattle and a puff of oily smoke from the jalopy, the merry party left me marvelling.

Zazy timed me perfectly and reached back for the tip of the cone as she walked. I was just wiping my mouth with the back of my right hand when I noticed a man watching us from the end of his lane. The steep bank hid everything behind him.

"What a fine horse!" he said as he stroked Zazy's sleek neck. "I'd like to take her into the stable and give her a feed of oats." He folded his words with care, like my Dad. "I am Tom Lewis." I gave him our names and we all climbed his lane. At the top, he sent me over to the house and led

Zazy toward the stable. I walked at leisure across the yard, savouring the uniqueness of this place.

Here was no appearance of wilful human conquest, no marginal ragged wasteland where nature had lost a battle. The forest seemed simply to have moved over to make room for the people. Green fields smiled up at the windows of the sturdy, modest wooden house. It too was green, battened vertically with daring black boards like saplings.

Mrs. Lewis met me at the back porch door, smiling. "Hello, I'm Mrs. Lewis. Do come in."

She was as English as Mom. I slipped off my shoes, stepped onto shining linoleum, and followed Mrs. Lewis into the dining room. She seated me in a leather-backed oak chair and set a tall glass of milk and a big wedge of chocolate cake before me. Tom came to join us at the table.

The walls and sideboards were alive with the faces of children, grandchildren, graduates, couples just married. Birthday cards on the buffet opened the family history only a crack. An oil painting took us fondly to the rich English soil of Oxfordshire.

I needed to understand how the Lewis family had prospered into a third generation, working so intimately with wilderness. Tom and Mrs. Lewis glowed as they showed me the trophies won by the experimental varieties of grain and potatoes they had grown. Wilderness was their friend; it buffered their virgin soil from plant pests and diseases common to crops grown in intensive farming regions. The tidy management of the cultivated land prevented its contamination with native plants that were potentially weeds. These two factors were essential to the production of certifiable seed.

We looked from the house across the fields now sown to oats and hay with seed varieties chosen for maximum production on this land and in the relatively short growing season. Humus built over decades in the soil was holding moisture, available for the seedlings and in reserve for the maturing plants. Around the perimeter, the boreal forest stood tall, thriving and diversifying and shielding the tiny patch of human endeavour from wind erosion, drought, and invasion. Now I understood.

Zazy was fed and rested. We left with a feed of oats in her nosebag.

— —

The next day, we travelled through ragged country that was neither wild nor well farmed. In a patchy settlement, a boy gave me leave to spend the night in a vacant barn. There we found a small feed of dairy ration, some hay, and shelter from mosquitoes. We hurried away at dawn. Vermilion Bay on Eagle Lake came up on my map as the last habitation before the sixty miles remaining to Kenora. I needed to buy oatmeal for the journey, so in hope I turned off the highway at the road sign to the village.

The general store was easy to find. Its white-board front faced small cottages across the main street. I left Zazy under a tree and walked across the yard to the store. A grizzled, half-grown pup was seated on the cement steps. He turned his muzzle toward me and quit his seat as I went to step past him.

"The Indians use them dogs to pull sleighs," an unshaven old-timer volunteered, leaning against a Pepsi Cola sign on the wall, pulling at a pipe. The pup had gone over to investigate Zazy. I felt an affinity for him that I refused to allow, remembering that Zazy and I were in a race with the flies. I loaded the oats; the pup ran off to play with the children. He scarcely gave us a glance as we passed them.

We left the village and crossed the highway. Something made me look back. Walking hesitantly toward us came the grizzled pup. I stopped, and he stopped. I knew he belonged at the village and not with Zazy and me. But there was something about him that unsettled my mind.

Gaunt, grey, and wolf-like, he stood at the corner, sniffed the raw-faced boulder beside him, lifted his leg and marked it, and looked into my face. "Go back, boy! Go back!" And I lifted Zazy into a canter. For a mile or more I pushed the mare on, never looking back until Eagle Lake was far behind us. The mare was hot. I slowed her to a walk, turned and saw. Far back, where sheer rock rose beside the road, a narrow figure came trotting steadily. The pup had made his decision.

Eagle stopped in his tracks a horse length behind Zazy, ears pricked, brush tail hanging straight down. It was my turn to make a decision. "Going our way, are you, boy? Come on then." The tail wagged low and the three of us continued together.

3

Eagle was barely ten months old, not hardened to travel, but determined to keep up. I would have to compromise on speed until he was fit. At noon we rested on a bed of pine needles, fought off blackflies, and shared two handfuls of Zazy's oats. Through the hot afternoon, we stopped at every stream and lake for Eagle to cool himself. Late in the day, I bought bread to fend off hunger and two sweet tarts to boost our energy.

At evening, a family at Richard Lake was just packing up the remains of a picnic. Eagle paid them a polite visit, and like a seasoned moocher, he came away well fed. I thought of catching fish for supper, and so I chose our campsite on a perfect little island separated from the road embankment by a natural rock moat. Zazy stepped across, stood while I unburdened her, shed her duties, and went foraging among the shrubs for grassy patches. I unrolled my sleeping bag in a moss-lined glacial trough sheltered by a boulder, and set down the pack. Eagle sat on his haunches, accepted a chunk of the bread, and watched me store the remainder.

Loons were yodeling far out on the water as I prepared to go fishing. I baited my hook with a white root, went round to the high side of the island, squatted on a block of granite, and dropped my line into the clear water.

Keeping very still, I listened to the splashes of fish jumping and watched small ones investigating my bait. At the first nibble, I gave the line a quick jerk, but failed to hook a fish. Interested shadows gathered in the water below my rock. Suddenly all the potential catch vanished. Eagle's reflection had appeared beside mine. We two sat still. Gradually the nosy company reassembled, and I pulled one fish clear of the water, though I failed to land it. Again the fish scattered. Zazy had come to join the dog and me. I drew up my tackle and led the way to the campsite.

Zazy finished the rolled oats in her bag and settled on a level place to rest. I crawled under the canvas of my sleeping bag and Eagle curled himself into a mossy niche. Weariness overcame mosquito worry and we all slept.

Long before dawn, I was aware that the mare was nosing the baggage.

The moonlight threw everything into silhouette. I raised myself on an elbow just in time to see Eagle spring for Zazy's throat. In the same moment, she reared back beyond his reach. Time stood still. Under the eye pressure of the dog, the mare withdrew from her pilfering. In my mind's eye, the profile that had flown past the moon was that of a wolf.

All night Zazy searched the island for food. I had no more oats to give her. Eagle received for breakfast the bread he had guarded. At half past five, we took to the road with my objective of twenty miles before flies would be warm enough to fly.

A porcupine crossed our path, plunged through the roadside shrubs, and began climbing a scantly treed slope. I knew I could kill the animal to eat, but how would I keep Zazy off the road while I hunted it, and what sized stick would I need to deliver a lethal blow? While I deliberated, my prey was climbing and Eagle was bounding after it. Did the dog know the wolf's trick of flipping the animal to bite the smooth belly? A yelp told the tale, and Eagle came to me with a bristling nose. 'Til then he had remained aloof from my hands, but now he stood before me and allowed me to pull out every quill.

I stopped at a creek that I thought might lead me to trout. Leaving Zazy grazing and Eagle guarding the pack, I went upstream until I was looking across a beaver dam at a pond alive with jumping trout. My cast spooked the fish, but I was sure that once the line was placed, they would return. I waited; the splashes came nearer. A sound behind made me turn. Zazy and Eagle were striding solemnly along the footpath to join me. As one they waded into the shallows, stirred the mud, and banished the fish beyond recall.

Lassitude was replacing my hunger in the heat of the day. At about ten o'clock we met a highway crew relaxing over coffee and sandwiches. Eagle trotted ahead and went the rounds, without a qualm and with great success. Zazy admitted her weakness for doughnuts and joined the feast. Near the end of the straggly line of men and parked vehicles, one man made bold to ask me if I were hungry. I hesitated; he pushed the rest of his lunch into my pack. I attacked the food while he looked on, half surprised and all smiling.

Before that day was spent, Eagle became lame. Fifty miles had bruised his puppy pads, and the hot pavement was burning them. He let me hoist him onto Zazy's back, but he was too tense to balance. A boy in a gravel truck tried to adopt him; he had seen us several times in passing. I was willing to let the dog go to relieve his misery, and the dog was willing to jump into the cab. However, when the truck put distance between us, he became frantic and had to be let out. He limped back to us, we rested, and then we three continued as far as the laneway into Whitesides' Guest Ranch. We were within four miles of Kenora.

— —

Eagle needed rest, food, healing. Zazy needed hay and oats. I needed money to meet our minimal expenses. Mr. and Mrs. Whiteside welcomed us unconditionally upon arrival, and they urged me to stay at least two days. Knowing there would be money at Kenora to pay the bill, I gladly agreed.

Zazy and Eagle were stabled in comfort, and I was free to set out on foot for town. A neighbour driving a horse and buggy scooped me off the road and whisked me to the post office well before closing time. Twenty-five dollars entered my wallet and I stepped solvent out of the little building that flew the Canadian flag. With letters stored in my pouch, I headed for a grocery store to buy provisions for Eagle and me. Oops, the day was Wednesday, and the sign on the door said: Closed at Noon. I was caught out.

I sulked my way back to the highway, carrying my cash intact and burdening myself with silent grouching. A mile along, three lighthearted Frenchmen in a beaten-up truck came by and squeezed me into their crowded cab. Laughing with me amidst the hilarious nonsense that our two tongues generated, they rescued me from my failed effort to control my future, and restored me to the joy of the present moment.

The driver of a gravel truck somewhere back on the road that same day had invited me to meet him for steak dinner at the Lake-of-the-Woods Hotel. I told Mrs. Whiteside and she picked up my enthusiasm. She found a clean shirt and jeans for me and sent me back to town to enjoy the evening. But first, she insisted on feeding me.

Walking along the road, I felt uncertainty edging into my happy expectation. Had I understood the man? Did he really mean to meet me? I looked fresh, ready to meet the world in my borrowed clothes. I found the hotel easily. No trucker was waiting there for me. No message had been left at the desk in the lobby, no way of telling whether I was too early or too late, or mistaken after all. I decided to step past the incident, and so I walked home, free of misgivings.

The extra day at the ranch was filled with opportunities. Mr. Whiteside fitted felt pads under the girth rings to protect Zazy's sides from galling. The blacksmith from Keewatin came to shoe the ranch ponies, and he took Zazy's size for front shoes. He promised to have the shoes roughed out when we would arrive at his shop the following day. Zazy enjoyed a short outing free of bridle and saddle. Eagle was willing to rise to his feet.

Mrs. Whiteside and I planted turnip seeds in a patch of newly turned ground. We laughed away the blackflies, hurried the job along, and covered the last row just before we had to run for shelter from the downpour that watered the seeded rows. A thunderstorm troubled the night but left the morning air washed clean.

— —

We passed through Kenora and around Lake-of-the-Woods on a pretty peninsula, came to Keewatin and stopped at Sven the blacksmith's shop. Efficiently, he fitted new shoes to Zazy's front feet, and we agreed that the hind shoes from the Austrian farrier would last well into the prairie. He commented discretely about the work of his predecessor, as the Austrian in turn had commented on the work of the farrier at camp. I found it was the way with these craftsmen, and I used it, as I travelled from one to another, to glean fine points about hooves and shoeing.

Having shod the mare, Sven invited me without explanation into his small black truck. It was as squat and square as he was tall and broad. First it brought us to the elevators of the Lake-of-the-Woods Milling Company. I knew that name. While oats were being weighed out for Zazy, Sven and I watched a man metering flour into printed bags. Mom used to get flour in bags like those, with a picture of the grain growing and the company name across the top. I used to imagine stepping into that wheat field and looking at the country around it. Soon I would see it first-hand!

Next the truck took us to a grocery store. Sven turned me loose to shop, but he paid the bill. Finally, his wheels took us back to his shop.

Zazy had been left in the yard to eat grass. Eagle had been closed in the house, at Sven's wishes, though I could not know how the dog would behave in a house. Neither of the animals did any harm. Eagle did not even disturb the geraniums in bloom at every window. Sven had expected the best of them; he had entrusted his home to them, and they had kept faith.

I put the food in the pack, slung the oat bag to either side of the pommel, and offered payment for the shoeing and provisions. Sven would receive only a share in my joy as I saw my bulging pack, the supply of oats, and Zazy's firm step restored. Cheerfully, he clasped my small hand in his great one, wished me well, and from his doorway, watched us on our road.

The evergreen forest closed around us, flanking the strip of black pavement and gravel shoulder where we trod, closing it at the horizon. Again we were alone, three comrades linked in a timeless dimension.

Eagle had bravely re-entered his vagabond life on tender feet. After Keewatin, his condition was only fair. All afternoon he kept up with Zazy's walk. At evening we climbed to hiding in woods high above the road. I examined the dog's paws and found that they were at last beginning to callous, although the heat in them told me that they were far from toughened for a pace of thirty miles per day. We sat together on the slope, looking down through the trees across the miles of forest, and Eagle put his young, grey wolf face into my hands, as if he would tell me what he could not express.

Miles of forest and lakes before our meeting with prairie. June 1950.

He was my soulmate as Zazy was. We needed to stay together.

Cold air quelled the mosquitoes so that we ate and slept in peace. We were on the road well ahead of the Saturday traffic speeding eastward to the lakes. At 7:40 AM the buffalo replaced the crown on the route signs, and the white middle line changed to yellow. We had just passed out of Ontario and into Manitoba. I sensed progress without joy.

Eagle's lameness cast a shadow ahead of us. As the sun heated the pavement, he chose the coolness of the light-coloured middle line. Motorists had to stop to avoid hitting him. Between letting the dog ride and walking with him where the shoulder was grassy, we passed safely into Whiteshell Forest Reserve and stopped at West Hawk Garage. I bought milk for Eagle and rolled oats for Zazy, and we found shade. When I tried to leave, Eagle sat on his haunches, whining, reluctant to follow. The proprietors could not let him stay, so I decided to give him my place in the saddle for two days.

In this way, we went on. Eagle's balance and his confidence improved, and I prayed that two days would make the necessary difference to his feet. We could not walk away from each other, so we played a game that I had to prepare myself to win or to lose. Around us there were no farms, no alternatives to continuing.

None, until a dark blue pickup passed us, slowed, and pulled over. The driver walked back to us, easily sizing up our difficulty as he came. He had heard our story from the garage keepers. "I'll take the dog on to Winnipeg," he offered. "I'll let him out near farms where he can find food. He'll make out all right."

I could not believe the man. I had passed this point in my life before, with a Dalmatian dog named Prince. He had adopted me, and his fidelity cost him his life. Yet I knew I had to choose between Eagle's welfare and Zazy's. If Zazy failed, we all failed. I had to let Eagle go. Unlike Prince, he did have a chance to survive.

The wolf dog offered no resistance to being set in the open back of the truck. The words North Star Oil Company engraved themselves on my memory, as a clue I might use to trace Eagle in the misty future. A minute later, the pickup with the small figure sitting in the back was gone from my sight. I asked God to provide for Eagle, for whom I could no longer provide. I was left to live with the shadow of the trust I had broken.

4

Had Eagle gone the way of Prince? Their stories were similar, their coming into my life by their choice and leaving by mine. I mourned Prince as dead. I grieved my choice but kept for Eagle a tiny flame of hope. Not that I watched expectantly for him, as I had watched for Rusty after his death in my childhood.

Zazy and I moved quietly through Whiteshell Forest Reserve. Trees and shrubs grew around us as if they had a right to be there, as community members in natural order according to their fitness to belong. All ages, from seedling to seed-bearer to hoary lichen-bearer, welcomed me. Each assemblage of species found its place, on a hill or at the margin of a wet meadow or by a stream or at a lakeside. Second growth commercial forests of spruce and jack pine, existing only to be harvested for money, were not part of the scene. The wholeness of this forest biome was bringing me healing and peace.

Along our way, we had a surprise visit from the First Nations agent and his wife. They drove forty miles from Kenora to bring us their greetings. The lady brought a bag of salted peanuts especially for Zazy.

Zazy had more tricks than tact. She spied the bag and began eagerly counting out her age with her left hoof. She mouthed the reward, enjoyed the salt, but acted surprised when she crushed the oily nuts. She spat them out indelicately, raised her head, curled back her upper lip, and burped. I explained that she used to burp her thanks to Connie for cookies, but there was no fooling this lady about the spat nuts. She tucked the rest of them into my pocket and we all laughed over Zazy's cheek.

The First Nations agent mentioned some spots of settlement ahead, and as the sun set, the mosquitoes drove me to find shelter. At Rennie where we passed out of the Whiteshell Forest Reserve, Zazy spotted a side road. It forked and narrowed to a baked mud track, and just when it seemed about to peter out, we smelled wood smoke.

In the gloom of the twilight, I could just discern a clearing in the bush, a house, and the outline of a small barn in a fenced yard. A cloud of smoke rose from a flameless fire, and around it hovered the shadowy

Boys at Rennie, members of a family living capably with dignity, close to the land on a subsistence farm at the edge of the boreal forest. We found there food, shelter, refuge from flies, and welcome into the family. June 1950.

forms of cattle. The smoking heap was a smudge like my parents used to light in the garden on summer evenings in mosquito season.

A dog came barking from the house. He was a reasonable hound. He escorted us with reserve through a gate, past a pump, and up to a board veranda.

"G'wan, Joe." A man's voice spoke through the screen door. I called a greeting, and began to ask pardon for my horse eating the lawn.

"Come in," the man broke in cordially. "The pony can't hurt nuthin' there." I hung Zazy's bridle on the pommel, and stepped across the threshold of my own hesitation into a lamp-lit kitchen.

"What's your name?" asked a weathered woman seated at the table. "Sit down and tell us yer story." I took the nearest empty chair and settled into the family circle. Two lanky boys came through a dark doorway, and a small girl straightened her skirt and stood listening beside her mother. We all told our stories.

In the last light of day, we moved Zazy from the lawn into the barn. The walk gave me a chance to discover politely what had been crawling out of my socks and up my legs. I looked and saw ticks, flat, dark creatures climbing by instinct, seeking a site that suited their sucking mouthparts. The ticks must have jumped off the grass onto my legs where I was met by the hound, and onto Zazy's neck where she was grazing. I picked off all I could find and hoped I had got them all.

At half-past ten that night, I was eating whitefish that the boys had caught in the river. The hound stood at a safe distance from the table, sniffing. Little Elsie, with mimic severity very real to her, warned him: "G'wan, Joe, else I'll give yuh a good'un." The big dog looked down at her and humoured her by retiring to a corner and stretching out, head on extended paws.

Savouring her authority, Elsie looked out from herself until she picked up the drift of her parents' political discussion with me. Away she floated into another role. Feet planted, palms upturned, she exclaimed: "Call that fer the good o' the country?"

I enjoyed being with these frank, self-confident homesteaders. They invited me not to hurry away in the morning, and I was glad to stay a while. Zazy fed on the lawn until we took our leave at ten o'clock. We had stumbled into another niche where people belonged within the fabric of wilderness.

Riding out of the bush road onto the highway, I was primed to see a dramatic sweep of prairie. The map suggested it, and Winnipeg was a prairie city, only two days' ride away, so I thought. Yet we were still in boreal forest, as we had been for the past seven hundred miles. I wondered if I had lost my way in this seemingly endless corridor of trees.

Zazy caught the news before me. She raised her head, pricked her ears, and broke into a trot. In less than a minute she carried me to the threshold of the forest, and there she stopped still. We were looking out on a flat, treeless expanse of grassland spreading in a semicircle to the horizon. So we waited, caught at the interface between forest and prairie.

The westerly wind was carrying strange scents to the mare, and she was busy reading the messages. I was held by the powerful pull of the forest behind me. In its domain, I had found kinship and begun to find myself. I was leaving a lot of love behind as I stood on the edge of goodbye.

Zazy broke the spell. She leaped through the interface, from pavement onto springy sod in a happy canter. The prairie opened her arms to us in a welcome wide as the limitless plain before us. A meadowlark sang a chorus from its perch on a highway sign. Zazy's speed blew away my tears as she carried me into newness.

A car roared past the bird and Zazy and me, but the prairie came back smiling, as if the dust and noise had never been. Another meadowlark stretched tall on a hummock, held its yellow shirtfront to the sky, and sang an encore. The westerly wind filled my lungs.

PART FIVE
Prevailing Westerlies

1

A kindly conspiracy between solar energy and roundness, child of gravity, allows Earth to continue to rotate. It invokes the westerly winds prevailing between 30 and 60 degrees latitude, to balance tidal and aerial forces that could otherwise drag Earth to a standstill and end our mornings and our evenings.

The prevailing westerlies can halt the westbound continental traveller, blow away her plan, test her fibre, and dare her to receive a new vision. They can bring her to smell and hear and fear human corruption born on the breath of greed. They can pause at evening from their motion under the sun, and allow the traveller to rest. They can bite her eyes with sand and hold her back in tears of rage, breaking her shells, daring her to open her eyes and see that the storm has passed. They can bring up puffy white-gloved hands to cover the sun, sparing her the burning heat. They can tease the traveller into persisting westward to the mountains at the edge of a continent.

Flat, open grassland prevailed to Whitemouth. The prairie had me to herself. She absorbed me like the company of a new friend. She surrounded me and led me in arcs of vision, no matter how we touched. She sensitized me to the interplay of details, beneath my feet, under my nose, before my eyes, beneath my body as I slept on the pristine ground. I reached for that nurture; it made me grow. Beyond Whitemouth the road passed through a short stretch of bush and entered cleared land where grain farming began in earnest. The farmsteads were miles apart, looking like oases, each with its cluster of buildings almost hidden within a square of windbreak trees.

We stayed at a farm near Beausejour. The woman who welcomed me said she and her husband kept a few cattle as a complement to grain. She did all the fieldwork with a tractor while he worked off the farm for cash. They grew oats as forage and fed them unthrashed to the cattle. Zazy gladly accepted this oat hay.

Oats would not be as easily found on the prairie as I had expected. After Beausejour I saw almost no livestock, and machine sheds replaced barns.

Welcome to a Manitoba farm near Beausejour. June 1950.

I kept hoping to find a small mixed farm, and meanwhile, Zazy could feed on the roadside cover of brome grass. I was dreaming of a full bag of oats to start every day, when we came to Garson Quarries.

The open pit of the quarry made me scrap my quest for feed and go on a fossil hunt. This was my first chance to explore Devonian rocks since I heard about them from Dean Hall at Sir George Williams College in Montreal. I grubbed around happily on the cut surfaces of the limestone walls, enjoying my Devonian holiday while Zazy fed at the cafeteria of green plants growing round the edges of the pit.

At Tyndall, not far beyond Garson Quarries, I rode into a neat barnyard enclosed between a whitewashed cottage and a small barn. A red hen was leading her chicks in search of food that their tiny beaks could grasp. Zazy and I stopped and waited at the edge of the flower garden in which the cottage was planted. A short, suntanned Ukrainian woman smiled at me from the back doorstep, and a young woman came beside her and spoke to me in English. Two friendly little faces popped up at the window. Everything about this homestead was friendly.

Mary and I exchanged names, and her mother smiled again and held her peace. Mary fed Zazy in the barn, and then she took me into the kitchen and gave me a meal that reminded me fondly of Connie's cooking. While I ate, the young woman told me her story: a plunge from the rural scene into the fast lane in Toronto, a marriage that failed, two youngsters and herself towed by society from the mainstream and left at the edge to pick up the broken pieces of their life. Now a single mother, she was safe at home but going nowhere.

Mary was my age, too young to be so limited. I urged her to keep looking for a good way to expand her options, but I could not change her situation. I could only share her sadness. I took her picture to keep her in my memory. I lost my lens cover in the process, and she assured me that she would find it and send it to me.

Time came for me to go. I thanked the elderly Ukrainian pioneer woman and she smiled again. Mary and I squeezed each other's hand for a moment, and said goodbye. She and the little ones were waving as I rode out of the farmyard.

— —

All the way to Winnipeg, I never saw my dog Eagle. The dwellings were so far apart and the terrain was so different to his home on the Shield, that I doubted he could have made a living or found a home. I wanted to think that the North Star man just kept him.

The Red River had been doing its devastating work to the city of Winnipeg and its environs while I was waiting out the battle between winter and spring at Camp 51. In June, I was seeing the aftermath of the flood as I followed the valley south from Selkirk. The river was a reddish brown torrent sulking along reluctantly in its course. Its earth banks had been scoured naked by ice and high water, year after year. Market gardens occupied the flat valley floor, and the fields were littered with debris and plastered with mud. As the water drained away, a few gardeners were beginning to reclaim their land.

The bridge at Lockport was passable again. Zazy took one look at it and suggested we change our route. The roadway was steel waffle-mesh, not good footing for a horse with metal shoes. We stood at the edge of the pavement, considering, while the traffic passed by. Tensely she put one foot on the open grillwork. I gave her time, the motorists slowed to a crawl, and over we went.

I watched in vain for a field where we could camp. We were entering the outskirts of the city, and night was upon us. The traffic became dangerous, and we could not hope to escape it until morning. As the western sky darkened from gold to red to purple, the glaring eyes of the cars worried the little mare. A vacancy sign drew me off the road. If Zazy could stay in the parking lot, then I would gladly pay the price of a cabin. I took courage and went into the office.

In the brightness of the room, both the woman at the desk and I became aware of my road dirt. She agreed to register me, asking only that I keep the tack on the floor. She gave me a unit with a window overlooking the parking lot behind the building.

Zazy spent the night safely, tied to the bumper of a grounded truck. She called to me a few times, I called back through my window, and she settled to rest. I enjoyed a shower, a sink in which to wash my clothes, and a fresh bed. I left the cabin clean.

The clerk told me of a bypass round the city that was reached from McPhillips Street. We took that route, and encountered a flagman at a freshly paved intersection. He surprised me by flagging us across the soft asphalt; Zazy was being invited to leave her signature in Winnipeg. When she had duly done so, the flagman waved us on our way out of town.

West of Winnipeg, unbelievably flat land carried the highway between prosperous farms. We stopped for oats at a large Jersey farm owned and operated by an assiduous German couple. The man asked me how I liked being a tramp. I felt a tiny barb in the question, and probably threaded a strand of independence into my reply. As this open-handed couple proceeded to feed both Zazy and me, I began to realize how easily I had mistaken the man's innocent quip. My self-doubt was at fault, and I would overcome it.

Mechanized cash cropping claimed most of the plain. Late in the afternoon, we passed hundreds of acres of sugar beets being weeded by foreign hand labourers. Absentee owners operated their agribusiness with hired managers. Here was neither wheat nor livestock, nor common ground that I had expected to find. There was no place to camp.

After a thirty-eight mile day, we came to a Durham cattle farm. Sleek red cattle lay at rest after milking, in green paddocks alongside the lane. We walked between white board fences up to a large house. A man came out to greet us. He received us with quiet warmth, expressing regrets that his family was abroad, unable to entertain me, and he took us to the stable himself. He gave Zazy feed and water, bedded her stall, and even helped with the grooming. In the big summer kitchen, he introduced me to the cook, a European woman who would arrange my accommodation. He left me in her care, again with apology for the absence of his wife.

After supper, the cook's helper took me across the yard to a row of bunkhouses and showed me into a unit at the end of the row. The girl set the lighted oil lamp beside the bed and left me, closing the door behind her. I unrolled my sleeping bag on the bare mattress, made a diary entry, read a few verses of the New Testament, rolled down the lamp wick, and fell asleep.

A sense of presence roused me. Three men were standing just inside the door. One had a flashlight making plain their nakedness. I was rigid with fear. "Do you want some company?" The man with the flashlight had spoken.

"No thanks!" I tried to muster up a disgusted rejection.

He taunted me. "Wouldn't your mother let you?"

I couldn't think. I heard words seeming to go from the darkness beside me. "God would not let me." I waited in silence, too scared to move. Time stood still. The men were shifting around, speaking low. Presently they turned, filed out, and closed the door.

Dawn at my window was my next visitor. I dressed, left the bunkhouse through the empty hall, tacked up the mare, and rode from the barnyard. I saw no one, except the cook, who noticed me passing the kitchen window. She called me in for breakfast, but I declined because I could not imagine how to handle the fallout if she learned of the escapade in the night and told the owner. I thanked her and rode away.

2

Traditional hospitality materialized all around us, totally healing the memory of the miscarriage of goodwill at the Durham farm. "Come in out of the rain!" shouted a woman from her porch. She easily outdid the noise of the thunder and wind as we rode through her town at the break of a storm. I shared her porch and her company, while Zazy ate her lawn grass.

"We want you to stay for tea," a German farmer said as I was paying him for oats. His small farm barely provided for his large family, but what they had they shared with natural dignity.

The expansive Main Street of Portage La Prairie caught me up in this lively tradition of windblown openness. Painted clapboard buildings, high-board storefronts boldly carrying the owners' names, hotels calling in all of society—this town was strung out like a line of covered wagons that had simply stopped and taken root.

A day's ride of forty miles across incredibly flat land brought us to low hills clothed with wind-stunted trees. As we rested among them, the westerly wind brought us the heady scent of wolf willows in bloom. Here humankind and nature seemed to have found a workable compromise. Ground-nesting birds, hares, and rodents had taken up residence where shrubs and grasses and flowers thrived together in the rippled land. Level tracts yielded to the twelve furrow ploughs of the wheat farmers, escorted by a cheering, flashing sky full of Franklin gulls diving to feed in their wake.

I lay down under a weightless blanket of emerging stars, while a persistent streak of sunset painted the horizon with the glory of a promise that will be kept. Zazy went looking for native grasses. Satisfied, she returned to sleep near me.

Three hot weeks of June had come and gone. The rains of the past few days portended change. The yellowish grey of the sky in the west was ominous on that morning when I would not listen to wisdom. "You'd better wait a while," advised my weather-wise hosts. "There could be a bad storm." The cloud was darkening. Still, I dared the day. True to prairie practice, they let me go, with food, oat chop, and their blessings.

We were barely on the road when the hot wind hit us. It whipped up an ugly brown cloud and threw it at high speed into our faces. In no time it gained such strength that Zazy could hardly move against it. A hard-won mile brought us into naked fields, bereft of sod or stubble to hold the soil. The wind grew dark with sand and topsoil snatched off the low hills and hurled against everything in the storm's path. Lone plants were being cut off at ground level by the flying dirt. We moved in a cloud of dirty grey air; the sky had come down around us.

Slightly shielded by a shallow roadside ditch, we persisted while the gale grew cold and beat harder against us. Sand found its way into my mouth, ears, tightly fastened clothing.

My eyes caught a fresh barrage every time I looked up, until I could see through my streaming tears only a blurred image of the ground. I had to trust myself entirely to Zazy. Surely she was seeing with her feet, and maybe with eyes shielded by her long lashes, for whenever the wind momentarily dropped, she strode forward with confidence.

Around midday, we came to a wooded gully. With its back rooted in a sandstone ridge, it stood for us against the storm. We had come only ten miles all morning, but I was so tired, so ready to quit the battle! I stripped the tack off Zazy, released her, lay down and slept until the crazy wild screaming of the wind stopped. Zazy went grazing out along the gully with her tail to the wind!

The landscape was visible again. I realized that we had passed through sand hills and were coming into fertile land. We travelled ten more miles before I began to think of oats.

I faced the impact of rejection that evening, as I asked to buy horse feed at a farmhouse near Douglas. The woman behind the screen door scowled, sent me away, and closed the inside door. I left, resenting her coldness. Continuing westward, I began to wonder what that middle-aged woman had seen at her door. All day I had not encountered a fellow traveller to hold as a mirror to myself.

We came to a farmyard where a man black with dirt was unhitching a pair of dust-caked horses at a water trough. He hailed me as we approached. He had been caught by the storm, out disking summer fallow. He took care of Zazy and sent me to the house. His young wife invited me in. Waving aside my reluctance to put my feet on the kitchen floor, she offered me a shower and led me through to the bathroom.

The visage that met me in the bathroom mirror made me laugh and set me straight about the woman behind the screen door at Douglas. A black face stared back through eyes ringed with white where the wrinkles had folded. Wrinkle-ways led to ears lined with black dirt. Around the face, greyish blond frizz stood wildly wiry. I peeled off my clothes and let soap and glorious water wash away my disguise and send it down the drain.

Clad in a borrowed bathrobe, I went as a different person to my place with the family at the kitchen table. The farmer, fresh from his turn at the shower, thanked God for our safety, our fellowship, and our food. The baby in her high chair gurgled for joy. We found fellowship as old as this wonderful, relentless land.

— —

The prairie tested our heat tolerance as we travelled toward Brandon. Never passive, she reflected heat from her surface as the sun poured it out of the sky. In this natural oven, we were wilting. If we stopped, we began to cook, so we kept moving. Just before the sun passed the zenith, clouds appeared on the western horizon and a gentle breeze rose to herd them up the sky. I croaked out a song. The clouds climbed until they were overhead, big white cumulus sunshades shielding us from the radiant blue. For the rest of the afternoon, they continued their leisurely drifting, shadow puppets at play on the undulating face of the prairie.

I stood on the high, steep bank of the Assiniboine River, thinking of Connie. Brandon was below, and Brandon had been Connie's hometown as a child. She had told me about her stepfather, and about the Ukrainian mother whom she had loved and left in her teens. Zazy and I went down, past the Dominion Experimental Farm, past the shady hospital grounds, down to the river bottom, where cottage dwellers transformed their small squares of alluvial soil into productive kitchen gardens, accented with flowers.

I wondered if Connie's mother still worked a plot there. And was the ghost of Peter, her cat, still on the prowl? Connie had told me Peter's story. The old tomcat had sprayed and wailed around her Mom's cottage once too often. She caught him up, dropped him in a sack, and threw him in the river. Walking slowly home from the execution, she struggled with her feelings, while Peter was busily tearing his way to freedom and swimming home. The cat was seated on her doorstep, meowing, when she returned. "Peter!" she cried. "I'll never drown you again!" Many moons waxed and waned before Peter died a natural death.

Downtown at the post office, I received a letter from Connie, and news with a postal note from Mom. Zazy was waiting tied to a lamp pole, dancing for the crowd. I tucked away the mail while answering questions from her audience, and we left the business section without further delay.

Zazy continued westward along a ridge above the Assiniboine River while I read my mail. She only caught my attention when she paused at the head of a farm lane marked by a Holstein dairy sign. Zazy had oats on her mind. We inquired at a cottage near the cross gate to the barnyard, and out came a jovial herdsman followed by his wife and several children. They were the Lawrences, and we were their guests for the weekend.

The swirl of activity in the household caught me up and carried me into the routine for Saturday afternoon. Housecleaning was finished, and now it was bath time for the children. Jimmy loved it and chortled as he was soaped and rinsed in the washtub. The two girls had their hair washed separately from their bath. After supper, Jean sat very still while I put up her straight blond locks in pincurls. She wanted to look pretty tomorrow because it would be her eighth birthday. As well, it was Sunday.

Zazy enjoyed a sponge bath. Her skin was tolerating the tack quite well, except where the girth rings pressed against thinning pads and where the saddle put uneven pressure behind the withers. That sensitivity on her back was my most disquieting problem, and I could never fully relieve it by artfully folding the blanket or pounding the pad.

My fingers made a gruesome discovery beneath Zazy's tail. I touched a grape-like object under the dock. Raising the tail, I found the whole undersurface disgustingly studded with engorged ticks. Eight days had passed since we left Rennie in the bush. These spidery creatures had been drinking Zazy's blood since then. I pulled them off and squashed them in the gutter. Had I known the volume of blood they held, I would not have done that, and had I known about the infections transmitted by ticks, and the irritation those embedded heads could cause, I would have asked how else to remove them. Mrs. Lawrence gave me Lysol to swab on the tail, and the ticks caused us no further trouble.

Jean looked pretty with her curls, on Sunday and her birthday. We had a special meal, with ice cream that I was allowed to contribute. A shadow passed over the household for the briefest moment as the owner of the farm drove by the window, going to see his prize cows. Then all was noisy, friendly give-and-take again. In between the children's talking, their parents shared their perspective with me on local topics, such as dairying on this rich alluvial land, Holstein breeding practices, and milking three times per day for intensive production. We also shared a concern about the oil drilling operation in progress in the wheat field across the highway. Like me, they had divided feelings.

June examinations at school had begun, and Ellen and Jean had to prepare for their spelling exam. After supper dishes were done, the girls and I sat down at the kitchen table with tattered spellers open. We worked over the words, sounding and spelling until I was not sure myself whether *potato* had an *e* on the end. The whole family retired early.

Leaving in the morning, I looked again at the big drill rig with its trucks and accessories on a hill in the wheat field. Crushed young plants lay wilting in the churned earth, forming a wide swath from the rig to the road. Back of the drill site, unbroken lines of growing wheat merged like strands of yarn on a giant loom into a living cloth reaching the horizon. Nascent potential lay in the drill rig and the young wheat. Yet whether or not the hole produced oil, reclamation of the torn, packed, polluted ground for wheat production would require years.

— —

Across the vastness of Manitoba, Zazy and I travelled slowly by most standards, thirty to forty-five miles each day. I was glad to be a guest of the prairie, to find myself in the hands of an ancient teacher. I learned her language, learned to dwell on the promise of a distant hill or a grain elevator, to celebrate our finding native grass underfoot and Saskatoon berries thick on the bushes that crowded the drainage along a creek. Sometimes we covered easy miles, cantering through flat wheat land.

So we lived the rhythmic roll of the landscape, crossing prehistoric sea bottom, meandering with the Assiniboine watershed, speeding over tilled flats that merged politely with rugged natural habitats. People before me had lived out full lives in this domain. Rambling slopes teased me: *Stay a while, we have all day to play.*

I turned aside, freed Zazy to graze the prairie wool at her will, and followed a footpath in the grass up to a pair of stone pillars. There was a cemetery, high and dry, a wonderful place for a pioneer to rest. I saw no dwellings for miles, yet the graves were tended and the gates between the pillars were closed against wandering cattle.

The bolt worked, the gate swung. I stepped inside and entered a past age. The markers bore neat etchings of names, dates, and comments. Lives of the dead buried there had been mostly brief, and many children never got started into life. It must have been the few who survived to old age who implanted their wisdom and technical knowledge into later generations, so well that family farms survived and gave me joy in 1950.

A man came walking up the track. "Hello! I noticed a loose horse. Are you okay?"

I slipped through the gate and closed it. Zazy noticed, and started to rejoin me. "Sure. Just enjoying the view while she eats." Zazy was near me; I felt secure. I could enjoy our visitor. He said he was from Winnipeg. The question leaped to my mind, had he seen a wolf dog roaming? Recalling the extent of the sprawling city, I let my question die.

"Where are you from?" the man asked me.

"I came from Brandon." I spoke with caution.

"I saw you crossing the Lockport Bridge. That's quite a pony!" And our story was out. He talked not like the usual point-to-point motorist, but as a fellow listener to the voice of the prairie. "You could leave the main road at Virden if you want to see the slough country. I love it, but I have to go straight into Regina on this trip. Where the highway swings northwest to the city, you just take the dirt road and keep going west."

I slipped Canada Section II out of my pouch and we found the junction at Virden. "Good luck," he said. "I'd best be going now."

"Thanks for stopping, thanks for everything. I'll take the dirt road." Our hands met, for me a vote of confidence, and then we went our separate ways.

Below the cemetery hill, a small cattail colony lived where the creek bed turned, just before the road began to climb again. A yellow-headed blackbird called from the top of a low willow, dazzling me in his black suit and intensely yellow head. And he had friends just like him! Watching the birds, I spooked a herd of deer. They leapt and went bounding along the slope, flashing their white tails. Afternoon changed into evening. Against a blue-green sky above the sunset, pearly-winged Franklin gulls journeyed with one mind to roost. We too needed rest, and the tiny town of Griswold took us in.

Zazy was housed in the stable at the postman's house. He suggested that I sleep in the railway station, and he pointed out the red wooden building with the coolie hat, down near the tracks. "Tram—" he caught himself halfway through the word, "tramps occasionally use it." This time I took no offence. I shouldered my baggage and hiked away toward the one-room building, noting that it was at a distance from the stationmaster's house. Under darkness I slipped in, bolted the door, and went to bed on the floor. My mental alarm clock was set to rouse me before the milk train was due to arrive.

At four in the morning, I vacated my quarters. By five-fifteen I had fed, groomed, massaged, and packed Zazy for the road. The morning was perfect for travelling, clear and fresh, and we were moving ahead of the heat.

Virden was asleep when we clip-clopped along its main street. Rather than wait hours for the grocery store to open, I left Zazy's lunch to our good fortune. The brome grass sown along the roadside was thick and heavy in seed, as good as a feed of grain, so local farmers told me. Zazy cropped it as she walked.

Following the dirt road out of Virden, we moved into slough country. I had pictured a slough as a water hole where thirsty cattle on dry range went to drink. I found instead a naturalist's dream come true, a focal point in the midst of this amber and green land where wild birds found food and drink, shelter and safety, a resting place in their migration or a nursery for their young. Now the sloughs were filled to overflowing with meltwater and rain. Each one had evolved differently from their common beginning at the end of the Ice Age. We toured them as honoured guests.

In a slough bordered by tall marsh grass, the invisible bittern called *punk-a-dunk, punk-a-dunk,* throwing its voice from here and then away over there. In a dugout slough with grass sod hanging over its banks, the open water was alive with ducks and grebes feeding and preening and talking together.

Willows stood tall around a slough hidden from wind in a hollow. I watched from their shelter. A flash of brown and yellow caught me up in the action of a crested flycatcher snatching a dragonfly out of the air and sweeping it up to the top of the tallest tree. From a hunting perch, the bird watched again, raising and lowering its crest with bridled excitement until another fly came in range. I stayed for three acts of the show.

In a wandering slough where colonies of aquatic grass channelled the open water into a maze, black terns swooped with the grace of swallows and the shrill voices of parents defending their floating nests. Back from the slough, back from the road, wherever food was to be found, Franklin gulls flew, now visible, now vanishing against the blue and billowy white sky.

No town broke the spell all day. I rarely saw a farm. Sometimes I wondered casually whether supper would happen to us. Little did I know that the spirit of the prairie was pussyfooting along behind me, holding her hands over my eyes.

She followed me up a certain hill, just to the top where the road bends, whispered in my ear: *Surprise!* and took her hands away. Below me lay her gift, Pipestone Creek valley, infusing its poetry into my soul.

It was a gentle valley, walled with terraced turf, grazed by cattle. Trails linked the terraces, fanning and fusing to end at the edge of the sky-lit stream that watered the valley floor. The sandy road went easily down to thread the slender bridge and wander away up the far side, a yellow-brown strand losing itself among the hills. We followed that strand and found ourselves in Saskatchewan.

3

The afternoon was passing and we needed food. Maryfield was the next place name on my map. Maryfield before closing time became my goal. We reached the town and stopped at the Red-and-White Store. Sure enough, it was still open.

Had Zazy behaved like a normal horse, we might have shopped, eaten our simple meal, and lain down to sleep in some cottonwood grove. Instead, the moment I went into the store, Zazy thought she had lost me, and went trotting up and down the sidewalk, whinnying. I ran to the door and called her. She stopped, turned, and came to stand with her front hooves on the top step of the entrance, looking in through the screen, nickering softly. Our shopping trip quickly became a social gathering.

James the hardware merchant and Shorty the cobbler from next door arrived. Bill, the grocer, invited me to stop overnight in their town. Shorty, James, and Bill hastily completed a parliament capped with a telephone call or two, and sent us off with Freddie to the livery stable. Already he and Zazy were friends.

Fred worked for Mr. Dixon, a neat middle-aged man with a steady horseman's voice. "Will she stand in a stall?" he asked, perhaps considering my English bridle. I assured him she would. He placed her next to a team of Belgian draft horses. I smelt cattle and spotted a pair of stanchions inserted in the row of stalls. In came Fred with two Jersey cows. They stepped into their places with a dignity that comes from belonging.

Fred was to take me to the Barnards' house. Mr. Dixon hurried us off lest the oil pipeline workers who were flowing into Maryfield for the night got there first. Up and across and along streets I hurried after my guide. At the edge of town, I saw a substantial white-board house, eloquently historic, surveying the open prairie from within its white picket fence. Freddie stopped in front of it, I thanked him, and in an instant he was gone at the run. I picked up the bag he had carried for me, passed through the garden gate, caught the breath of night-scented flowers in the border, and crossed a wide veranda.

Mr. Julius Barnard answered my ring. He stood tall and straight in the doorway, greeting me in a few quiet words flavoured Norwegian. His wife joined us in the wide polished hallway, and there the couple received me with practical warmth into their home.

The Barnards were expecting me, for Shorty had phoned. Mrs. Barnard took me into her shining kitchen. I had to rejoice aloud over the view from her picture window above the sink. In no time she had a meal ready for me. As I ate, she began with polite restraint to feed my thirst for the story behind this team of retired farmers.

They had come from Wisconsin, homesteaded, and raised a family when the prairie was without roads, fences, or trees. In those days, the common fuel was buffalo or cow chips, meaning dung dropped on the range and dried by the sun. Settlers who chose to burn wood had to take a team and wagon and fetch it from a mountain fifty miles away. Was it the Wood Mountain on my map? I could not risk spoiling the flow to ask.

Looking beyond the garden to the darkening landscape, I reached out for more stories. Mrs. Barnard stirred the embers deeper and deeper, and she began to speak.

Mrs. Barnard drove fast ponies. One afternoon she set out to visit a neighbour. Perched on the seat of the rattling buckboard, reins in one hand and an arm around Baby Gladys, she was singing in the wind. Halfway to the speck that marked the nearest homestead. The rhythm suddenly changed. The buckboard was lurching, the team bunched into the neck yoke. She knew in a moment: the pin had jumped out of the whippletree!

Seizing that moment before the team leapt out of control, she grabbed Gladys by the pants and lowered her to safety on the ground. Away went the ponies, taking the buckboard bouncing and rocking, with Ma balancing the whole outfit while she worked the ponies back into hand, reined them in, and quieted them. Then from her bag she hauled a sturdy cloth diaper, stepped down, and bound the whippletree into place, centred on the draw bar as before. Confident as a prairie crocus in a gale, she drove back to where Baby Gladys sat howling on the grass, gathered her into her arms, and proceeded to visit the neighbour and beg a new pin for the return drive.

Mrs. Barnard and I sat in twilight, filling the kitchen with runaway laughter.

— —

Saskatchewan! I sat on my bed in an upstairs room, making a final entry into another tattered volume of my diary. In the account on the back page, I wrote: bread, peanut butter, cheese (Maryfield), and in the expense column, I entered: paid by a drunk. A hint of injustice nudged me again, as it had done when the man came up to the counter in the R&W and insisted on paying for my groceries. The clerk had dismissed my dilemma with an approving smile. My anonymous friend had sent a wave of warmth my way in his shy smile. Simple acceptance of his gift overwrote my uncertainty, and now the memory of his smile freed me again. Two logs, one flame!

Finally, I pulled out my map to check our mileage. We had travelled forty-five miles that day. Zazy had earned her massage, full feed, and a soft bed. I slept content.

— —

Zazy was ready for a new day. She had found comfort in a stable that was probably one of the last of its kind in Canada. I was tacking up when the cows strolled along the alley and out to pasture with slack udders. The draft horses were already at work, delivering water in a wooden tank from door to door. Mr. Barnard had told me that every house had a well or a rainwater reservoir, but many people preferred the water pumped from the spring outside town. We met the team on the main street.

I stopped at the R&W in passing to thank Bill and his pals. He gave me a large bag of biscuits to cheer us at noon. As I was adjusting the pack at the edge of town, a truck driver stopped and called out: "Have you got any trouble, Ma'am?"

"Thanks, we're okay," I called back. With a smile and a wave, he was gone.

Saskatchewan! Even the birds seemed to make personal contact with us. A magpie walked elegantly along the road ahead. Cooing doves challenged me to find them screened in the cottonwoods. Small flocks of brown pigeons with shiny green necks flew low along the shoulder, searching for spilled grain. Prairie chickens were having a siesta unseen under shrubs when I went looking for a shady spot. Out they flew from their cover, and where they came to earth, they vanished into a camouflage of colour.

We passed through the green valley of Wawota, where travelling Plains Indians used to stop for water. We stopped at Suitsme Farm. The words had weathered well on the board above the gate. Two sleek saddlebreds galloped down the lane to invite us in. They paused a second, wheeled and were gone, tails high as their spirits. I followed on foot with Zazy, and Mr. and Mrs. Coe came to meet us. They had been watching us from the wide porch of their bungalow.

Zazy was their first concern. They gave her fresh water from the pump rather than slough water. They put salt before her to lick while they sponged her back and massaged her legs. Meanwhile, they were asking me all about her.

These people had ridden the trails through the Cypress Hills for decades as park rangers. Their horses were dear to them. Now they were taking Zazy's condition seriously, and I listened for every bit of wisdom I could glean. After all, we agreed that the skirtless saddle was the culprit behind the irritation on her back, and indirectly behind her overnight stiffness after travelling forty miles or more. I was doing all I could to maintain the mare, and none of us suggested dumping the pack and going bareback.

The Coes showed me pictures of the Cypress Hills, giving me insight into their uniqueness from ancient times, because the last glacier had never overrun them. I would ride in those hills some day. "Watch to the south as you are passing the Maple Creek turnoff. You'll see them," called Mr. Coe as we were leaving Suitsme Farm.

That morning of June 30 was dry and torrid. We endured, needing the sunshade clouds to make their appearance. They came, and they rose on waves of heat reflected from the land, gathering head until they dumped a deluge of cooling rain on us. A noisy thunderstorm broke overhead, made me notice the absence of cover, relieved the electrical stress in the sky, and subsided, leaving us unharmed. Intermittent showers kept us cool until sundown.

A ball game was in full swing, regardless of the showers, in the park at the edge of Peebles. We stalked unnoticed out of a vast solitude up to this spot of human playfulness, stepped round it unnoticed, and passed out again.

Where was reality? I stood at the intersection of road and railway,

Neil Ennis on Zazy. Glenavon, SK. We stayed at that home for a long weekend.
Pinto took me for a ride. 12 July 1950.

looking back along the line. Peebles had become not a sound, not a speck on the plain, only the upended rectangular silhouette of a grain elevator, silent as the brooding sky. I looked ahead up the line. The next town was no more than the last. Zazy's hooves rang hollow on the planks of the level crossing. And then we too became a silent, insignificant speck moving through the vastness.

Our road jogged north and west, touching towns that the railway linked in a beeline. Kegworth's elevator became our marker. We approached it steadily; it retired before us. In time we overtook it, passed it, left it behind. We actually were moving!

The final shower of the day fell from the troubled sky onto the muddy road we trod and the absorbent sod around us. We were off the flat and among low hills. The sun was sinking like a big red tomato into undulating wheat fields. Ahead our prospects for finding shelter were nil, so we tried a side road. We crossed a trench bordered by heaps of gumbo clay, the burial site of another segment of the oil pipeline from Alberta. A mile from the highway, we came to stand at the back door of a big house.

Alice and Gilbert Ennis welcomed us, muddy as we were. They stabled Zazy, fed and watered her, and bedded her down to rest. Teenaged

Ruth set my wet baggage to dry, and young Neil came into the kitchen to say hello, and disappeared. He came back for tea with the rest of us before we went to bed.

Mr. and Mrs. Ennis urged me to stay over Dominion Day to avoid the traffic, and I agreed. I met their married son, Clifford, and his wife, and joined in the busy life of this extended family. Based in two households, putting their special interests together, they ran a successful family farm. Ruth and I visited round, churned butter, laundered my clothes while I wore hers, and did all sorts of farm jobs together. Zazy rested her legs.

Late in the afternoon, the cattle and horses gathered to drink at the windmill in the field below the barn. Among them came the notorious fence jumper, Pinto. He was a tall red and white gelding, bold and merry. He dared me to ride him. After supper I jumped onto his broad back.

The prairie in twilight always spoke poignantly to me; the company of Pinto carried the message even deeper. This was his home, these wheat lands green now and varied by groves of darker green willows and silvery poplars. This was his home, these range lands with ridges crested by hardy grasses, draws traced out by bluish wolf willow pouring out perfume into the evening air, hollows pregnant with roses in bud.

We startled a jackrabbit and watched it go springing away, floating by magic above ground in fifteen-foot leaps. We climbed a hill to catch the last trace of sunset. I watched the afterglow until the drone of an aircraft drew me to see the faint silver bird, blinking green and red as it sped straight to the darkening blue-green that hung, perhaps over Calgary, perhaps over the Rocky Mountains.

Within twelve hours, I was thanking Mr. and Mrs. Ennis and saying goodbye to the family. Alice said: "Come back again. Your bed is always ready." I would return, because of her perennial invitation, and because of the evening that Pinto shared with me.

It was very late in the afternoon of July 2, 1950, when a nameless imminence prodded me. The silhouette of an elevator was peeking over the edge of the world, distant beyond our present day. Zazy was uneasy. Casually, I was watching a thin line of darkness broadening above the northeastern horizon. Sky events were like grain elevators; they came and went in our life.

Zazy was not so casual. Her agitation mounted as the darkness advanced. Without warning, an invisible wall of air under high pressure blasted us almost to the ground. Zazy drove her canter obliquely across its path. A sheet of greenish water hanging between cloud and land was sweeping toward us, blanking out its wake. Zazy galloped for the lane ahead, wheeled in, raced for the barn.

The wall of water hit us halfway there. Zazy threw herself against the storm and ran while the lane changed to mud beneath her hooves. Clinging hard to her, I glimpsed faces at the windows as we charged past the house. Zazy fetched up at the barn, I pulled open the door and drew her inside. There we stood, beyond the storm, panting and drenched, when a figure swathed in black waterproofs struggled into the doorway.

"Put this on and go dry yourself in the house," he directed me. "The hurricane is past; you'll be safe now."

Zazy ate and slept, sheltered from the rain that tailed the storm. I found myself added to a family of nine that shared the spacious house. There was room for all my wet things behind the kitchen range, without disturbing the dog. The boys gladly helped me to unpack while their oldest sister ran errands to the pantry for her mother. Two impish little girls were bubbling with excitement, in the care of their good-natured brother. Father came in and the little ones subsided into the delights of a secret bit of nonsense. The Holy Family looked down approvingly from the picture on the kitchen wall.

Father, Mother, and I found common roots. She was from Quebec. We both remembered the smell of the wind off the open St. Lawrence at Laprairie and the calls of the redwings in the marshes. Her husband I guessed to be French, from the tang of his speech and the ring of his name. He was native to Saskatchewan, of pioneer stock from French Canada. His family had survived the Dry Thirties, when a fifteen-hundred-pound beef brought fifteen dollars, a two-hundred-pound pig, five, when dust storms buried the fences and cut off the crops at ground level. Now he had achieved a modicum of prosperity.

Sometimes whispers from the nurturing land sifted through the fond reminiscences of people like these, still working heritage farms. All too often I had heard a farmer's regretful conclusion that he had no choice but to join the march to the marketplace, borrow money, streamline his operations, and get a job off the land to pay the mortgage. This family believed in their way of life. Now the father was offering his experience for the benefit of the community as a councillor.

The household awoke to a rain-washed prairie. The older children were starting two weeks of catechism now that the regular school term was ended. I shared Zazy as far as the schoolhouse with the girl who had shared her bed with me. On the way, I asked: "Do you ever see baby ducks?" We were watching a mallard swimming away from the near bank of a slough.

"Oh yes!" She hesitated before adding, "We've found a nest . . . but we mustn't touch the eggs." Her childish impulse to show her secret, or simply her trust, overcame her caution. When the other children were well past, we left Zazy at the road and I followed the girl through the long grass toward the slough. She parted the sedges just as a matronly mallard slipped off her nest on a tussock, revealing her eggs. A momentary peek was all I was allowed, and then she closed the sedge curtains. I left her at the school and kept her secret.

4

Sunset etched Regina's profile on the horizon. Only Regina! And it was still due west of us! I had hoped to be many miles further on, hoped that our long days were adding up to time saved to spend in Lethbridge having the saddle overhauled. For the moment I had lost sight of the Red-and-White Store and Pinto and the duck nest, those spiritual river crossings I had taken time to make. Now memories rose and rebalanced me, and poised me to see the sunset colours before my eyes.

We turned off the road where the grass was heavy in seed around the ruins of an abandoned homestead. I ate bread and peanut butter from my pack, under an arbor of willows and wild roses. Zazy was free to graze. Only the resident kingbirds and chipping sparrows voiced objections to our presence, and since it didn't drive them away, I felt right about our staying. Mosquitoes I ignored. As stars shone through the interlacing boughs, Zazy and I lay down and slept.

Brightly striped ground squirrels were up with the sunrise, stuffing their cheek pouches to the limit. At our approach, they would spring up on their heels, straight as sticks, and chatter. I envied them their adaptations to this climate: indifference to heat and independence of drinking water.

Through glassy heat waves, I watched Regina grow from a line of blocks and smoking pillars to a city spread like a creeper on the face of a treeless plain. West of the junction of the bypass and Highway #1, wheat dominated our world. As far as I could see, all day, a sea of waving green heads covered the land. Rarely, it yielded an island of ground to a town or a clutch of farm buildings or a row of simple frame granaries.

A distant sound, a distant speck crawled toward us, gradually taking the form of a fat-bodied insect with outstretched wings, metamorphosing into a power sprayer. I talked with the operator recharging his monster from a tank truck. He told me that the hundred mouths on his machine spat herbicide and pesticide together over a swath forty feet wide. He could protect two hundred and twenty acres of crop in one day. He warned me that chemicals toxic to horses drifted onto the grass by the wayside.

The prairie's voice was muted and the land had grown harsh under the heel of rank, profit-driven business. The five-foot stands of brome in seed were potentially toxic, yet farmers were making hay from them along their frontages. Zazy needed their seed in place of grain, so I had to hope for her safety and allow her to continue to crop the brome and cool her legs in its shade.

Hazards underfoot added to my anxiety. I was constantly on the watch for broken bottles and jagged cans tossed from motor vehicles. They tended to collect partly hidden in the belly of the roadside grade. To avoid them, I chose to travel up along the edge of the wheat whenever we could.

Where the verge was covered with sod instead of brome, ground squirrels had moved in and dug holes. Zazy quickly learned to spot them or the runways that led to them ahead of her footfall, but eventually she cantered into a hole. She recovered her balance and went on, but only at a walk. When I asked her to canter again, she would not. Soon she was walking lame. I led her to the shade of trees by Sunrise Farm.

Zazy was so lame that she lay down. Massage and liniment were of no help. She rose to her feet painfully stiff, and I was at a loss to do more for her. Just then a young woman came down from the farm, and she took us home for the night. The immediate rest, treatment with flowing cold water, and more massage and liniment healed the strained tendons. By morning, Zazy was cautiously roadworthy.

We were making for Moose Jaw, along with suntanned farmers in cars and trucks boiling over with eager youngsters. Something was in the air. A billboard explained: the Moose Jaw Exhibition was opening that night. Everyone who could spare a few hours from work was on the way to town. I elected to stop short of the city and pick up mail in the morning.

We crossed a creek stinking of urban sewage in the summer heat. It seemed to have lost contact with its headwater, lost its vital structure, lost its potential to cleanse itself. At a small farm along the creek, we waited out the night. The people who lived there asked me to stay, and we talked about the farm and their life and the life of a traveller like me. They were a family in distress, caught somehow in no-man's-land between city and country, falling through holes in the matrix of family life. I was conscious of the fragility of domestic accord on which hung the survival of that home.

Zazy danced through town without a sign of lameness. She wound her rope around the pole at the post office and defied the RCMP to enforce the law about horses on the sidewalk. I stuffed the copious bundle of mail into the pack and retreated to a ballpark.

Under the shade of a caragana hedge, I unsaddled the mare, sorted from the pack some dispensable items, and wrapped them ready for mailing in the inverted paper off the parcel from home. Now there was space for the new food! Our pack was trim again, except for the ungainly parcel. I tucked it under my right arm and we rode from the park. No sooner were we on the road, than the driver of an oil truck slowed beside us and offered to mail my parcel. Saskatchewan, again!

Intuition goaded me to water Zazy before we left Moose Jaw, but I was finding no water. Finally I trespassed into the grounds of a prestigious school, hoping to alert a caretaker. An elderly man came around the side of the building and spoke cordially to me. He gladly searched out a pail, filled it at an outside tap, and held it for the mare to drink. She drank well, and I felt blessed.

That drink was one to remember as we moved into a region where drought was the rule. Jim Prowse's prophecy at Longlac came to mind: "You'll never cross the dust bowl in July." The date was now July 6!

West of Moose Jaw, the few surviving farms looked forlorn. Buildings were aging, lone cattle searched scant pastures, raped wheat land was staggering through rank weeds, groping for its true identity as grassland. A decade of crop failures explained the defeat admitted by the voiceless remains of abandoned homesteads, weathering thin and grey beyond the mercy of wind, rain, and snow. No sloughs relieved the parched land, and dugouts were rare. Toward evening, rain fell while coyotes raised their voices and howled on the desolate prairie.

The cacti were the winners, spreading their spiny lobes over the woolly turf and opening waxy yellow faces to the sunshine. Little cactus pincushions crouched tightly to the ground, hidden in the short grass until they too saw the light and opened their crown of shaggy, deep pink flowers. As the sunlight touched the prairie's dress to colour, so it tanned my skin and bleached my hair and changed Zazy's coat from black to auburn.

We stopped for water, and by common practice we were also offered shade. It was a perfect gift, because the pavement was so intensely hot, and roadside litter was forcing us to travel on the road. Fencing cut off our escape to friendlier ground. Like an unexpected holiday, an unopened stretch of highway between Parkbeg and Secretan gave us miles of clean footing on the hard sand, and respite from speeding cars. Beyond Secretan after sundown, we regained the old road and went toward Chaplin.

A jackrabbit materialized from pale pasture land, a silver-grey phantom, airborne, bounding like an impala in great elastic arcs. Through the throats of birds hidden in grass, through the vibrant wings of crickets, through the brush of the breeze blowing free over the miles, the prairie sang her evensong.

Midnight was two hours away. The long-distance vans began to roll on the highway. It was time for Zazy and me to strike out across country and find a campsite, our first on absolutely bald prairie. But for the cover of dusk, I would have felt naked to the world.

We wandered over one rise after another, and settled at last in a trough between two ripples no more than three feet high. I unsaddled the mare and unrolled my bed without so much as a tall stand of grass to hide behind. Zazy emptied her nosebag, then she fed to her satisfaction on the short prairie wool. Soon she came to drowse beside me. A chorus of coyotes sang close by, and mosquitoes were in close touch too, ensuring that I did not sleep through the changing beauty of the night.

I peered up, planets peered down, stars twinkled. I knew some of the stars by name, and the basic astronomical laws that governed them. Dean Hall had taught me to know and helped me to see beyond knowledge. Lying on the living ground of native prairie, I simply knew the presence of God, up between the stars and infinity, down here around a mote like me, as present to me as Zazy, who dozed by my side.

At midnight I noticed a glow in the east and watched a big misty lantern rise behind a thin veil of clouds. Mosquitoes drove me wild, and I remembered the heavenly nights under the fly bar strung out between real trees! Zazy had some protection from her sheet and her long tail.

Lightning silvered a black cloud in the west and changed the picture again. The storm moved up to the zenith, painting a sulky sky with blue and orange light. Rain poured down, and for a couple of hours, both heat and mosquitoes were gone. We slept relieved, while all our tack except the sleeping bag remained dry under the plastic sheet. At dawn Zazy ate grass while I packed, I ate a chocolate bar, and then we were sharing the road again with truckers just finishing their night's work.

"You look lonesome." A sleepy driver had slowed beside me. "How about having breakfast with me in Chaplin?"

"Great idea!" I thought, though I said something less to the same effect.

"You put your horse's front feet in the window of my truck when you come by, 'cause I'll be asleep." And he drove off.

Inside my skull, the battle was on.

"Sure I'd enjoy his company."

"Does he mean to pay? I can't afford to pay. How can I ask?"

"Is he trying to pick me up? How could you get picked up in a restaurant in broad daylight?"

"I feel intrusive waking somebody up."

"What if I wake up the wrong guy? Why didn't I think to note his license number?"

"I feel like a loser, chickening out."

An hour later, with persistent misgivings, I rode quietly through Chaplin, leaving my friend snoring in the cab of his truck under a big tree. I ate salmon off the blade of my knife, from a tin Mom had sent to Moose Jaw. It was delicious; Mom always sent the best.

Salmon for breakfast was not the best choice, however. In the rising heat, my equilibrium began to fail. I watched for the sunshade clouds, wished I had fasted, felt faint and nauseated. Zazy took me to Ernfold, where a kindly English storekeeper revived me with iced ginger ale. He also arranged for us to rest at a farm an easy hour's ride to the west.

I went where our provident friend sent me, and found myself happily immersed in a southern Saskatchewan family. Zazy enjoyed shade and feed in the stable, and I recovered to join the family for supper. I tried to say how rescued I felt. Grandma spoke for them all: "I guess we've seen too much to turn anyone away."

We sat together on the cool porch and told stories. This region was a

Saskatchewan prairie. Grain elevators marked the distance of a day's haul with a loaded wagon from the surrounding farms. SK. July 1950.

tough place to ranch. The prickly pear cactus that I was admiring was no friend to cattlemen, with its thorny lobes. People burned off the thorns with flame-throwers when there was no other forage for the cattle. I wondered if Zazy would have to eat burnt cactus some day.

Jimmy was eleven years old, full of questions about travelling with a horse. He had horses and rodeo in his veins, and a creative, rational kindliness about him. As I passed the corral, I watched how he followed the movements of the half-grown steer that he was riding. He finished his ride, and we talked. His goal in rodeo was to ride ever better, not to defeat the animal. He was drawn more by adventure than by prizes to be won.

Zazy and I moved on in the cool of evening. We enjoyed another magnificent sunset, and bedded down on the prairie, back from the road, just as the stars were coming through the blue. At midnight, a crash penetrated my sleep. I sat up in my mummy bag as a flash of blue-green light painted the southern sky. Again a storm was moving up and over us.

I was too caught up in the drama to prepare ahead for the teeming rain that would inevitably escort the storm to the zenith. I found myself in the downpour, lugging our equipment to a barbed wire fence corner. Having slung the plastic sheet over the brace posts, I pushed the saddle and kit under the roof and covered them with the groundsheet. Then, encased in the mummy bag, I wriggled myself under the edge of the shelter. Zazy enjoyed hours of cooling rain on her back. Meanwhile the tack, including the saddle pad, remained dry.

The intense heat of the next afternoon parched me. We must have been sweating and constantly being dried by the hot wind. Maybe I was losing too much salt. Outside Morse, I yielded to swamping weakness and lay down. The heat without the fanning breeze weakened me all the more. I rose unsteadily and rode with a light head.

Did my map really show a lake ahead? Reed Lake? The blot of blue near the name fixed itself in my mind, but it faded with the miles of sameness. Reed Lake had dried up, and so had the community.

Toward evening, two young men in a truck stopped to visit. One was from Montreal, heading for Vancouver. The other, from Ontario, intended to sell the truck in Vancouver and fly to New Zealand. Three pilgrims at heart, we stopped by the way to celebrate our journey in storytelling. Were we all following the same star?

We didn't want to lose each other. We hoped to meet again. We had to go. Bob from Ontario reached into his small store of keepsakes and handed me a picture of himself and an army buddy. He would get in touch with me by mail; I gave him my home address. We all waved, the truck came to life with a snort, and they were gone.

The whistle of a train called me into the present moment. The train crawled into view along an invisible track marked by a string of telegraph poles, so distant that they looked like a flimsy fence. As the rail cars came abreast of us, they seemed to be travelling three feet above the ground. Through the glitter of heat waves that danced on the dun face of the plain, the bright colours told me that I was looking at a circus train. It led my eye along our own course, straight to the vanishing point beyond the speck that was Herbert's elevator.

I looked back along the way we had come. The low sun was linking the power poles with heavy shadow, creating a solid wall that followed the contours of the prairie. Very far away, between wheel tracks shining in the hard-packed clay of the road, the dark central crest of dried mud mounted like a thin column of smoke to vanish in the air. I stared at the mirage, until a flock of birds flying higher than the smoke delineated ground from sky, releasing me.

Twilight was dimming out detail, but the flight calls of the gulls showed me their travel path. They were moving from food to rest at a place they knew. I knew only that there was a place somewhere for Zazy and me.

We stepped off the road as the first heavy transport truck of the night passed. I watched another circus train rumbling westward, the gaudy advertising on the coaches illegible in the twilight. This train was travelling on the ground. Yellow lights shone from the windows. Were the passengers discussing the last performance in Moose Jaw, or the next; perhaps in Medicine Hat, or anything but circus? Behind their coaches came animal cars, and flatcars with awkward loads in silhouette. Last of all came the riotous caboose. Then the circus was gone.

I went in search of oats to the only habitation in sight. It was a small house with a couple of sheds, well back from the road. I found two Chinese market gardeners and a white man, all bachelors together.

The Chinese men gladly fed Zazy and offered to keep her for the night in an empty stall. When I asked if I could camp there, they offered me a room instead. They were gentle and sincere, and I wanted to accept their offer. I wrestled with my cultural ignorance and the flickering tongue of memory, and ended up in a cheap room in the Herbert Hotel.

The luxury of a bath and a bed put me in the mood next morning to have breakfast in the Tuxedo Café. Cornflakes and milk were a treat. The pancakes and sausages came with the deal and they tasted good, but I ought to have known to stop short of them. I paid the bill without regret and set off for the market garden, feeling comfortably fed.

I found Zazy also well fed, and ready to travel. She walked steadily along the wide, baked roadside. The temperature climbed with the sun, and soon I was weakened with nausea. I rued the choice of sausages and pancakes, while I hung onto the saddle horn. Zazy never failed.

I craved water. I reminded myself why I had none. I could not carry enough for both of us, and Zazy was as thirsty as I was. George at Longlac was right when he rid me of the sense of duty to carry a water bottle. Now sloughs were a memory; we were in a dry land. Windmills reached up water from deep wells and pushed it into farm homes and stock troughs. I knew we must find a farm.

The heat intensified. By mid-morning, the usual sunshade clouds failed to come riding up the sky. I tied on my headscarf. Sagging in the saddle, I caught sight of a windbreak, then a windmill on the horizon. Zazy continued her even pace; I clung to the pommel with both hands and hoped for water. Finally we were at a farm lane.

We followed that lane between poplar hedges into the yard and stopped at a windmill standing over a large stock trough. The sail was stilled, the mill was disengaged, the trough held a few inches of green water. Zazy declined to dip her muzzle; I turned away in disgust.

I lowered myself from the saddle and walked weakly to the house. No person answered my knocking. Probably folks were at church. Neither dog nor cat came to inspect us. I went to the shed at the base of the windmill; there was no manual pump. Swept by indifference, I hastily unbridled Zazy and slacked her girth, staggered partway down the lane, and sank into a sliver of shade under the hedge.

Aware only of Zazy grazing, and of shade from the sun, I lay out of touch with the rest of the world while hours passed. The cycling sun erased the shadow and shone full on me. Zazy came and roused me. No one had returned to the farm. I found that I could stand again, walk again. I would be able to ride, and we would target a grain elevator and go to it, and there we would find water. I checked my map. Rush Lake was merely fifteen miles west. A lake! We would swim.

The temperature rose, but I knew I could endure it. I had made up my mind in childhood, one overwhelmingly hot day in Mr. Shaw's hayfield in Quebec. Gradually, my body had become heat-adapted. Now it saved me from collapse.

Zazy walked in her unhurried way, measuring the fifteen miles along the grassy depression beside the road. The breeze freshened and fanned us, and now the big white clouds were sailing high, patched here and there with grey. Ahead of us, a storm was gathering. Fragments torn off by the wind came cruising overhead, letting down showers so refreshing that I found myself singing, hoarsely but happily.

Rush Lake proved to have no lake. As we drank at the well of a kindly woman on a farm, she explained: "There used to be water in the lake in olden times. It dried up in the Dirty Thirties and the lake grassed over." All that marked the town now was the elevator.

As the storm consolidated itself overhead, a strange chill slipped into the wind. Showers changed to deluges, deluges coalesced until it was hard to breath air. Within seconds, we were drenched. Zazy drooped her ears at a comical angle to shed water from the tips. Lightning dazzled us, jolted us, took my breath away while the thunder crashed and crushed us close together. I shuddered at the thought that we were the prime targets on that featureless plain.

Through the teeth of a fresh deluge, I caught the blurred image of a railway section house and a pile of ties by a tree. I dared to pause for us to catch our breath there. Was the tree more of a hazard than a haven? As if in answer, lightning split the clouds overhead and thunder rocked the ground beneath us. We quit our shelter and fled, chased by stinging hailstones.

The eye of the storm moved eastwards, leaving a belt of rain and hail. Wheat stems tried in vain to hold up their fat heads against the barrage. Near Fauna's mile sign, we turned down the lane to the section house. I found shelter there for the night with the section man and his family. Zazy was offered the comfort of an open garage, but there was nowhere to tie her, so I had to leave her loose. As soon as I had freed her of the tack, she strode out to feast on green wheat! I hoped for the best and left her. As darkness fell, she was still out there. By morning, she was near the house, sound, and smugly satisfied.

All night, the rain was cooling and healing Zazy's back. I walked through the morning to prevent irritation from the wet saddle pad. We were only a few hours' journey from Swift Current, and our friends at Fauna had told me of an excellent saddler there.

Zazy's intermittent discomfort had haunted me like a latent disease all the way from the Lakehead. At last in Swift Current, I found expert help. Leaving Zazy eating oats in an obsolete dairy barn in town, I carried saddle and pack to the shop of the saddler. He quickly verified the root of our trouble, the lack of skirting to distribute the weight. He took steps to reduce rotation of the saddle, replaced my outworn army haversacks with real saddlebags, and fitted a second girth to tie them down. He also added new lacing to secure the pack to the cantle. Under the girth rings, he slipped sheepskin-lined leathers to prevent further galling.

Having done all he could in an hour to fix our problems, he handed me a tin of gall salve to apply in anticipation of more galling. In payment he would take only eight dollars. I tried to thank him, and I was prepared to leave when the saddler stood back, thought a minute, and said: "If you can stay over another day, I'll put sheepskin-lined skirts under your saddle for ten dollars." I knew he was offering me a gift. If only I had stopped to think! Of course, I could have stayed over another day in the dairy barn. If only I could have seen! I had no idea where I could stay in town, and I doubted that I could afford the cost of stabling. Foolishly, I passed up the bargain.

We rode out of Swift Current more comfortably than we had arrived, with the sleeping bag now fastened across the front of the saddle and the new saddlebags secured snugly behind the cantle. Yet intuitively I knew that Zazy would be sharing with me the cost of a bad decision.

— —

The rain that fell in the afternoon did not seem to matter. Zazy was comfortable, so I was happy. Clear of town, we left the road and stopped to open the parcels and letters from home and Camp 51.

"Keess Zazy on the nose for me, because she is bewdeefull!" came Connie's orders. Zazy had a mouthful of prairie wool just then, besides a muddy nose. I held out a cookie, one of Connie's 'oatmealers'. Zazy crunched it and watched for the next one.

This loafing on a clouded hillside might have bored casual friends, but for Zazy and me, having come up from the past together and always stepping into the future together, this moment was a little glimpse of heaven. Had we hurried on, we would have gone right past the wheat farm of Mrs. Legate. She saved us from spending a night in the pouring rain.

Mrs. Legate was an elderly pioneer widow who was still very much in charge of her farm. She offered us dry beds in the vacant stable and bunkhouse. Thoughtfully, she invited me to join her for breakfast. While the steady rain on the kitchen windows accorded us morning leisure, Mrs. Legate shared her wonderful story with me. From a rather austere first impression, she emerged as a lady who had lived through all the hopes and successes and frustrations that were the gist of human history on the Saskatchewan prairie. She liked my ride story, and I left her home with the gift of her lasting friendship.

Rested, but windblown and shivering in damp clothing, I moved Zazy quickly over the good sand road through Beverley. A hard shower chased us again toward the shelter of a section house. While Zazy was measuring her first step down the steep bank, a freight train came. At the challenge of the iron horse, Zazy threw up the whole idea and scrambled for the road. Meanwhile the shower caught us, soaked us, and went its way.

Rain softened Zazy's hooves, making them more open to the oil I applied against the drying effect of the heat. Rain blessed the thirsty ground here in the Palliser Triangle, where natural cover had long ago been stripped from the soil and nothing had grown in its place. One dry year after another had bankrupted many grain farmers.

Hardships had all but overcome the young couple that sheltered us that night from the teeth of a driving drizzle. They and their three small children welcomed us without reserve, despite their poverty. The turkeys, goats, cow, hens, and vegetable garden barely fed them. The father, despairing of reaping a wheat crop, had turned to doing custom work with his tractor and local jobs on the railway line. He was saving up to free his family from their hopeless situation. Where could they go? He said he had cut pulpwood at Kapuskasing in northern Ontario, years before. "Once you've been in the bush, guess it's always in you. You always want to go back." I knew just what he meant.

After supper, I went to find oats, and the grain elevator seemed like the place to begin. The door was open, but only an echo answered my "Hello-o-o." I saw my chance to explore this towering rectangle.

The emptiness was eerie. I ascended the wooden stairs, flight folding back on flight within the tower. By the light of each window, I looked up at the cable elevator that raised the grain from the weigh scale on the ground to the lofty intake of the huge storage bin. I wondered if I would meet the attendant up there. Or was he out, and would he return and lock the door at the bottom? Curiosity had got me to the very top, and now it forsook me to an urgent desire to get out of that gloomy shaft, where I had no right to be. I trotted down quickly and stepped into a downpour.

I ran back to the farm through the rain. After the storm had passed, the farmer walked over to the elevator and somehow got oat chop for Zazy.

Saskatchewan's emblem, the sheaf of ripe wheat, was out of place here. We had reached the margin of the once great wheat belt. We had travelled nearly off Canada Section II, the middle part of the map that showed me roads and rivers but withheld details of geography and personality for me to discover. I folded the map on the floor. The next morning, I milked the cow, ate my share of pancakes, exchanged the warmest of good wishes with this courageous family, and rode into cattle country.

5

We left the naked, thirsting, dying prairie, a defeated partner in a bargain with sod-breaking farmers. The farmers were gone; their relics of mutual defeat remained—leeward leaning barns, tattered curtains flying in broken windows, ploughs and rakes and binders abandoned to stand silent above the weeds. The barely breathing prairie was waiting, dormant, alone at last, hiding life in its seeds, until the slow cycling of weather patterns would bring round another cycle of germination and growth.

Among hills, the native grasses and low flowering plants thrived where contour and cover conserved water from spring thaws and June rains. Within clever plant tissues, under stones, in creek bottoms shielded by steep shrubby walls, water was present to meet the needs of the plants and animals that belonged there.

These gentle outlier hills created on rippled bedrock caught us in their folds. They fed and watered us, sheltered us, and lifted me above the shoulders of past errors to see the high landforms encircling the southern horizon. We were coming in sight of the Cypress Hills.

We travelled under a cool and cloudy sky over long reaches of open range. Zazy's interest sprang back to life. She had oats and stem-cured grass. I had food from the pack. Surface water was rare; the map could not help us. Gull Lake, like Reed Lake and Rush Lake east of Swift Current, was dry land. Instead we watered at a windmill pump. The sky cleared in the afternoon as we followed a quiet road to Tompkins.

I stopped in town to ask the way and stumbled into a noisy house party of young people. Zazy and I were not allowed to leave until we had eaten. A girl about my age slipped out to the elevator and bought oats for Zazy's supper, and filled her nosebag for another day. She even offered to pack food for me. I went away tremendously cheered, besides being informed about a road allowance where we could go far on grass.

At a bend in the gravel road, we entered the road allowance. It was a straight strip of public grassland wide as a country road, fenced off from privately owned grain fields on either side. What a perfect way to get to Piapot, with no cars, no dust, grass underfoot, and safe, unlimited grazing for Zazy! The sun bowed out in a blaze of gold, and as darkness deepened, I looked back affectionately at the white beacon lights shining from the tops of Tompkins' elevators.

Zazy was restless, maybe confused by the unfamiliar fencing. Lest she stray into the barbed wire while trying to reach for grain, I fetched her early and tacked up. At bedtime, there had been starlight; at 3 AM, we travelled under a bright moon.

A few miles from our campsite, we were stopped by a cross-fence. I was about to engage with a Manitoba gate. It was a portable structure of fence wire and light posts, anchored to one field fence, stretched across the road, and hooked to the other by two wire loops. The bottom loop, I noticed in the moonlight, was attached to a fence post. The top loop was the key that I had to learn to operate.

I had to get enough slack in the gate to let me lift the loop off the post. A few minutes of trial and error reminded me that a lever turns a weakling into a hero, and that I had a lever built into my left arm. I just had to crook it round the terminal post of the gate and use my left hand to pull the fence post toward it. I pulled hard, and the gate gave. The loop went slack and I raised it off the post with my right hand. The wire gate sagged away and I had only to lift it from the bottom loop and carry it aside. We were free to pass.

Zazy watched my strange work, standing well away as the tight wire tried to recoil. I controlled it so that we passed safely through, and reversed the steps to close the gate.

By the time we came to the end of the grassy track where it opened on the gravel road, I knew well how to deal with the Manitoba gate that let us out. Cattle tracks in the roadside dust made sense of gating a road allowance, and of the country code of conduct: Close it!

We drank at the cattle trough below a windmill. From the top of a power pole, a brown hawk watched, motionless but for the slow turn of its head. Cattle gazed as we drank, and stared after us in a phalanx of white faces as we left.

— —

Alberta was near and I had a great urge to be there. Hoping to escape the bruising gravel and perhaps find a trail across cattle range, I took a sand road. Three miles in, we stopped at a wide gateway squarely arched with wooden rails, from which hung the words Buffalo Head Ranch. The way was barred to animals by a Texas gate, a pit dug across the gap and bridged with iron rails spaced more than a hoof-width apart. There had to be a way for a rider to pass. Beside the cattle guard, I saw a short wire gate closed by a loop. A Manitoba gate in miniature, I knew how to deal with that! But I wasn't quick enough to please Zazy. She grew impatient. I noticed her leave, and frowned.

Zazy walked back to the Texas gate, measured it with her eye, and cleared it with a standing jump. Inside, she stood waiting for me while I humbly refastened the partly opened side gate and teetered across the bars after her. I mounted and rode to the house.

A real ranch! Tack hanging in the porch, busy folks in jeans taking time to cook breakfast for me and visit a while. All my romantic notions of a ranch lined up behind me and I watched wide-eyed to see the real thing. A powerful sense of acceptance and fulfillment made me strong as Zazy and I left the corral to find the trail across the range to Piapot. My dream with the Irish setter of my childhood rang true. "I made it, Rusty! It's as wonderful as we knew it would be!"

The morning was hot, as the ranchers predicted. They had let me know that they would not be out riding under the midday sun. We went anyway; I just couldn't wait.

Zazy easily held to the trail, whether it was a clear wagon track or a mere difference in the texture of the grass, where years of passing hooves and wheels had altered the earth. A breeze freshened the air. Flowers in cream, yellow and orange, pink, red and purple painted the turf. Iridescent blue-green magpies with elegant black accessories on white bodies spooked around the old sheep sheds. We wandered happily over the hills while the voyages of the prairie schooners moved from my imagination into the historic reality etched into the ground beneath us.

The trail rejoined the road at Piapot. Not knowing where range gates would allow us more off-road travel, I left a blackbird to his song on a fence and accepted our pedestrian route along dusty Highway #1. Almost unbelievably, near the road a stream was flowing between lush banks. It led us to its confluence with a similar stream, and there I stopped to feed and bathe Zazy. I intended to sleep there, but horseflies scuttled that plan. Cooled by the creek, I rested while Zazy had a short feed, and then I was ready to ride.

Before evening, we longed for shade. I knocked at the door of an apparently vacant farmhouse, and found an elderly couple living there. They put Zazy in a shelter, and insisted that I join them for supper. They had farmed in Ontario and survived the Dry Thirties in the Palliser Triangle. I was tempted to stay and hear more from them, but wisdom told me to travel in the coolness of night.

Rain came with the sun and gave me a feeble excuse to turn into a ranch in sight of the Cypress Hills. At last they were in view! The young family whom I met was as excited to hear about our journey as I was to learn about their lives near the Hills. They fed my mare and laid on breakfast for me, and we all sat round, a shirt-and-jeans company, trim Mom and Dad, their teenage son, and me drying out in the warmth of the kitchen.

The boy eagerly scooped up details about maintaining a 'horse on the road. I asked what he rode, and he glowed! He told me about his mare, Trinket, that he had ridden to Junior Championship in the 1949 Maple Creek Light Horse Show. As he fetched down the trophy from the shelf, his dad's face broke into a smile, and his mom suggested he introduce me to Trinket.

From a small corral near the barn, a copper chestnut mare about Zazy's size saw us and called. Her burnish glowed even through the raindrops on her back. The boy slipped between the rails and rode the mare around with only a hand on her neck and his perfect balance to guide her. He took me to the tack room. "That's my dad's saddle." He pointed to a wear-darkened, double-rigged, supple old stock saddle resting on a trestle in front of a smaller model. "This one's mine. Dad has a new one that he won roping last year." Reverently, he lifted a Navajo blanket off an unblemished roping saddle honoured with a separate stand. The boy was proud of his dad.

He told me his plans for the summer as we took Zazy back to the house. He laid out the steps he would take to educate his horse in mind and body: dressage for agility, roping skills to make him and Trinket a team, sliding stop for safety at speed, and obedience without fear. The show season was coming; he would be busy getting Trinket ready to compete. "I'll be helping Dad with the cattle, too," he assured me with a ring of pride.

At noon, Zazy and I were alone again, loafing on the shady side of a granary beyond Maple Creek. I sat with my back against the weathering boards, looking across a field of paling winter wheat to the grey-green range that blended with the blue Cypress Hills. Across that distance, those hills seemed to be sending me a promise of a time when I would know them personally. I thought of the boy and Trinket, and of freckled Jimmy riding the steer at Ernfold. There was room in this country for a kid not only to watch and dream, but to do and be and grow.

Zazy asked for a cookie as I reached into the box from home. "One for you and one for me," I told her and we crunched together. Then it was time to go.

Reluctantly, I saddled the mare. I hoped in vain that the blanket in the last parcel would ease the pressure on the tender spot behind the withers. No blanket could replace restructuring. I had missed my chance at Swift Current. I had no second chance.

I did what I could to help my friend. I unsaddled her several times in a day to cool her back, and I walked many miles beside her. I walked the soles and sides of my canvas shoes into holes. The soles of my feet thickened until stones ceased to bruise, except by direct hit through a hole. Dust entered at the sides and left through the holey soles, or stayed to be ignored. Only foxtail awns and tumbleweed spines could make me retreat to Zazy's back.

Against all the misery stood the certain fact that daily we were moving toward the Rocky Mountains. Reaching them would be a milestone in my life.

But first, there would be Alberta! I watched a herd of cattle fanning out on a hillside as they went up from their watering place at a creek. The sinking sun was sending long shadows after them. We were so close to my goal! We camped in the hills a stone's throw from the border.

Early on Saturday morning, July 17, we entered Alberta. The road was marked Route 3 below a line of snow-capped peaks; the terrain was more or less flat. Almost immediately, we were in Walsh. All I saw of it was the stockyards just coming to life. Guys were sitting on the top plank of the loading chute, waiting for something to happen, when Zazy and I came along. A cattle dealer stepped out through the office door, took a look, lifted the cigarette coolly from his mouth with thumb and forefinger, and shouted across to me: "I'll make a deal with you on that pony!" He got a laugh from the audience on the fence.

That started the fun. Questions came flying my way, and I was silly enough to feel obliged to answer. "Why do you shoe your horse?" "Why do you need two reins?" I caught on slowly. I was feeling slightly under attack, and definitely superior about my undervalued horse. I also felt stupid for being too slow to fire back. I left the scene with an airtight grudge against Walsh.

"Watch out for rattlers around The Hat," warned a rancher who gave us a late breakfast. He was not joking. Since I expected to pass through Medicine Hat that very day, I left wondering how to go about watching for rattlers.

Still east of The Hat at nightfall, I camped with never a thought of snakes, in a remote fence corner. It was rain that took me by surprise. The first cold, heavy drops woke me to the fact that the ground around us was quickly changing to mud. Once again I scrambled out of my bag, groped for our belongings, and piled them against the fence wire. I fumbled until I had a hand on the barbed strand above them, used it as a ridge-pole, and draped the plastic sheet like a tent over the whole kit. Satisfied with the bivouac, I curled up so that most of me fit under a dry corner, and slept out the storm.

Zazy spent a restless night looking for oats. Already I had learned that Albertans don't stay home on Saturday night, and that not every store sells oats or even oatmeal. The mare was still looking hopefully at the pack when I saddled up at 4:40 AM.

—

We were in The Hat before Sunday had properly begun. As I rode down the coulee into the city, my childhood picture of The Hat as a sombrero with bricks and pottery all around it came to life. I saw the clay banks, Medalta Pottery works, piles of bricks and tiles, and the gas wells that fuelled the furnaces. We slipped like period characters past the dormant motels mocked up in Old West style.

The day rapidly changed from cool to hot. I wanted for Zazy relief from the pavement, and for myself a drink. She had drunk from a trough the night before, and rain had wet her pasture. The one person I met in The Hat perfectly filled my need. From his milk wagon he handed me an ice-cold pint bottle. We talked as I drank down food and drink combined, leaning against the shady side of his wagon.

Beyond town, Zazy cooled her belly and legs in the long grass at the edge of a golf course. Two young boys on saddle ponies stopped for a word, left the highway where leisure traffic was building, and headed across the open range, free as the white cloud above them. We came to the airport, where I saw pronghorns for the first time, looking at us from a safe distance behind the fence. Brightly tawny creatures with bold white patches and black facial lines drawn down from their spiky horns, these six shy grazers drew me deeply into the community of the open plains.

Looking again for water, I met an elderly farmer in his barnyard. He invited us into the coolness of his low red barn, and gave Zazy water and a feed of oat chop and hay. For me he fetched a tall glass of ice water from the house. We stood talking in the shade while Zazy was feeding.

The antelope, as local people called them, had drifted down from the bombing range to the north with their kin during heavy winter snows. Searching for food, they had walked over the snowed-in fence, and these six had become trapped when the snow melted.

Farmers welcomed the antelope far more than the personnel from the Department of National Defence. The army had moved out the farmers and confiscated seventy-five hundred acres of land for military training during the Second World War. The war ended in 1945, but the army kept the land for defence research. The conflict between the deposed stewards and DND was as raw in 1950 as any war scar. The passion of the farmer for his lost land touched to flame the fabric of the prairie community being woven into my memory.

The farmer showed me how to spot a road allowance on my map, and he set me on the trail to Seven Persons. I won a fight with a tight Manitoba gate that freed us onto springy sod, gentling us away from the hot, hard haste of the highway. The living prairie, millennia old, subtly inscribed with bluish grass in memory of prairie schooners, forever renewing herself: she comforted me as I believe she comforted the aging farmer. His story is terminal; her story is open-ended.

I looked down on a colony of blue pentestemon flowers, each holding to a stem as thin as a hair. They lived in a patch of sparse grass half the size of Zazy's midday shadow. Respectfully apart from the colony, a shock of creamy vetch burst eight inches above their cushion of fuzzy grey-green leaves. Drought survivors all, the plant colonies of the virgin prairie led out my vision in ripples. Each plant community belonged on a different surface. Bare gravel scrapes hosted frosty green felts of seedling pussy-toe rosettes. Their close-pressed mature kin raised hand-high forests of flowering stems. Fuzzy pink blossom pads proclaimed to the wind the success of the family as a whole.

Away from our track and the disturbed soil around gopher diggings, grasses secured the surface with their distinctive colonies. I walked among them, carrying Zazy's bridle. Thin soles allowed my feet to sense the sod. Truly I trod holy ground.

Another Manitoba gate let us out of the road allowance and onto the highway. Although the day was Sunday, I found a store in Seven Persons where I could buy rolled oats. I asked the storekeeper where the town got its name.

According to the storekeeper, the hamlet was named by a railway construction crew for seven human graves they found. Blood and Cree tribes were said to have clashed there and seven Cree were killed. Was I sharing an ancient site sacred to my forbearers as I lay sky-watching by the creek?

The westerly wind laid its cool hand on me as I tramped thoughtfully along the top of the coulee. Beside me Zazy walked with a twenty-pound bag of oatmeal laid across the front of the saddle. We stopped where a steady breeze was hindering the horseflies. I freed Zazy to search out the satisfying native grasses already bearing seed. As for myself, I loafed on my back on the turf, making fantasies out of cloud shapes, with a yellow-skirted coneflower looking me in the eye.

— —

In a day or two, we came into arable land shared by ranches and farms, south of the South Saskatchewan River. Now oats were available, but water was a serious problem. I saw neither streams nor sloughs. A farmer never refused us water, but the farms were far apart and sometimes the water drawn from deep in the ground had a bitter flavour. One day I found out what that taste meant.

We had been travelling through suntanned range. We were not parched, but certainly thirsty. Across a pasture, I spied a windmill and a bunch of cattle standing around a trough. I hurried over, unwise to the meaning of the white rings around depressions on the ground. Clear blue water was brimming over the trough, rippling in the breeze.

Zazy barely touched her muzzle to it, and stepped back. I tried it. It tasted and felt like soap. Alkali! It clung in my mouth. I went to a farmhouse near the pasture. "There's water at the pump," said the woman who answered my knock, "and if you want a really good drink, go draw a pailful from the well over there."

I took her pail and rope to a covered well in her field. Zazy came too. I let down the bucket almost to the end of its tether, heard it splash, felt it fill, and drew it up. Zazy immersed her muzzle and siphoned up that pailful, then another. I let down the pail again, drew it up dripping, dipped my face into its icy delight, and drank, slowly, sensing its coldness all the way to my stomach. I sloshed the rest over my face and arms and legs.

We walked back to return the pail. How could I thank the woman? How can you thank anyone for a sacrament?

We came to fenced range and good fields of wheat bred for resistance to sawflies and grasshoppers. A horde of ravenous insects met us on the few square feet of ground where I set our camp. They brazenly nibbled at me and embroidered the edges of the leather with their mandibles. As we left, they projected themselves in a rustling bow wave ahead of our feet.

Hoping again to have the saddle fixed, I watched for a chance to get work. Around Bow Island, I saw crops being harvested, so I stopped at a farm to inquire. The couple that ran the farm quickly took up my cause.

"My cousin might need help," offered Mary. "I'll phone. Please come in. Sally, will you take care of the pony for a minute, please?" Zazy went happily with the twelve-year-old girl. The question went out, the cousin would ask his neighbour, and Mary would ask another neighbour if the canning plant at Taber was hiring help. Randy would keep an ear to the ground for work I might do, and I was to stay overnight until answers came.

Sally and her two younger sisters took Zazy and me to the barn. They watched intently as I removed the saddle and pack, then they fed the mare, talked to her, sat on her while she ate. They talked about everything, including the pimples around her ears, muzzle, and tail head. They helped me lug her tack upstairs, out of reach of the calf. They filled her manger with hay for supper, and sat in a row on her back while I led her to a small field where Mary said she could spend the afternoon.

I needed to buy a few items in town, so Mary directed me to the general store and lent me her bicycle. Zazy watched in distress as I wheeled away.

Shopping in Bow Island was a social event. The storekeeper engaged me in a friendly chat before he even hinted at my business. It seemed not to really matter whether I bought anything, so long as we had a visit. He stocked no running shoes, but he did have film, and Lysol for the pimples. I found Mary's bike where I had parked it, unlocked, of course, for this was Bow Island!

Zazy saw me coming and called from afar. Mary said she had paced the fence all the while that I was away, even ignoring carrots.

Lysol made no difference to Zazy's pimples. I discussed the cause with Randy, and the suspects were chicken lice from an overhead hen house in a barn where she had slept, and alkali water. After two more ineffectual spongings, I blamed the water and let place and time solve the problem. I made the judgment while sitting on the edge of the salvaged antique steamer wheel now holding the mildly tainted water that Zazy was drinking.

Little Doreen and Mary Ann proudly took me to see the polished dance floor in the renovated loft of the red barn. Now that the loft was no longer needed for hay, it was rented for dances.

No jobs came to light while I stayed at the Bow Island farm. Though I drew a blank on employment, I learned what fun farm diversification really could be. It just took a wide-angle view of present resources and emerging markets.

— —

Hot, dry terrain was the order of our day. At high noon, I was walking beside Zazy when a man yelled out from a highway crew: "Hey! Where ya goin', kid?"

I stopped. "Montreal to the coast," I said.

"Watch out for them rattlesnakes in that ditch! Ya don't get them around Montreal!"

I looked down at my holey shoes. My feet suddenly felt naked and every tussock became a sunshade for a sleeping snake. I went an uneasy mile. Gradually, reason began to insert a word or two. After all our miles through snake habitat with never sight nor sign of a snake, why should every bush now shelter a rattler? That guy was teasing. I quit watching and began to enjoy the patchwork quilt of pink, white, and blue larkspur laid along the railway embankment.

While my thoughts were gathering wool, Zazy was watching her every step. *Look out!* Something shot tension through her easy pace. She took a wild leap diagonally across a wide ditch, landed on the road shoulder and bolted away, carrying me scrambling to recover my seat, and wondering.

At sunset, Alberta's famed mosquitoes came out in force after blood. Somewhere near Antonio, we turned up a lane, hoping for shelter. Two dogs came running down to escort us back to an old farm. A tanned, wrinkled woman with a woven headscarf and pendant gold earrings rose slowly from an armchair beside the house. She smiled at me. Her husband smiled too, continuing to recline on one elbow on the sunny hatch of the cellar. The couple remained mostly quiet, and I asked simply for horse shelter and feed. They seemed to be trying to make sense of our presence, so that I wondered if they spoke another language, maybe Italian. When they came to understand that I did not expect or want to be a formal guest, that I was more like a gypsy, we all were at ease.

After Zazy was fed and settled in a corral, and the son of the family came home from work, we all sat by lamplight in the kitchen, talking in a blend of Italian and English. We told about adventures in the wide world, their immigration, their farm, and the irrigated area through which I had been moving. They said I would surely find a job at Taber, either on a farm or in the factory.

Zazy fared well on the little Italian farm. I stood aside in awe as she ate a third of a pail of rye in lieu of oats for supper and almost finished the pailful for breakfast. The only effect that I could see was her high spirits for racing with the sleek black pony that the son rode. He and his pony saw us on our way along a dirt track as far as Purple Springs.

At the village, we had to return to the paved highway. Again we were picking our path along the shoulder between broken bottles and jagged cans. The grass on the other side of the railway fence looked cleaner and greener than our littered way. We stood on the planks of the next level crossing, considering how to outwit the cattle guard.

The cattle guard was designed to allow only a train to pass the gap in the fence. An array of narrow boards was set obliquely on edge and cunningly spaced to turn a hooved animal. The guard was too wide for Zazy to jump from a takeoff on planks. I tied up her reins and waited to see what she would do.

She was free to return to the roadside, but instead she set about solving the problem before her. First she placed a hoof tentatively on the guard, felt her toe slip into a gap, and stepped back to ponder, or perhaps to recollect an event in her history I might never know. Again she tried to step, this time placing her hoof flat. It stayed steady. Finally, placing one foot after another flat across two edges at once, she stepped deftly to the far side. I jumped on her back and we went sliding through the blue vetch down the cinder bank and cantering along the right-of-way.

At each level crossing, Zazy honed her skill. One train passed, but she had plenty of room to dance away from it. We covered carefree miles before a man came along the tracks on a handcar and advised me that I was breaking the law. A policeman slowed his car and called from the road to enforce the warning. I called back my reason for being there, but it did not alter my option. At the next level crossing, I felt compelled to quit our safe path, and soon a patrol car came bringing an officer to see that I had complied.

Factory chimneys rose on the skyline. Like magic, a luxuriant field of corn appeared, growing right up to the edge of the dry land. We had reached an oasis called Taber Irrigation District. Back from the highway lay the huge blue reservoir lake, feeding the canals that fed the ditches that let the water onto the land. Crops thrived in the midst of drought, and farmers prospered. Sugar beets and market vegetables, acre after acre, drank up the water that rained from huge mobile sprinklers while the sun shone.

Out on the pea fields, machines harvested the vines and heaped them on trucks. Every truck that passed us on the road to town swamped us with the smell of the succulent crop. Zazy fell in behind a slow-moving truck and merrily pulled out peas to munch. Outside the cannery, the round stacks of discarded vines grew hour by hour, fermenting for silage while the peas went into cans. The chimneys billowed black smoke and the boilers generated sterilizing steam.

Did I really intend to ask for a job there? Zazy would have to be left in the hands of strangers while I was at work. A farm job would make more sense to me, but would it pay enough to merit the delay? We had a goal to reach, hundreds of miles ahead, in a month's time.

Was I just finding excuses to keep going west? Something intangible was drawing me toward the mountains. Zazy's back was comfortable; she was going with renewed vigour. I was eager for a new day to unfold. I never even drew rein at Taber.

At nightfall I stood on a hilltop, at the door of a cottage, asking for shelter from a storm that swept a wild open range. A household of Mormon people welcomed me in. I was thrilled to find myself among them, all ears to hear their story firsthand.

Barnwell was their place of birth; their ancestral roots were there. The mother was writing a history of the community. The children knew that their paternal grandfather was one of the four founding fathers, and that their parents placed the future of the community in the children's hands, within the boundaries of the Mormon Church. Sharing the family's story, I felt as if I were looking into a strangely attractive valley, walled not by rocks but by the social force of heritage. The bottomlands nurtured the familial roots, feeding the vines that reached so competently into the world outside. My roots were not in their valley, but our kinship in Christ was real.

I rode into a calm, cloudy dawn time. As light developed, I began to notice stands of trees on the landscape. Trees? At midmorning we were resting from the sun under leafy poplars growing in a ditch. How did all these trees come here to change the complexion of the prairie? What force tamed those prevalent winds that elsewhere set limits on the height of a sapling?

The arrow flight of a flicker led my eye to see the big picture. The bird connected our shade trees with the crowns of a row of sturdy poplars that stood round a pasture field. People had been cultivating rows and rows of trees like the windbreaks around prairie homesteads. Here, nurtured trees were creating tree habitat, as surely as an eroding riverbank created plant cover. Contours, natural or man-made, were taming the relentless westerlies, guarding the youth of a sapling, enabling it to stand up and become a tree.

Reluctantly, I passed by the experimental station of Canada Agriculture, while all my latent questions raised a furor of objection. I could not stop; I was going to the mountains.

Next the stockyards came up with a second, Walsh-like assault. Idlers on whitewashed plank fences heckled me: "A hundred and fifty dollars for the outfit!" "Hey Charlie, why don't ye trade 'er yer ol' Chev fer that horse?" We were in Lethbridge. Stop and work in this hot, hard, unnerving city? How could we possibly fit? We stopped at the post office, then we left town.

6

The road wound down through a deep coulee into the Oldman River Valley, over a bridge, and steeply up onto the flat plain. We climbed aside to a shoulder of the coulee. I unsaddled the mare, unpacked the heavy parcel from Mom and Dad, paid Zazy for her patience with a marshmallow, and saw her drift to grass. I opened an orange, buried the peel in the loose brown earth, and savoured the juicy fruit while I pored through the news from home: the latest rose to bloom, a girlfriend's holiday at a resort, a neighbour's illness, the painting of the new church.

Sky and breeze and warm earth wrapped their presence around me, filling me with a sense of order and balance. I folded away the letters, fitted the new food supply into the saddlebags, and compacted the wrappings. In a shallow bowl scraped in the soil, I burned the paper bit by bit until nothing was left but fine grey ash. Finally I levelled the soil as it had been.

Yet there remained a mark at the centre where the fire had burned. Nothing was left but a centre. I felt I was on the mark, expanding from that centre into the cleared space around it, and outward, limitless, at the pleasure of sky and breeze and warm, brown earth.

From the top of the coulee I looked intently to west and southwest. What of the jagged bluish clouds I had seen lined up along the horizon? From that coulee top, in mid-afternoon, I saw no mountains. The round shoulders of the Oldman River levelled away to dry range. Where the river meandered near to the road, it gave us a sheltered campsite. That evening, the bluish forms reappeared, more substantial than before. At dawn the overcast hid the horizon.

I knew we had encamped near the historic base of the Northwest Mounted Police, and as we came near to Fort McLeod, I recognized the remains of the buildings from Miss Porrit's Grade Six history lessons. I saw the historic roundhouse on the Canadian Pacific Railway line, and noted it to Dad in my next letter.

We ended the day in a pretty valley sheltered from wind and the view of many people. There lived an old couple and their son. They had good hay for Zazy and a comfy cot in the brooder house for me.

Long before the sun looked into the coulee, we began climbing the dewy hillside. Just as we came over the top, the sunlight touched my shoulder like the hand of a friend. I looked up and saw that it was splashing gold and pink and snowy white paint on the peaks of real mountains! Those painted peaks challenged me to believe what I had seen. Right before my eyes, they were fading into their foreground as the rising sun drenched the plain with light.

All through that shimmering day, we travelled in a land whose beauty lived in every river threading its way between coulees, in each afghan-striped field that breathed of fallow land and growing crop. Here the right to till land imposed on the farmer the duty to conserve exposed soil. Here the ground was alternately cropped and rested in bands following the contours of the land. Here earth still clothed the hills and gently fed the rivers with its surplus water, as in time past, when it shared with unbroken sod the close embrace of mutual need, before the ploughman came.

At mid-morning, I drank rich Dutch coffee with a farm family, while Zazy ate oat chop in the stable. Our hosts were eager to hear about Montreal, which they had barely glimpsed on their way to Alberta from Holland four years before. I wanted to know about their life in the west with their four children, aged precisely two years apart. I missed meeting the fourteen-year-old son. His mother showed me his collection of carefully blown birds' eggs. She explained, "Sometimes he's away for days, studying birds and animals."

I wished I could have gone hiking with him, to see what he saw in the Porcupine Hills.

For now, the horizon was drawing me toward those ephemeral Rockies. When the sun once more sighted low across the prairies, it pencilled in a line of dark blue forms no longer as clouds, but as mountains.

I rode that evening with a man on a palomino horse. He was searching for a bucking mare that had strayed from his pasturing rodeo band. We listened to each other. He considered that the good feed and rest between rodeos compensated for the rough handling the horse received at work. I saw the sport as cruel. A Peace River rancher had told me that raking with spurs was the measure of skill of the rider. I had seen the bucking straps pulled tight around the loins just before the horse sprang out of the chute. It seemed unfair to me that a rider could choose to play the rodeo game, but a horse had no choice. The man's informed viewpoint gave me food for thought. Opinions aside, the defecting mare would be caught.

Our horses moved in quiet companionship. At a side road, the wrangler and I disengaged from our differences and parted company with a friendly "So long." The palomino cantered lightly over the level crossing and engaged with the dirt road in full stride, attended by a small cloud of dust.

Dew cooled Zazy's back as we slept out the darkness. In the first light of morning, the frosty caps of the Rockies seemed to float detached from solid ground, white wizards playing a game with optics. Through the day, we measured out the miles over windswept grassland, stride by stride, aiming for those mountains. I could easily have been blinded by anticipation, had not the prairie sent out a messenger or two to get my attention. She had more gifts for me, folded in her sun-bleached mantle.

Two Native men appeared, riding across open range on the Peigan Reserve. Seeing us, they turned and came down to the highway to greet us. They were as friendly and curious and shy as I was. We talked little. They seemed easily satisfied with my answers, and I did not know how to explore their space without intruding. We just rode together.

They mentioned the annual Sun Dance on the Blood Reserve to the south. My enthusiasm seemed to embarrass them. Perhaps they spoke from Inside while I cheered from Outside, cheered for my hope someday to see inside their culture. Uncertainty clouded their faces. They roused their ponies, and Zazy took that as a cue to race. So it happened that we all came galloping dusty and thirsty and laughing into Brocket.

We tied our sweaty horses to the hitching rail at the general store. The Natives greeted friends in the row of observers smoking on the board veranda. I felt like any stranger would, as I walked up the plank steps. My smile to an expansive woman puffing her pipe near the door fell flat. I went inside.

My eyes reached into the dimness, following a line of dark faces: women, children, and men scrutinizing me from a bench. Beyond them, indistinct figures leaned against counters laden with bolts of cloth, boots, shirts, and hardware. A white man rounded off his conversation across the grocery counter and leisurely went about supplying me with bread, cheese, and oatmeal. He told me that the town's drinking water came from the tap at the base of the railway water tower.

I went with Zazy for a drink. Warm water fell from the tap into my cupped hands and boiled off the cinders around our feet. We wet our mouths, stepped away, and took the steep road down through the Native village to the river. Zazy drank her fill, and we eased into lunch under the shade of a cottonwood tree.

I watched the action among the cabins opposite us across an open field. A lean pony plied the beaten paths, immune to the random techniques of the kids who took turns riding it. Indifferently, it received the heavy hands and heels of the man who jumped on its back, apparently to impress the youngsters.

A buckboard came rattling down the hill behind an unshod team and swayed past us to the ford. For a fleeting moment the horses paused, then they splashed into the water and drew the wagon across the stony riverbed, followed by two fans of shining water thrown up by the wheels. The outfit rattled non-stop up the far bank, tilted and settled over the crest and was gone.

An oil truck laboured down the hill against its gears and ground to a halt at the ford. Half a dozen children and a small black dog gathered to watch the driver fill his radiator.

I was beginning to pack when the bushes parted and two dark-eyed, barefoot girls stepped out. A colourful roll of candies spoke their language. They took the gift politely and vanished. Soon the bushes parted again. Half a dozen youngsters stepped out, frankly expectant, labile as deer. I surrendered the last of my Lifesavers to them and watched the innocent company melt into the leafy screen, sharing the sweets as they went. My friend Amy, who sent those Lifesavers, would have smiled. The children reappeared to watch us leave their green and tawny river bottom.

All afternoon the prairie hummed of crickets under cactus clumps, of grasshoppers skimming on paper-dry wings, of yellow-headed blanket flowers fanned by a breeze. When the sun dropped behind the mountains, we were at Pincher Station.

Pincher Station was the point on the Canadian Pacific Railway that served the foothills ranching area. For that reason, the station house was also a livery stable. Few travellers used it in 1950, but the station master told me that a group of riders had recently stayed there. We were welcome to stay and to use the hay and oats they had left. Yes, I could sleep in the loft. Would I like to hitch a ride with his family into town?

Zazy stepped into the first stall she came to and checked it for leftover food. She attacked a salt lick in a corner of her oat box while I went to the loft and dropped hay through the chute into her manger. She was well into her meal when I left for town in the station master's van.

Pincher Creek was a spot on my map, but certainly not a town on the landscape. It was hiding in a coulee completely below the surface of the prairie. Flat land flew past my window, while the children sat silently trying to figure me out. Abruptly the car dived with the road over the edge of the coulee and angled down to the bottom. A whole town was tucked into a pleat of the prairie's skirt.

I left the family at the top of Main Street and nosed along to a shoe store. I bought a pair of boys' canvas shoes with laces and wide toes, for $1.75. The salesman urged me to try them on. Knowing how dirty my feet were, I assured him that the shoes would fit, paid him, and left the store with a parcel under my arm.

Twilight lasted for me to find my way up the coulee wall. On top and alone, I sat down to try on my new shoes. To the accepting prairie I could show my grimy feet without shame. Looking at the tattered remains of my old runners, I could see the perplexed look on Mom's face, and hear her voice: "Barbara, what will people think?"

"No one to see, way up here, Mom." I unwrapped the replacements and tried them on. They fit just about perfectly. I rewrapped them and wore the old ones back to the stable.

I felt a twinge of nostalgia when I came down the loft stairs in the morning, new shoes on my feet, cast-offs hanging from my hand. We had broken new ground together, at Camp 51, at Port Arthur, through hunger and flies and quicksand, losing and winning through to the prairie, pushing against those westerlies in heat and dust, wild storms and weird human ways, and resting in a pool of wolf willow perfume, celebrating the glory of everything on the back of a great pinto horse, persisting forward until the snowy Rockies appeared on the horizon. My good, spent shoes, I left them side by side beneath the bench inside the door, where stablemen year after year had sat and chewed their plug and swapped tales with travellers.

Zazy and I were alone. Thanks had been said the evening before, no payment was accepted, and our host wished us well. I filled the nosebag with the oats Zazy had left in her box, pulled the manure back and shovelled it into a wheelbarrow, tacked up the mare, and left on foot.

I walked all day beside Zazy. The road wandered across open range, down through creek bottoms walled by plates of brown rock, up the shoulders of rounded hills to outlooks on a land with a story written on its face as beautiful as the story on the face of an elder who has found peace. I bent to feel the familiar grasses, mixing here with lupines and milk vetches going to seed. To the west, the hills reached for the sky.

At 9 AM on Sunday, in the third week of July 1950, the breath of a mountain forest stopped me in my tracks. My tired pony lifted her nose to the wind. My nose searched the corridor of scent.

Wait. Don't move. Don't miss the message.

Ask again, ask the birches and balsams and firs what they mean. The forest was speaking. *Remember, remember.*

"Forest breath, throw the bridge across. Make me stand again where I knew you first, in my time of affirmation, when the birches and balsams breathed your message to me, back in the *brule* on the farm in Quebec.

"Zazy, it comes back to me, that dewy morning in the woods above the spring, where Charlie sent us on our first solo ride! Breathing trees, lift the magic bridge between a time of filial love and an unborn future. You Rocky Mountain forest, you are luring me."

This time I wouldn't be afraid to let go. The prairie had prepared me for this parting, for change as she was forever changing, toward a new point of balance.

Banner Clouds

A matterhorn mountain peak standing in lofty isolation, ground to a point by ice lobes, can make a banner appear in the sky. It can cleave an oncoming air mass and divert the two streams into its lee side. Sheltered downwind, the streams of air recoil against their former direction and mount the lee slope of the mountain, until they are sucked up into a vacuum near the top. Suddenly the invisible water they carry changes into droplets, to be caught by the surrounding air as a cloud and carried out like a banner from the peak.

A banner cloud shines like a snowfield cut loose to dance in the sky. It celebrates the action of unseen forces on unnoticed events, to create a great prospect, a new dimension of being.

Zazy and I walked down a wandering trail in forest shade, then out across open shoulders where yellow flowers smiled frankly at the sun and grazing cattle started and stared. At noon, thirst urged us toward a scintillating stream held deep in a steep valley. Halfway down, above the trail, a hollowed log, bearded with moss and brimming with spring water, invited us to drink.

As I cupped my hands under the flow, a woman wearing an apron came down the stony path. She handed me a tumbler and invited me to follow her to her log house, half hidden in the trees. I was to share the roast that her husband was just then carving. Zazy was welcome to make herself at home.

The Leskosky farm drew from me a deep *yes*. Its chinked log buildings nestled in the hillsides. Zazy moved about, grazing as if she belonged there. I sensed a natural balance, not of rich or poor, modern or ancient, but of fitness and wholeness, *shalom*. After Sunday dinner, Emily set Baby Joan in a field of daisies and I photographed her. I noted Emily's mailing address. We talked to the tethered milk cow and agreed on the joy of having a food supply at the door.

Emily told me about the Frank Slide that had engraved the grey scar we could see on the face of the mountain across the valley. Midway through the afternoon, Zazy and I stepped down the path past the log trough and onto the trail that would lead us to scar-faced Turtle Mountain.

The earth road took us in its own way to the floor of the valley. We passed over a plank-and-log bridge and up and out on the grade, where we began our first long climb. For an hour I worried about Zazy's sore back, while my feet complained about going twenty miles in new shoes. Quite suddenly, we passed from living mountainside onto dead rock. Pain was eluted by the unworldly hush of the Frank Slide.

Motion had ceased; Nature had paled and lost her voice. All was grey, silent stone: the road where Zazy's shoes shuffled the dust, the raw limestone height joining earth to sky, the mute expanse of giant and pygmy boulders lying in disorder to the horizon. While long shadows fell across the stony world, we moved slowly up the slope. In the last light of that day, I breathed in the scene once more and read its history inscribed on the bronze plaque beside me.

> Disaster struck here at 4:10 AM, April 29th, 1903, when a giant wedge of limestone 1300 feet high, 4000 feet wide and 500 feet thick crashed down from Turtle Mountain and destroyed the town of Frank. Seventy million tons of rock swept over two miles of valley, taking 66 lives, burying numerous homes, the entire mine plant, railway sidings, and 3200 acres of fertile land to a depth of 100 feet in 100 seconds.

An eerie whisper invaded that sensory vacuum: The last word had not yet been spoken by Turtle Mountain.

— —

Darkness and cold were upon us; we needed to escape the road. We hurried past sleeping Maple Leaf, past Bellevue, where the noise and dazzle of a refreshment booth shocked me out of the sombre spell of the slide. In a park at the edge of Blairmore, we found quietness.

Warmth was a quality of the past. I snuggled deeply into my sleeping bag while mountain breezes hunted round me for any way to get in. Their icy touches told me that we had climbed to the clouds. How I thanked my sister Joan for that eiderdown bag! At earliest light, I rolled and packed it with care, washed in a stream, and got myself moving.

Blairmore was sound asleep when we stepped side by side into the green rift between the hills. Workmen with lunch pails came from cottages to walk the road we walked. A miner's wife drove two tawny cows home for milking, through a narrow buttercup meadow between road and railway. Just as we reached Coleman, the colliery whistle piped in another day.

Beyond the last cottage, we began climbing in earnest, while the sun expanded the dew and changed the cool morning into a hot July day. Each curve of the road set us on a snatch of the way ahead while the mountain closed behind us. Rumblings rose from the depth of the canyon. Zazy tensed; I swung onto her back for our safety. The dirt road narrowed, clinging like a goat track to a ledge high on the mountainside.

A train sent its whistled song ricocheting off the rock walls. Zazy broke into a canter that carried us smartly over the last quarter-mile of the grade. At a bend, we looked straight down into a railway yard. Engines made noise and billowed up columns of smoke and steam as they shunted rolling stock into train lengths. Zazy broke and ran. I glimpsed the words Crow's Nest Pass, Continental Divide, and we were gone before I could read the altitude. Already we were descending, powered by the height, the airiness, our speed, the drop-off, the peaks ahead. The pass bent, levelled, handed us over to forest and to the meaning of the moment. We had just crossed the Great Divide!

Oat time overtook us. Zazy was watching for a turnoff when a lumber truck nosed out of a side road and gave her the clue she needed. Within half a mile, she found her dinner in the stable of a logging camp. The barn boss sent his helper to show me the way to the dining room for a regal dinner with the kitchen staff. This was British Columbia!

Before we left that hospitable camp, I showed Zazy's 'sit-fast' to the stableman and asked for advice. The gall was circumscribed but deep, and below it the veins stood out ominously. All around it the skin was tender and hot. The stableman took it seriously. He gave me cold water to bathe the area, and he suggested that the RCMP at Natal might direct me to a veterinarian when we stopped for provincial border inspection.

During our walk of five miles to the twin villages of Michel and Natal, I resolved to do whatever was necessary to end our misery. At my request, the police called in an adviser.

A seasoned horseman came late in the day. He examined the gall carefully, stood back, fixed me with his eyes, and stated: "You can't go any farther with that horse. The sore's a sit-fast. It's like a boil. She's straining her muscles to keep the weight off it; that's why her veins are up. Bathe it with salt, put on your green salve, cover her back to keep out the flies, and it should come all right in time." He handed me a small cotton bag full of salt, accepted nothing but my thanks, wished me well, and walked away.

I knew exactly what I had to do. I tucked the salt into a plastic bag, against the rain that cut short the light. Then I tacked up for the last time and led Zazy back to the railway station we had passed at Michel. The freight agent found two sacks for me, and he helped me to stuff the bulk of our possessions into them on the platform while the rain overflowed the eavestroughs and poured down my back.

The deed was done. The agent dragged the sacks indoors, tied them, and tagged them Express Collect to Charlie Dobson at St. George's Indian School, Lytton, BC. I signed the waybill, tucked a sheet under my arm to cover Zazy's back, found space for a few treasures in my pouch, and profoundly thanked the agent for his help.

Released like a king crab cut loose from a drift net, I plunged back into the rain. I crossed the street and rejoined Zazy, standing naked and slick in the circle of light under the lamppost. I laid the sheet over her body and fastened it behind the sore with the light string girth from Swift Current. My belt bag was stuffed with gall salve, knife, comb, wallet, miniature New Testament, and Canada III. With the salt bag in my left hand and the reins in my right, I led my friend out of the light.

— —

The black night claimed us. Only the glaring red mouths of coke ovens and the yellow glow of colliery lights defined the mountain beside us. Zazy's feet guided us off the main road onto a drenched trail and kept us from the edge of the canyon wall, feeling a way to safety until we reached a fork in the trail. There we could rest until the light would come again. The rain bathed the back of the mare as she grazed. A leaning tree made room for me under its evergreen boughs, and the wet sheet conserved my body heat while fatigue plunged me into sleep.

Before dawn I was stiff with cold. I dragged myself on unwilling legs out of the shelter and looked around for Zazy. There she was, standing asleep with one hind leg slumped and her head over the gate to a ranch that I had tried and failed to find in that dark night.

Shivery and wet, we made our way back to the main road and set off down the Elk River Valley in the mist of an infant day. One truck came by, one conversation broke into our lone march. Hours later the sun was bright and high. We stepped down into a riverside meadow, where I bathed Zazy's back with the salt. Afterwards I coated the sore with salve, tied the sheet round her body, and left her free to graze. Then I lay full length on the warm ground, totally surrendered my body to the power of the sun, and slept.

The sunshine limbered my joints and dispelled my fatigue. Gradually, I awoke into the awareness that we were freed of the things my Latin teacher had called *impedimenta*. The rain and the sun in turn had restored us. No rheumatic pain came to haunt me from my childhood. We were free, moving into the promising uncertainty of the next hour, the next day.

Walking beside my friend, I looked happily ahead. Never again would Zazy wince under the pressure of the saddle, nor would I waste time trying to devise new ways to fold a blanket. Packing time would be negligible. Rain would hold no threat, because we had nothing that rain could spoil. As for comfort, we could always travel ahead of our chills, knowing that the sun would shine again.

Grey, saw-toothed mountains looked down at us. A miner told me that mountain goats lived among the crags, wily ones that always kept a chasm between themselves and the hunters. I watched for goats as we followed the Elk River into this new country.

The prairies were a world and a light year away. We had left the take-it-or-leave-it open road. Now we followed a trail that sometimes clung to the face of a precipice, a road inescapable except where water and wind had widened the way.

The mountains welcomed Zazy and me with pockets of grass and flowers and spring water in rock clefts, with luscious berries, black and red, that fell cool into my hand from bushes hanging to the rims of canyons. Truck drivers welcomed us with a smile and their care, as they passed us on narrow heights and curves.

Before darkness fell, the grade gentled into an arable slope, and we entered a secluded farmyard. A kindly, reserved couple offered us food and shelter. Their mentally challenged daughter reached out first to Zazy. There in the yard we all paused, unhurried by socially obligate words, moving gently to the edge of each other's comfort zone. I stood in my only clothes, holding my salt bag, wearing a pouch at my belt. Zazy was unbridled, free to enjoy the trusting touch of the girl. Beneath my freedom from burdens, something new was resonating, the freedom to be, like these people, totally and simply ourselves. We settled Zazy in a box stall, went across to the cottage, and spent a pleasant evening together and a peaceful night.

Gradually, Zazy and I were leaving the Rockies, following the way the Elk River had found down from its parent glacier, south and west between ridges, emerging at Elko into the Rocky Mountain Trench. There our road turned north into a level valley flanked in the distance by the Purcell Mountains.

In only two days since our unloading at Michel, Zazy's back was rapidly healing. The cold rain of the first night had quelled the fire in the tissues, and the pain was gone. Already, I could ride her.

Zazy did need new shoes! She had outworn the flat shoes that Sven had nailed on at Keewatin. Now she would need heels and toes to raise her hooves above the gravel, and possibly leather sole shields as well. I hoped to find a farrier in Cranbrook. Meanwhile, the search was on for an accessible stream in which she could soak her bruised feet and drying hooves.

Galloway, I noticed on the map, was located at the bend of a river. Galloway Forest Products said the sign at the entrance. Two young girls ran to meet us, offering to sweep us immediately into their town and their homes.

"Zazy needs to soak her feet. I'm looking for a stream," I explained. That news didn't even slow them up. They led me to a creek flowing beside the stable. Nature's hydrotherapy! I accepted the children's invitation to be their guest.

"Stay over tomorrow," urged their families, and I was more than glad to remain near that creek! I slept at Alein's home and we visited back and forth at Jean's house.

The Galloway welcome felt like being taken inside a human microcosm dependent on the surrounding forest. My hosts at this company town were among the harvesters of the forest that had already drawn me into its wild heart. The dual experience brought comforting balance to my fragmentary fears for the future of the forest.

On two mornings, Zazy and I stood in the stream, up to her fetlocks and my shins in icy water. The cold reduced the inflammation under her soles and the moisture softened the horn to absorb hoof oil. I tolerated being frozen to the knees, only because Zazy balked on the bank and said quite plainly: *Not unless you come too!*

Zazy sheltered in the stable from heat and flies, and when she chose, she had the freedom of the town. I rested from the responsibilities of life on the road, falling in easily with everyday life around me, but especially with the adventures of the children in the security of their microcosm.

— —

The mill was the hub of Galloway's big timber operation, and the girls were eager to show it to me. Returning from the general store, we took a daring shortcut under the creaking, dripping jack ladder above the pond. Just then, a hoist began to swing a massive log off a truck onto the toothed conveyor to the first saw.

"Run!" cried Alein, and we ran. Far behind us, we heard a huge thud. That evening we learned that the log had jumped the track and fallen to the ground. It lay unmoved when Alein took me back to explore the mill after working hours.

The men had gone home. The machines had stopped in their tracks. We climbed to the head of the jack ladder, passed a carriage bearing a log that had yielded one slab to the big saw, made our way among the sorting tables, where miscellaneous boards had been moving into orderly piles when the action stopped. The edgers and tail saws all were asleep. The planer mill with its neat pieces of finished lumber looked smugly at the rough, misfit newcomers. The boiler room was still murmuring of a day past and a day to come as we emerged from its doorway to cross the yard to the pole plant.

The pole plant's machinery selected straight trees, peeled off their bark, deeply perforated several feet of their butt ends, and hoisted them upright into a tank of boiling creosote. Hours later, it hoisted them out and swung them onto flatcars, ready to be moved by rail to sites where they would be replanted, already soaked in preservative derived from wood, in the ground from which they had sprung by the slow process of tree growth.

Evening at Alein's house was a wonderfully homey time. Jean joined the family of eight girls and a boy, a mom and dad, and that night, me. We ate, we talked and listened to each other, we laughed together and sang around the piano. Only the toddler had to leave the party early. Before he went, Alein played his favourite song, "The Anvil Chorus." "Oh the blacksmith's a fine sturdy fellow," he sang with the rest of us at the top of his lungs.

I could not stay to see the mill coming back to life. Zazy's need for shoes was too urgent, and time was short for us to reach a farrier in Cranbrook by Saturday. We were ready to leave Galloway. The salt from Natal had done its work; her back was healed and the bag was empty. My belt bag was groaning with foreign objects it had received at Michel; now the salt bag accepted them, along with a bottle of oil from the barn boss.

The stream had done its work; Zazy walked away from the stable with a firm step.

As we came by the houses where two families had shared my care, out came Alein and Jean with a card they had made for my twenty-second birthday. They had got to know the date the night before. "We'd have made you a cake if you'd stayed," they said. I felt sorry to miss the party!

Pressing on toward Cranbrook, I tired of the mud on a dirt road under drizzle, and took to a logging trail that seemed to be going our way. The grass pleased Zazy, the sod underfoot was restful, and we agreed that the Saskatoon berries among the rocks were perfect. For a couple of hours, we wandered happily over ridges and into green pockets, but when the trail petered out instead of rejoining the road, I moved out of the trees to get my bearings.

I found myself on the flat rocky brow of a steep talus slope, standing in awe. Far below, the asparagus-green Kootenay River waltzed between islands and scalloped banks. It filled the valley for miles, braided around treed islands and grass-fringed points. Cloud shadows were dancing on the passive green flow. Away to the south, I could see a toothpick bridge carrying the road across the river to Wardner.

We had to go down that bank or back the way we had come. Cautiously, I tested the footing. Zazy watched, with the updraft blowing back her forelock. I found sliding shale on a doubtfully secure base. I had to decide, knowing two things. First, I could venture a little farther and still be able to get back. Second, Zazy was wise enough to discern the risk and to refuse if descent was unsafe. I scrambled back to her side, removed her bridle and scooped all our belongings under my arm. So I started down, tacking and sliding as far as the first terrace. I looked up just in time to see Zazy act on her own decision.

Very slowly, confidently, she lowered her head, sank on her hocks, and lowered herself over the edge, avoiding momentum. She tested the talus as I had done then, taking her time, she began tacking back and forth, sliding very little, straying casually to strip Saskatoons off a bush. I relaxed and joined the feast. So we each moved safely to the bottom and met on the trail to the road. We crossed the toothpick bridge into Wardner, where Zazy topped off her Saskatoons with oatmeal before we entered the hilly parkland west of the river.

Through a showery afternoon, we travelled across open, mostly empty range. A passing rancher warned me to watch out for wild horses that would come from nowhere and lure Zazy into their herd. The showers ended by evening, and smoky yellow clouds hung below summits highlighted against a clearing sky. A shadowy vagueness crept up the peaks, as if they were dissolving into the wreath of clouds.

We made camp in a pine grove on a slope. I fed Zazy the rest of the oatmeal, watched her beginning to forage, drew the damp sheet over myself, and shut down. I expected no wild stallion to disturb my peace.

In the fullness of time, Zazy came and settled close beside me. Dreams passed. Suddenly something very hard struck my head. I woke to the flailing of legs above me. In the next instant, I rolled clear. A moment later, Zazy was on her feet, bewildered as I was.

My head cleared. I deduced that she went to sleep lying on her sternum and later laid down her head, intending to stretch out. Being on a slope, she began instead to roll. I finished the night in a spot shielded by closely grown trees, and resolved never again to lie downhill from a horse.

At dawn I was stretching stiff limbs, and Zazy was foraging. I had no grain to offer her, so we went in search. We found food at a dairy farm just outside Cranbrook, and we both were ready for it. The farmer's daughter served me a full breakfast; her father fed Zazy in the stable. While Zazy finished her hay, he showed me through his bright barns and creamery. There, milk was processed from cow to delivery wagon. He also directed me to Ellis Sweet, the blacksmith, and told me where to find the post office.

I headed straight for the post office, expecting to pick up the money order from Camp 51 that would replace the cheque rejected in Dryden. There was no money for me at Cranbrook. I counted my small change. Lacking by far the price of the full shoeing that Zazy needed, I made for the farrier's shop at the run.

Mr. Sweet talked me out of sole pads and oakum, for the sake of hoof health. He ignored my financial report and insisted on shoeing the mare all round, complete with heels and toes. He encouraged me to stand Zazy in every creek we came to, and he replenished my supply of hoof oil. After all that, he handed me a bill for $2.65, to pay when I could.

— —

Beyond Cranbrook we were well within the Purcell Range, travelling easily over moderate hills, across farmed valleys, beside the lake, following the wide pass of the Moyie River. I nursed along the idea that I would pick fruit and make money in the Kootenay and Okanagan valleys, a stone's throw ahead. Pickers were always in high demand, I recalled from overheard conversations of teenagers in Quebec. I rode in Scotch mist, daydreaming of earning enough money to pay Mr. Sweet and be solvent for the rest of the trip.

The mist broke in a downpour, just as we came to cleared land with a board fence and a small barn. While I hesitated on the road, a young couple skirted by a trio of little children walked out through the rain to meet us. Greetings tumbled out among the raindrops: "Hello! Come in! Where are you going? Where have you come from? Come stay with us. What's in your bag? Come meet our friends!"

Zazy was ushered into a box stall that supplied all her needs. I moved among the family across the gravelled yard to the cedar ranch house. A springer spaniel left his dry bed on the porch and wagged us indoors, where the sun seemed to be shining out of the mellow tones of polished wood. We circulated until we came to rest around a table populated with snacks and coffee cups, and lit from picture windows.

"You must stay with us tonight; our friends will be coming." Wanda refilled my cup from the Thermos flask. "Here comes my brother Lyle!" Wanda turned as a lean cowboy ducked under the lintel, hat in hand, and stopped a stride or two from us. "Lyle, this is Barb. Her horse, what did you call her? She's in the barn. They're on their way from Montreal to Vancouver. Bareback!"

"Glad to meet you, Ma'am." He had a reaching smile and his weathered hand met my own in a strong grasp.

I felt sure of myself. "Happy to meet you, Lyle."

People began to arrive. Conversations threaded their way between toddler, youth, adult, granny, and grandpa. I found myself caught up by this lighthearted crowd as an adult, not as one of the kids.

Wanda put an arm round my shoulder and led me to meet Jenny, a teenage girl with stars in her eyes. She and her parents dove into the prospect of my riding from that ranch house to the Pacific Coast. I knew it was possible, I knew surely as sunrise that Zazy and I would do it, but how? I could say only: "One mile at a time."

That was good enough for Jenny. "Can I come with you? I have a good trail horse and I could be ready to leave here by morning."

Her courage and candour won me. "If you think you can take the travel, sure you can come, if it's okay with your folks. Anyway, you could try it for a day or two."

We left the matter at that, and the evening went spinning on its course. The rain cleared off, the crowd did likewise, and Uncle Lyle and I fell heir to the three smallest youngsters to mind while their parents went out to dinner.

Uncle Lyle was a bachelor who had drifted in from Cache Creek. I enjoyed him; he was fun, and he expanded my vision. "If you once get into the Cariboo, you won't ever leave it. I've known girls that have gone up in there just to see the country. They've all got married and settled there." I can still hear the soft drawl of the prophet.

We spent a lively hour minding imps who appeared at every turn. Right after supper, we all walked to the spring above the creek. While the children splashed around, Lyle showed me how to make a desert cooler. It was so simple, a food box set on stilts in the stream, and a wick of sacking draped over the box with its ends in the water! Capillary action raised the coolant, and evaporation did the cooling.

We herded our charges home and settled in. Lyle worked on a rawhide quirt while he told Cariboo tales around the photographs he handed me. "Hey look, Bawbwah!" Alfie was hailing me from a doorframe, where he hung like a spider, long and skinny in his swim trunks. "You try it!"

I didn't take Alfie's dare; I was too carried away by images conjured by his uncle, this traveller, guide, trapper, ranch foreman, lumberjack.

I left alone. Overnight, Jenny's parents had decided that the trip would be too risky for her. I was sorry but not surprised. The questions that rolled around in my head, looking for answers, were about Lyle and the likelihood of my meeting him again in Cache Creek. How would I go about finding him? Would he notice me? Would he even be there? Why didn't I ask him? All I could do was to head for Cache Creek.

Cache Creek was on the far side of several mountain ranges and an arid plateau. Close at hand were valleys famous for their bush and tree fruits, a job market in my unrealistic sights. I pressed on expectantly, while the sky clouded and the day grew cold.

The pass had narrowed to a slit clutched between sombre mountains. Toward evening the air took on the immanence of frost. As chills infused the long tree shadows that lay across my shoulders, I turned Zazy down a side road, crossed the log bridge over a rocky stream, and came into a farmyard.

Not a person was in sight. The dog barked from its chain to no effect. I knocked on the house door, but no one answered. We waited in the yard until night came. I shivered, remembering my night in the boxcar at Hearst. If the residents returned now and refused us shelter, where could we go? Necessity spoke louder than my respect for private property. I led Zazy into the empty stable, fed her the oats that I had carried and hay from the barn, groped my way up the ladder to the loft, and settled into a light sleep.

Much later, I heard a truck and the voices of people mingled with the greeting barks of the dog. A conversation took place in the barnyard, but no one entered the barn. I rose before day, cleaned the stall, and arranged our simple tack. We stepped into the first light of dawn, retraced our steps over the corduroy bridge spanning the steaming stream, and regained the highway, apparently unnoticed.

Before we reached Yahk, a truck bearing a name I might have seen at the farm overtook us and passed slowly. I felt that I was under suspicion, wondered if I should have left a thank-you note. No, it seemed safer simply to have trespassed.

The Moyie River met the Goat at Yahk, very close to the United States border. There we crossed a divide and left the chilly dampness behind. Following the Goat west and north, we came at noon, hot and thirsty, to a farm at Goatfell.

I was glad to join a party of children and their auntie heading for a swimming hole. We all straggled across a flowery meadow, and stopped at a creek that must have come straight from under a glacier. In went the children, paddling among the boulders. In strode Auntie, finding depth for swimming in midstream. In went my right foot and out it came by a will of its own. I tried again. At knee depth, my leg went numb. I thanked the children and waved goodbye to Auntie, stroking and drifting in the current. She flipped over and waved back happily.

We entered the Kootenay Valley at Erickson, and there I promptly had my delusions about working brought in line with reality. I stopped at a raspberry farm, offered my services to the German owners, and learned that everyone was too busy picking to train a rookie. Special techniques were needed for a picker to work fast enough even to earn her board, much less to feed a horse. I would have no cash to take away. I heard my balloon pop, and decided right away to push on to Lytton, via Cache Creek, of course. If the good grazing and wild fruit continued, we should survive on our remaining $1.83 to the end of the ride.

The couple that had told me the hard facts about berry picking insisted I spend the night with them. They made space and found hay for Zazy in their small barn, and invited me into their cottage for homemade bread and raspberries. They led the conversation frankly to the central point of their faith as Jehovah's Witnesses, cessation of violence, and the advent of world peace. I replied that my hope lay in trying to reflect the love of God as I saw it expressed by Jesus Christ. They did not discredit my faith; we found common ground in the subsoil of our lives.

Later, I climbed the ladder to the barn loft with my arms filled with a soft wool tick to keep me warm. Through the hay window, I could see the splendid lines of the Selkirk Mountains silhouetted in moonlight. Within, I was free to see beneath religion toward accord.

Early the next morning, I was riding through white and flowery Creston, above the rich alluvial Kootenay Valley. The river had doubled back from its trip through Montana and Idaho to feed its lake. My eyes were searching the hills to the west for the draw that was said to mark the start of a trail thirty miles long, across the mountains to Salmo. How I wanted to ride that trail! Fortunately, I checked out my wild idea at the forestry office.

The officer behind the desk extracted a report from the file, and read aloud: "last crossed in 1948 . . . trail obscured by flooded streams . . . trail choked by windfalls," and finally, "impassable to a horse." On his advice, I chose the Kootenay Lake Road.

Orchards claimed the irrigated flats along the lake, and wild fruit trees and all kinds of berries fed us from the cliffs. The lake rippled opaque green like its parent river. No chill swept this valley at sundown, for the water and flanking rock held the heat for slow release. I planned to sleep under the stars, if only we could find a place to exit the road.

A friendly couple stopped their car to greet me and assure me that their friends just up the road would gladly let me camp in their orchard. I would find it easily, in a small green pocket indenting a long stretch of steep cliffs. We went there, and waited just inside the gate for the owners to come home. It was dusk when their car turned into the lane.

They noticed us, and the woman began directing the man behind the wheel. He got out and greeted me. I told him what had brought us into his orchard, and asked if we might sleep there to escape the road. The woman eyed us with suspicion, mustered the courage to follow her man from the car, and cut across his courtesy with curt words ending in a warning to me to move on. The man walked away in shame as we left the premises.

We were at risk on the narrow road in the darkness. The valley wall was steep, but I noticed that it was it was shelving and gentled by erosion. Scattered pockets of soil offered footholds to woody shrubs that in turn supported us, as we climbed to a tiny landing well above the road. I was able to feel out a level spot just large enough for a bed for Zazy. I improved it by kicking away loose stones, and tied the mare to a shrub lest she step off her bed and slide down the hill. Then I kicked stones off a smaller area, curved my body around the fixed bumps, and slept in a dimple in the hillside.

By daylight we slid down through a net of Oregon grape and sword fern onto the road. Not far on, I saw the green triangle of the Canadian Youth Hostel at Grey Creek. It reminded me happily of hostelling with Joan in the Monteregian Hills of Quebec, and it invited me to return some other day to Grey Creek.

Continuing north along the gentler western slopes of the Purcells, we came to a farm lane that drew us aside. At the head of the lane, I saw a woman and a child sitting on the grass, shelling peas. Maybe they would know more about my friends the mountains. As we came into view, both mother and child waved us in. I freed Zazy to graze and settled to shell peas with them, invite their stories, and listen. As I had hoped, the mother named the mountains we could see all around us, and went on to make sense of the switchback route that patterned our passage through the Western Cordillera.

The Purcells held the height between the Kootenay River and Kootenay Lake, where the Moyie River had passed us through. I recognized those forested domes from where we sat. Looking northwest, we saw the steep side of the Selkirk Range, avoided by most travellers by their choosing the southern pass from the Kootenay Trench over into the Columbia River Basin at Nelson. The line I had drawn in ignorance on my map went that way, through a draw we could barely glimpse. The old-timers used to use the sheep trail that I had dreamed of trying. Peaks alight with snowfields in sunshine were peering over the hills to the north. I would have a choice to make that afternoon. We picked up our peas and went into the house.

At lunch, the woman's husband told me about local soils and climate, the clearing of the cottonwoods and conifers and the founding of this farm, the challenges of life, and the value of belonging to the land. He gave Zazy a bag of oats for the road, and the whole family gave me a deeper intimacy with the region than I ever could have had, but for stopping to shell peas.

I rode along, smiling. Now for sure I knew the surrounding ranges by name, the rounded hills dark with forest, the sky-climbers white with snow. Before ferry time at Kootenay Bay, Zazy and I were swimming at the feet of these friendly mountains.

3

Zazy and I were the first passengers to board the Balfour ferry that afternoon. The mare stepped with confidence across the ramp and onto the steel deck, took her place near the chain across the bow, and planted her feet. Standing beside me, she casually noted the arrival of three cars and a bread truck behind us. The ramp was cast off with a clang and we were away on our first BC ferry ride.

Immobile relative to the deck around and beneath us, we watched the water slipping past us and the mountains rising higher. As we angled across to the Balfour shore, the Selkirks' shining peaks backed out of sight. I knew they were still there; I felt magnetized by them, drawn to enter them, not to merely pass to the other side.

A deckhand came to visit us. I asked him about the road marked by my reluctant pen, to Nelson, Castlegar, and Trail. Mom's words in a recent letter played into the prospect: "Stay away from the Doukhobors. They're in the news, protesting and burning schools in Nelson. They're thick around Castlegar." The myth in our town was that the Doukhobors lured people into their communes. I didn't mention Doukhobors to the deckhand, nor did I pass on the myth.

He said, "The easiest way over is straight along The Arm to Nelson. Trail's smoky, but it's not so bad just to go through. The other pass is really steep, and high! And that way's a lot farther to go."

I could see from the map that he was right about the distance. Balfour to Kaslo to New Denver to Nakusp, and over the Monashee Mountains to Vernon, did look like the long way round. We landed. Dismissing social prudence and the traveller's common sense about distance, I turned north from the ferry, like a compass needle, toward those magnetic Selkirk Mountains.

By evening, we were well up the west side of Kootenay Lake. My dream of tranquility beside a sleeping lake under a starry sky measured out by a silver moon was, however, in unseen peril.

We stepped from the road into a tiny meadow on the flat above the high-water level of a sandy beach. Zazy fed well while I pulled cedar boughs from an abandoned shack and arranged them as a couch on the wiry grass. Zazy finished feeding and joined me to sleep.

After an hour, vague discomfort prevailed over my sleep. I awoke to the burning of one fiery dart after another penetrating my skin. I thought of bedbugs and moved my sheet onto the sand. The torture continued. I discarded the sheet; I rubbed each searing point; I tasted futility! Zazy slept on, untouched by the no-see-ums. I alone was the victim of these sandflies.

The night wore on. Scrambling sounds snapped me from a drowse into Red Alert! I was sitting straight up, calling, "Zazy!" after the pounding sound of hooves retreating on sand. In the faint light of dawn, I saw the mare stop by the lakeside. I went to her, calmed her, and brought her back to bed.

Again the sandflies won the field. I cleared my foggy head in the lake, groomed Zazy with the edge of a rein, jumped onto her back, and left the flat. In the soft sand by the roadside, clawed feline feet almost as big as Zazy's hooves had left the signature of a cougar. Perhaps it had come to drink, and my calling had scared it away. The trail led across the road and up the talus slope, but I was too late to see the big cat.

Kaslo, BC, August 4, 1950. I wrote in my journal:

> We are the first guests to arrive in town after our busy night with the sandflies and the cougar. The grass in this village park is pleasing Zazy, and this picnic table fits me just right for writing and eating. I found a bakery shop already open, so I have a small loaf of fresh bread to enjoy in chunks. Only twelve cents! No one is abroad. Oh, except for that small boy coming across from the street to look us over.
>
> "Hello."
>
> "Hello." He stands thinking. "Are you hungry?" he asks after he has thought.
>
> "Yes, I am having breakfast."
>
> "You don't have butter."
>
> "No, but the bread is very good."
>
> He stands thinking again. After he has thought: "We have ham at our house. I will bring a slice of ham. You wait here."

The curly blond child disappears around the near corner, full of clear intent. I tuck the remainder of my bread into the salt bag and begin to groom Zazy.

Minutes later, the boy is before me, holding a huge wrapped sandwich. "This is for you." And he hands the package to me. I receive it, catch the glow in his face, try to speak. But he is gone. I eat within the covenant, as a rabbi told me that a Jew will eat, guarding every crumb in celebration of the gift of manna in the wilderness.

— —

Rain clouds stepped quietly out from behind the peaks and poised themselves in a body over the valley. Their downpour caught us within running distance of one of the laden cherry trees that lined Kaslo's streets. Seated on Zazy under the sheltering branches, I picked cherries while my moving ladder grazed. We dashed to a tree bearing tangy pale red cherries, next to a feast of sweet, black Bing cherries. Replete, I loaded my pockets and we ran for the shelter of a row of spruces on a bank by the cemetery.

From our natural grandstand, we watched the last solid rank of storm clouds moving across the lake and melting among the mountains to the east. Down came the sunshine! I sprang onto Zazy's strong back and we were away, up a narrow ribbon of road terraced high on the flat face of the Kaslo River gorge. The world in the wake of the rain set me singing, and the peaks around us seemed to catch up my song and share it.

I had shared that song one noon in chapel with Kurt Gilpin, a tall black senior student at Sir George Williams College. As I hiked and sang, his smile came and rested again round my shoulders, like the glory of the snowfields above me.

. . . gratefully sing his power and his love,
. . . whose robe is the light, whose canopy space.
His chariots of wrath the deep thunderclouds form
And dark is his path on the wings of the storm.

Kurt's resonant baritone voice was part of every storm that crashed around me, the sound of strength to survive the storm.

The earth with its store of wonders untold
Almighty, thy power hath founded of old,
Established it fast by a changeless decree
And round it hath cast like a mantle the sea.

That noontime in the chapel, Dean Henry Foss Hall talked to us about evolution and creation as full partners in the operation of the natural world. As an astronomer, he celebrated the dynamic order and perfection of the process. At worship, he hallowed it.

Dean Hall taught Natural Science 101, a survey course to be taken by all first-year Science students. He led me into all the disciplines where I had touched down in my childhood zeal to understand life in process around me: astronomy, geology, palaeontology, botany, zoology, genetics. He built for me a matrix to hold my random ideas and observations, and he drew them toward synthesis within the various disciplines.

Dean Hall affirmed my choice to be a veterinarian, and he set it into a limitless context. Kurt gave me a song for the road. Now there I was in British Columbia, singing my way across the mountains, in company with Kurt and Dean Hall and all the saints that God only knows.

The sun laid gilt patterns on the gravel road and spangled each well-washed leaf and berry and flower. White steam rose from exuberant waters rushing down to leap into the gorge. A stray white cloud passed over the face of the mountains like a memory.

The road ran for twenty miles or more, arrestingly beautiful, dangerous to share with a passing car or an overhanging buttress. Rocks loosened by the rain were falling from the face of the cliff above us, and a jagged piece landed two feet in front of Zazy's nose. It disappeared over the edge of the road and sent back no sound. I peered after it. Very far below us, a thin ribbon of churning grey water threaded the canyon's floor.

Zazy at times might shy for fun, but she knew when to take life seriously. She soberly teamed with me all through this high pass. A false step could be fatal, especially in the dark. I had no idea how far we had to go to get off the road. We could not hurry at that altitude; we could not see far ahead; we could only go on in hope. Before darkness fell, the road dipped and we came to a tiny settlement. Here were space, grass, and safety. We left the road.

People in Retallack came out to meet us and make us part of their tiny mining community. One family adopted Zazy, took her into their cowshed, and gave the children the fun of fetching feed for her. The Jack and Ruth Vine family invited me to stay with them and rest over the next day. The climb had been tough, and the stretches of crushed rock on the road wearied us. I was only too glad to stay with the Vines.

Zazy was set free in the morning to explore. She tracked me to Ruth and Jack's white cottage and announced her arrival with nickering and the thud of hooves in the porch. I hastily moved my writing to the back steps, where she went to sleep with her muzzle just touching my head and the odd drop of grass juice landing from relaxing lips onto my letter home.

Half a dozen youngsters took me up the mountain to pick berries, and a small dog and Zazy came too. The children led the way to the best Saskatoon sites, usually on ledges above the trail. Zazy was expected to graze by the trail, but when she smelt our berries, up she sprang and landed beside me and gathered her share. Ruth turned our harvest into Saskatoon pie for an evening snack.

Jack arranged for a chemical engineer to take me through the surface level of the mine. He showed me the flotation tanks where silver and zinc were separated, and explained the laboratory analysis of smelted metals for purity. Guiding my view of the steps between crude ore and pure metal from our vantage point, he made sense out of the sloping covered ramps, the jaunty towers over the vertical shafts, the piles of crushed rock, the loads being trucked to the road, and the grey foam on the river.

Our Retallack friends parted with us like family members leaving home. We were rested, fed, and provisioned for days to come. Somehow nine dollars had found its way into my wallet, and nobody would confess. Our journey was secured by all their caring.

— —

We continued to journey in the high pass through the hard-rock Selkirks until we came down into the north–south slot that held Slocan Lake. Ruth's salmon sandwiches and brownies tasted better and better as the day matured. We followed the lake north up the narrow valley through

New Denver and Roseberry, went on beyond the head of the lake, and found ourselves in early evening climbing into another pass.

Zazy needed grain to maintain her energy. Hoping to buy a supply, I rode up the steep lane to the back of an unusual chalet-styled house with a barn nearby. An expansive Russian farmer greeted me with a smile. He had no grain to sell, but he gave Zazy a feed of hay in the barn and extended the welcome of his household to me. I soon realized that I was the guest of a Doukhobor family.

Sam Podeyski introduced me to his wife, who spoke no English, his two school-age sons, who were excellent interpreters, and baby Mary in arms. In the background were two quiet women, aunts in the extended family. They all encouraged me to stay and I was happy to do so. For a few minutes we all stood round in the kitchen, doing our best to get to know each other. My appearance off the road without belongings seemed of no importance to them; simplicity was the keynote of their life. Even without a common language, we all felt comfortable together.

I even felt free to ask how the single light bulb that lit the kitchen was powered. In answer, the youngest boy, maybe thirteen years old, took me out to see the electric generator he had built from junk and installed in a man-made waterfall in the creek. As we stood talking, along came his big brother, riding a chugging hybrid tractor, also homemade from junk. I began to see how these resourceful people maintained themselves on minimal cash income, away from mainstream society where they could live by their own values.

We closed off the day around the table, where Mrs. Podeyski had spread the evening meal. We all found places along the benches. Baby Mary was fed in the security of an aunt's arm; there was no high chair in sight to depersonalize Mary's life. The borscht in the large bowl was the richest, most delicious soup I had ever tasted, with thick slices of warm bread and fresh butter. Practiced hands cleared the table after the meal, and we all went to bed by candlelight.

My bed was a spring and mattress in the hallway out from the kitchen. I was sitting there reading when everyone but Sam had gone by. He switched off the electric light, and paused in passing to ask me what I was reading. It was the tiny New Testament that Joan had given me. He hung there for several moments, thinking, said good night, and went away with his candle. I curled up under my quilt, aware that Zazy was safe and satisfied, at peace within myself.

We met around the table by early morning light. Mother set down hot buttered cornmeal mush and eggs, and Father shared them out. Through the morning we were busy at chores indoors and out. I learned to scour the table with homemade soap. One of the boys was working with the tractor, not a debt-laden monster like I had seen at work in the wheat fields, but an affordable machine capable of pulling and lifting and powering as required for this family's farm. Their second tractor, a big grey gelding, came out of the bush to call for Zazy, and the two horses went off to explore the woodland pasture.

A trip to Nakusp was scheduled to follow dinner. The aunts tidied up the dishes, while Mother, neatly maternal as always, adorned Mary in a pretty sunbonnet and dress. She outshone all the rest of us, though with a few simple operations, we fitted ourselves quite adequately for town. Then we piled into the ancient car.

The car had grown on the farm like the other implements. It was styled after a buckboard, topless, with a seat at the front and space behind. Mother and Mary sat in dignity beside Father at the wheel. The boys and I clung to the space behind, while the car bore us bravely over the precipitous road for seventeen miles to Nakusp.

In town, we made a number of calls. At the ferry office, I priced a ride down Upper Arrow Lake. For the sake of seven whole dollars, I was quite content to go by land. At a butcher shop, Sam bought a beef heart. Mother and I waited in the car, at a loss for a common language. The boys returned exultantly from the junkyard with the parts they needed for the tractor. Then we rattled and roared back to the farm.

Purchase of the beef heart was a life-changing event for the family. Mother was vegetarian by heritage; her family went meatless by default. Mother did not know how to cook meat. At breakfast, Father decided to broaden the menu. I would teach Mother to cook beef heart, and she would teach me to cook borscht. I think the language problem had hung on both of us as we waited for Sam at the meat shop.

There must have been some Russian magic in that kitchen, for Mother and I quickly discovered that words just got in the way of demonstration. One of the boys stayed in the kitchen to break any impasses, and the farther Mother and I went together, the more easily came understanding. At the usual hour, a tasty meal of red cabbage soup and meat and potatoes was served to the family.

Sometime during our trip to Nakusp, the horses left the farm. We missed them when we returned, but since no one except me seemed to be concerned, I acquiesced until the meal was over. Then I was about to begin tracking Zazy on foot.

The elder boy, pleased to have his father offer him the use of the car, persuaded me to ride. We sat braced for the lurch; the driver turned the key; nothing happened. He drew a heavy spanner from a tool chest under the seat, whipped up a metal floor plate, and pounded vigorously at a few chosen spots in the mechanism below. Satisfied, he replaced the flooring, stored the spanner, turned the key, and drove onto the road.

In the twilight, we could still see hoofprints, heading down the long hill to Summit Lake. The boy relaxed, as if he knew where the horses would be. He pointed out a dried marsh producing tall grass heavy in seed. This was one of the farm's hayfields. The crop would be cut with scythes, gathered by hand, and brought to the barn with the tractor. We continued down the hill. At the bottom, the hoofprints led off the road onto the railway following the far side of the lake. There we saw the two wanderers, dwarfed by the mountain behind them, coming toward us along the tracks. Zazy rejoined me gladly. I jumped onto her back and both horses made for home at a snappy trot.

When I fetched Zazy from the barn the next morning, Sam was in the garden, admiring his maturing potato crop. "Them potatoes," he said to me, "are going to stay in the ground until you come back and take them out." So the invitation stood. Though I could not accept it that year, I knew it was perennial, and I valued it highly. Here was enterprise tempered with contentment, mutual respect and healthy self-confidence, openness to an alien like me, and peace held in common by the whole household.

—

Under a clear, cool sky, Zazy and I moved briskly over the top of the pass, down again to Summit Lake, and on to Nakusp. A cheery woman operating a model dairy farm gave Zazy a welcome feed of grain. By early afternoon we were out of the pass and into the valley of Lower Arrow

Lake. The going was smooth and we made the most of it, coming within easy reach of Needles ferry by sundown. Ranchers busy at haying hailed us to come in and make ourselves at home.

I turned in and rode across a pasture field to water Zazy at a creek. An antlered stag stepped from the ferns and stood watching us. Uncertain, he moved out for a clearer view, and I was able to come within thirty paces before he turned and trotted away. He rose at the fence, floated over, and stepped onto a pulpit of rock at the edge of the woods. We watched each other until twilight crept between us. Zazy drank, and the stag melted into the ferns.

The haying crew used up all the daylight before they stopped to eat and rest. I left Zazy fed and corralled for the night and went to listen to people in the kitchen. They told me about the Monashee Mountains ahead, with their rugged eighty-three-mile pass over to Lumby and another jaunt to Vernon in the Okanagan Valley. They advised me to look for a truck to take us over, because they doubted that we would make it on foot. They said I might get a ride in a livestock truck at the ferry dock.

I went to sleep informed about the way ahead, but not convinced that being trucked was imperative. In any case, I ate a hearty breakfast and packed a lunch before heading for the ferry at Fauquier. Hours later we stood on the deck, watching the mighty Monashees coming closer and closer. They were dark and round-shouldered and high. I felt thrill and sober awareness at the prospect. There had been no truck. A driver told me there was no likelihood of one's coming along unfilled or unsealed. It was up to Zazy and me to cross the pass on our own feet.

4

The ferry touched shore and we were the first passengers to cross the ramp onto the landing. The little store at Needles, where I had meant to load up with rolled oats, had closed for lunch. Two hours was too long to wait; I sprang on Zazy and we started up the first hill. A hundred miles to Vernon!

One hill led to another, higher, hill. Level stretches rested us; deep descents only added to the next rise. I recalled the words of a cowboy: "If you want to save your horse, ride uphill if you like, but walk down." I did that, and proved the truth of his words.

Cars and trucks sharing the narrow trail were again our prime danger. Sounds of their approach were lost to me around the nearest bend or blown away by the wind. Surprised while on foot, I had to choose instantly, either to move Zazy over to hug the canyon wall if we had time, or to jump on her back and hold her steady if we were caught near the edge. The view was spine-chilling: sheer drop-off into airy canyon, tree tops screening thin air, roots clutching narrow shelves. We exulted and dared and clung to our foothold. Every motorist gave us reasonable consideration, and the truckers took the greatest care to safeguard us as they threaded that winding road with their snaking semi-trailers.

Night would challenge us. Through the whole afternoon, I had seen few recesses in the sheer wall. Zazy was finding tiny colonies of grass where springs had washed away the stone and fostered plants, but we could never stop safely for more than a minute. Despite such realities, I watched unworried for a place to rest, calm not because escape from the road had always been easy, but because inevitably we had always come to a safe place to rest. We had just to go on and find the blessing.

Surely we found it. Before night filled the canyon, the pass widened and the road ran down into a valley. Here in the middle of the mountains, a small ranch had been established. Zazy and I found friends, lush pasture, oats, and for me a fine supper.

Buoyed on good-night wishes, I carried quilts and pillow under my arm across the pasture to my bedroom. It topped a haystack built on the ground and set between four poles that supported a roof a few feet above the hay. Zazy watched me climb the ladder. I bedded down and sensed the night. Sounds were subdued to whispers. Starlight fell on stray tufts of hay, on the dewy grass below, and on the little mare dozing near the ladder.

— —

The rigors of the road tested the tie between the mare and me. Hour after hour, she plodded along, as one reach of canyon unfolded on another. I couldn't share with her the beauty I saw, or the mysteries hidden in this rugged wilderness. I wanted to go exploring, but wherever the grade relented, a tangle of shrubbery blocked Zazy's way. We were entering a different climate zone, and the plants marked the change. I celebrated it; Zazy was not impressed. She confronted me with this hard fact ever more eloquently as the day wore on. She slowed to a snail's pace, at times hardly moving. I felt frustrated by her indifference. She seemed to have soured on mountains.

The steeper the hill, the narrower was our road. Danger grew large. There had to be a laugh somewhere on this solemn mountain.

We were working our way along a naked promontory, inching up the trail, hugging the wall in deadly earnest, one bend from the top. Suddenly a great roaring filled the canyon, bouncing from wall to wall. Nervous tension drew my tired horse into an unpredictable power pack. The pitch of the noise rose. We crowded the wall, immobile, for long seconds. A huge van gradually reared itself over the height, hurling *Death Dodgers* in black letters in our faces from its white brow. Grim reality froze my blood as I sat the mare. Now the daredevil act was beside us, filling the road, creeping like doom.

The whole van gained the level road; the roaring engine rested; two male faces in the cab relaxed. Zazy and I came unglued from the rock face. A cab window opened, and suddenly laughter broke loose, filling the space between us, comrades all, treading the knife-edge of life. A merry sort of peace found random words for wings, filling the moment with fellowship.

— —

Feeling for width, the road twisted down to cross the flat, stony bed of the Kettle River. We stopped on the wide bridge under a clouded sky, just to inhale open space. A lumber truck drew alongside us and the driver reached across and rolled down a window. Our conversation led to his offering me a job cooking at his camp seven miles farther on. "Drop in for dinner, anyway," he added.

Then he was gone and we were climbing the far side of the Kettle Valley. As forested mountains closed around us again, the veterinary college that I had never seen, the west coast that I had never seen, even Vernon and the Okanagan Valley, seemed very distant and unreal. Real food, real shelter, a job, and a chance to enter the life flow of these mysterious mountains came nearer with each reluctant stride that Zazy took. Thinking back, I saw Sam in his potato patch, inviting me to return. After Christmas, perhaps I could work on the Doukhobor farm until spring.

But, could I believe in the offer made by the lumberman? I had gone a long way down the garden path believing in Jim's offer at Longlac, before reality blew up the road! I would watch for the turn into the Kettle River camp and simply show up for dinner.

Thunder woke in the grey sky, rumbled, boomed, and rolled to a crashing climax overhead. Peel broke on peel, shaking the land and dwarfing Zazy and me into obscurity. Big drops of rain led the way from black clouds into the scowling chasm. Kurt Gilpin was singing again! Then came the main downpour, laying sheen over the rocks and leaves and Zazy's sun-browned coat. The dust underfoot became mud. This "frail child of dust" was rapidly becoming a mud-blob. Zazy drooped her ears to let the rain run off and plodded forward. I wondered how far seven miles was by a lumberman's standards.

Over us swept a deeper darkness cut by knives of light. We trembled with the trees in the noise of the crescendo that spent itself, only to return for encores. Through a lull in the chaos, my ears caught the sound of a buzz saw, and almost at once I saw camp buildings veiled by rain. Zazy stepped up her pace. We scanned for the turnoff.

A noise on the road behind made me draw the mare in against a dripping bank of Oregon grape. A truck stopped beside us; the driver yelled through the downpour: "Can I give you a lift to Vernon?"

Five seconds later came my: "Sure can, thanks!" My speculations had vanished into the mud.

The driver stepped into the deluge, let down the tailgate, angled the rear of the truck up to the bank, and made room inside for Zazy behind the beer cases. Meanwhile, she and I had been ripping our way through the Oregon grape, and feeling out a footing on which to poise ourselves. At a word from the driver, I spoke to Zazy and she stepped dexterously down into the van. No traffic came, the tailgate went up, the driver and I sprang for the cab, and we were wheeling away toward the Okanagan Valley.

The trucker knew the road well. He said he had passed the summit when he saw us. Up and down we went, at speed unusual to me, while he regaled me with the story of every wreck site we passed. When the road dropped rapidly, snaking around hairpin turns, I was at the mercy of a well-fed imagination. More than once the driver had to pull up against a blank wall at a bend, then back the truck and work it into a recess to allow the front to follow the curve for the next lap down. We left the rain behind us.

Surprisingly soon, we were below the steep places, coming at ease in sight of the first hilly gardens and orchards around Cherryville. At Lumby we stopped while the trucker conferred about vegetable crates with a Chinese market gardener. In afternoon sunshine we drove the seventeen miles to Vernon. I arrived in time to pick up mail, and I was able to pay the very modest price of the lift from a cheque that Peg and Charlie had chanced to send to Vernon. Then we drove to the edge of town, where the driver could back against a grassy ditch. Zazy jumped nimbly from the floor of the truck onto the slope, the trucker closed his van, we shared a hearty handshake, and he went out of my life.

5

Zazy and I moved with fresh enthusiasm from the challenges of the Monashees into a mellow Okanagan evening. She liked the grass; I liked the idea of heading for Lyle's territory. We crossed the river at the foot of Swan Lake and found a small, unused cow stable by the roadside that I was permitted to occupy. Zazy had feed growing in the barnyard, and I had a bed in the loft. Before bedtime we walked to the river in the balmy air. Three horses trotted up from a hollow to converse with Zazy. The little mare was happy again, and I was deeply aware that I had made a good choice to turn north at Balfour.

At dawn we were heading up through hilly ranchland for Falkland, the South Thompson River, Kamloops, and Cache Creek. This was dry, sandy, sunburned country mantled with shallow sod. Pale wiry grass held to life in the open and prospered under ponderosa pine trees. I had never seen such long pine needles and huge cones. They crunched under Zazy's hooves, and the hot air among the trees carried up a brown scent.

All the green was on the Salmon River flats below us. We stopped for grass near Falkland at a road construction site, and there the engineer caught the spirit of our wanderings. He told me that the high land I had chosen to travel was very dry and barren at this time of year, but there was another way that he was sure I would not want to miss.

"Take the west fork at the town, and that will lead you to Westwold." He paused to mark my map. "Follow this road southwest from Westwold and go into the ranch at the end. The owners will certainly make you welcome. There's a trail that carries on beyond the road. It'll take you onto the rangeland of the Douglas Lake Cattle Company. Takes a couple of days to ride across."

Fancies of Cache Creek scurried in and out of the clear picture the engineer had given me. I was seeing through his eyes the chance of a lifetime! I let go of a shadow for substance; I took the road to Westwold and the Douglas Lake Ranch.

We were well on the way when a cowboy rode down the sidehill to greet me. He happened to be driving a few stray cows back to the very ranch the engineer had earmarked for me. He and his buddy were in charge of the place while the owners were absent. "They'd certainly put you up if they were home," he assured me. "You're welcome to put your pony in and stay with us if you like." I was happy to have his quiet company the rest of the way to the ranch at the end of the road.

We found his partner sitting with his back to a tree, enjoying a beer. He got to his feet, had a word with his buddy, shifted his bottle, and shook my hand. "Have you eaten yet?"

"No, but I don't need anything until morning." No more was said. I went with the rider to stable the horses.

The cook went to the kitchen. We returned to a spread of thick venison steaks, fried potatoes, peas, bread, butter and jam, and clear tea. It was agreed that I would cook breakfast.

I smelled a challenge. There had been some casual talk about the hens and the attack-rooster that guarded them. We would of course need eggs for breakfast. These guys reminded me of George and Jim at Longlac, joshing while we hid from the bullets of the bear hunters. Undaunted, I followed my ears the next morning to the centre of bustling hen activity in a small log building. Already there were plenty of eggs in the nests. I gathered up a dozen into my shirtfront and merrily started back to the house.

Not so fast! Within ten paces, something flew against my leg. Before I could look, it retreated. I caught sight of a flurry of orange and black feathers coming at me again with spurs extended.

"All bluff!" I faced my attacker with a stern: "Get lost, *you!*" The rooster rose in fury to my eye level. I guarded the eggs with one arm and tried to fend him off with the other. Now he was fighting mad, flying in, striking, dodging the stick I had taken up. I made for a pile of tin cans, flailed behind the knees as I trotted with my pinny full of eggs. Standing on the ammunition dump, I fired cans and insults. The rooster dodged every volley and returned every insult. In time, he lost interest and returned with his dignity untarnished to his harem, while I humbly observed that my eggs were still intact.

Cooking with Connie had not fully prepared me to cook for cowboys. To my offering of cereal, eggs, bacon, toast, and coffee, the cook added potatoes and venison steaks. We did not leave much on the table. Meanwhile Zazy was busily refuelling in the stable. She was in horse country again! We left the ranch restored and with bright expectations before the sun had raised the dew.

Our trail ran along an overgrown hillside. A small white cottage stood beside the way; the rustic fence around its tiny flower garden peeked up over the edge. As we approached, a small figure dressed in soft leather stepped through the gate, with hiking staff in one hand and water jug in the other. Like a spirit of the mountainside, he paused, radiating good wishes from the tip of his green cap to the toes of his brogues. He spoke: "Good morning," crossed the path and went in among the ferns.

We followed a high wall of rock made homey for delicate plants by centuries of erosion. In the confusion of greenery below us, I heard the rustling of a berry-picking bear. Zazy pricked her ears and I strained for a glimpse of the forager. Our road angled down through a lush daisy meadow, and we paused to reflect and drink at the creek. Then we were ready to cross the log bridge and begin the climb to the plateau. We never saw the bear.

The way was steep and rough. Zazy had to step over and around heaps of rock that lay where they had landed after blasting. A cowboy going east assured me that we were still on the trail. We climbed ever more steeply until the road was doubling back and forth to gain the sandy brow of the rock face. On the skyline at last, we caught the breeze and I looked in amazement down on a pristine world.

Douglas Lake Ranch spread as far as I could see, a green plateau watered by a chain of small lakes threaded on the Salmon River, dotted by woodlands, protected by two ranks of distant mountains. Our trail was a faint track dwindling to a thin line and vanishing beyond a rise. I rode from the brow of the hill as in a dream, down a long grade onto the plateau.

Before noon, we came to a clutch of ranch buildings and I stopped to water Zazy. The woman at the house invited me in, gave me a drink and a sandwich, and told me that I was at Salmon River Ranch. It was one of several units where part of the twenty five thousand cattle in the Douglas Lake herd would winter. The home ranch was on Douglas Lake to the south. I hoped to meet the owners there. For the coming night, she suggested I make for the haying camp at English River.

There was a mystique about this whole place. I rode along reflecting on what I had just heard and what was unfolding before my eyes. I seemed to be moving again within a microcosm. The cycling of water between snowfields, lakes, and plant cover, the seasonal grazing cycle, the home bases of people who were embraced by the natural rhythms, all spoke to my search for integration within the biosphere. I wanted to be part of this very place, to ride the summer ranges, to share in the gathering of the cattle, to follow them home for winter.

In the midst of my glorious breakthrough, a mundane event pulled me up short. After four thousand miles of riding, the last four hundred bareback, with never a hint of galling, suddenly I became scalded. Inflammation was flaring in the skin between my buttocks. Within an hour after we left Salmon River Ranch, I could neither ride nor walk without sickening pain. I stumbled into a grove of trees, threw myself down, and lay still. The pain eased until I tried to move and found myself tearing adherent galled cheeks apart. I lay still again, knowing I must find a way to move, and thinking over the supplies in our salt bag.

Bickmore's Gall Salve, be sure and work the horse. I read again the words on the battered tin of greenish salve given to me by the saddler at Swift Current. It had worked to heal Zazy. If it did no more for me than prevent adhesion, it was worth a try.

It did much more! It felt like salt on the raw flesh. I tried in vain to wipe it off. I lay still, sick with pain. Gradually I sensed a change. The pain was lessening, the weeping of the galls had stopped, and I could cautiously move again. I raised myself on an elbow and saw Zazy grazing near me, knee-high in a heavy stand of woodland grass. That grass had been feeding my horse, hiding and shading me in my misery, and growing to feed the cattle come winter. I left my small, flattened patch of it with a sense of personal gratitude. The gall salve reapplied during the afternoon continued its rapid healing without more burning. In the cool of evening, I was able to ride in comfort into the haying camp.

At English River, the men and draft horses camped during the haying season. There was room in the stable for Zazy, but in the cookery where I was sent, the staff needed all the bunk space. I offered to sleep outdoors or in the hayloft, but that was considered inappropriate here.

"Well, there's an extra cot and mattress," thought the cook aloud after some meditation. "You could set it up in the dining room after supper, if you don't mind moving it out before breakfast."

I met these easy conditions and had a good rest. Before we left, I tried to reciprocate for my bed and breakfast by helping to prepare the vegetables for dinner. It was fun to be part of the antics of cookery life again. It was also a good chance to find out how the feeding system for the cattle would work in winter.

Riding in the midst of expansive fields in the well-watered lands along the river, I had seen baled hay being hauled and stacked in the shape and size of cottages. I learned at the camp that in winter, when woodlands and meadows were depleted of forage, or in case of heavy snow, the cattle would be yarded and maintained around such feed stacks as these.

The undulating plateau carried us south, in company with our thoughts, the maturing grasses, and the seedeaters at home on the high prairie sod. At noon we came to Douglas Lake. The low buildings of the home ranch lay as if by permission within the rhythm of the hills. I left thanks with the caretaker, to be extended to the absent owners. This man was our only human encounter in that whole daytime journey.

Before the sun had set, Zazy and I stepped flat-footed over a Texas gate, passing through a wide-open rail gate hung beneath a crossbar. I turned to read on that sturdy log, Douglas Lake Ranch.

The Quilchena Inn, beloved, deserted, clothed in weathered boards, stood in the glory of its windows aflame with red-gold light. Loons were calling across Nicola Lake as we came down onto the winding lakeshore road. We crossed the pebbled beach and waded into the water, while the magic of the encircling mountains came down in cool breaths. I bathed my Zazy and me in the bright water. It was a time of holiness.

The legendary loons of Native lore accompanied us in our walk along the shore, until we crossed the Nicola River at the foot of the lake. Then we were heading for Merritt, looking for a campsite before the long summer evening closed down. Just past the village of Nicola, a car overtook us. "Have you a place to stay?" asked the driver. The young lady beside him added, "We saw you pass through town a while ago and thought you might need a place."

I was glad to follow these people back to Nicola. They led me to the hotel, presently out of operation but still the residence of the owners. Zazy and I received all the courtesy of invited guests.

Obviously we had been expected. Zazy was stabled in the barn of a family friend. I enjoyed the luxury of a shower and shampoo, towel-dried underwear and shirt. Finally I was ushered into a fine dining room furnished with a polished wood table graced by lace. A single place was set with china and silver, and there I was seated.

It was then that I realized I was joining a house party that was well underway. People were coming in and taking chairs ranged around the room. Tea was set beside me in a silver service. The lady of the house, and her daughter who had met me on the road, then began bringing in covered dishes of hot food, ending with a freshly prepared salad. I was urged to begin while my hostesses seated themselves with the company.

Everyone was asking about my journey, and I did my best to answer their questions. I was well into the salad before I realized that I was not alone at the table. On my plate, sitting sedately on a leaf of lettuce looking out on its green kingdom, was The Worm. The Worm was only an inch long, unobtrusive in its green suit, reserved in its manner. I had no wish to depose it. For now there was plenty of lettuce for both of us.

"How many sets of shoes has your horse worn out?" I looked toward the speaker and replied. The Worm moved to the edge of its leaf. I trimmed a piece off the other edge, folded it on a square of ham, and put it into my mouth.

"What would you have done if your mare had gone lame?" The question came from the man who had stabled Zazy. I paused to chew and think, and to watch The Worm hump up, rear on its terminal legs, and poise itself on the edge of the leaf, scanning its horizon. I gave some quick reply to the guest, and hastily sliced off a third of The Worm's dwindling kingdom to go with my last piece of potato.

Comments were being exchanged about hazards on the road. The Worm, meanwhile, let itself down into a shallow pool in the centre of the plate. Probably for the first time in its life, it felt the goad of discontent. It drew itself from the water and headed for higher ground. I went the rounds of the delicious casseroles for a second time.

"Is there anything more we can get for you?" asked my hostess. I faced her to reply. The Worm gained the upturned margin of the salad plate and set out to circle the world. I was now but a few mouthfuls of lettuce and tomato away from dessert. I refused to embarrass my hostess by leaving food, as if defective, on my plate, or worse, by leaving a worm in full view. It was a moment for mental multi-tasking.

The Worm, perhaps bored by the endlessness of a circular path, tried to sally toward the lettuce each time round. Anticipating its move, I would sweep the lettuce away for every cut. Sweep and cut, sweep and cut, the tension mounted. A question nearly cost me the field. One mouthful remained.

A man was explaining to me how to avoid the business section of Merritt. The Worm seized the advantage and skid home. I caught sight of its round head rising above the edge of its tiny island. My shining knife clipped the last bit of greens in half. I ate one. Beneath the other, half in the pool, back to the kitchen went the little green Worm.

I rode away from Nicola with a new banner cloud floating in my sky. The shadowy fallacy infused into my childhood, by whom, God only knows, the fallacy that snobbery accompanies refinement, was forever disproved and dismissed by these open-hearted people. The best of their possessions and the evening they had planned with their friends they shared graciously without reserve, with Zazy and me, two strange wanderers who happened to pass their door.

— —

Two more days of good travel should bring us to Lytton, where Peg and Charlie would welcome us. I expected no more adventures to befall us on this final stretch. I rode pleasantly to Merritt, on a sandy shoulder beside pinewoods, and then by a clear salmon stream that was the Nicola River. I ate wild apples from my pocket, and Zazy reached around always at the right moment to receive a generous core from my hand.

Before the sun was overhead, we were climbing into the Cascade Mountains. Lest the way become wilder, I took time out from our forward push to find hay and grain for Zazy. She ate well at a little farm near Canford, and there I learned that we had a tougher and longer road ahead than I had foreseen.

At evening we were in a high, remote wilderness. Clouds hung around the peaks, and light rain showers passed over us. Again we were walled in, by rock on one side and chasm on the other. Perhaps an hour of daylight remained, and the road was still rising. We needed to get over the top.

Where was the top? I spied a piece of board nailed to a snag. It seemed to point to a path, and as I got closer I read: J. Seymour, Chief. Zazy had already spotted an exit and she was making for it. She turned down a steep stony trail. I guessed we must be heading for an Indian person's home, and that if he were a chief, he would be able to tell me where I could camp.

To save Zazy's feet on the stones, I got down and walked beside her. Suddenly we came in sight of a cabin. At that moment, out from under the porch and around from the back raced a pack of lean and hungry dogs, hackles up and teeth bared. In a split second I was back on the mare with my legs over her neck. Zazy was not the target! No one came from the cabin, so we left the guards behind and continued on. I unfolded, and stayed mounted.

Around the next bend, the bush fell back and we came into a clearing where several cabins stood. This place also was deserted. Not even a dog showed its presence. The path turned and dipped and brought us at last to the villagers. They were gutting a freshly slaughtered steer on the grass by a stream. Everyone was absorbed in the process, and everyone except the smallest children had a job to do. A little dog saw us and ran up barking. I rode on down to the edge of the circle and dismounted. A woman near me smiled, but she did not speak in reply to my greeting. Instead she spoke in her own tongue to two girls nearby, and they ran up to me, smiling and greeting me in English. So we talked about who I was and what I needed. I asked if I could camp on their land.

The girls relayed my request for a campsite to a young man who was adjusting a block and tackle to a tree branch behind the beef. Zazy and I waited, and the girls returned and guided us to the corrals. A towering black stallion with a curly mane and tail saw us coming and fixed his eyes on Zazy. The girls told me to put her into the adjoining corral, where she would be given hay after the butchering was done. I complied and Zazy promptly made for the far fence, leaving the stallion pacing the dividing rails, tossing his head and squealing.

At the stream, my presence made the villagers uneasy. The girls grew shy and left me to attend to a baby crawling on the grass. How I wanted to speak their language! The beef was trussed and ready to be hoisted. I caught hold of the rope and heaved with three or four men and boys. The carcass went up and people around me relaxed.

The two women by the water looked up from their delicate task with a smile for me. They were threading sticks through yards of intestine to lead the flowing water to flush the entrails clean. Another woman made a friendly gesture as she brought the tripe to the water's edge with the help of a boy. If only I could greet them in their own language! Always I had felt akin to the people I knew as Native, people who lived close to the land. I wanted to know how they understood the natural world. Now on this special night of my journey, I would be quiet as they were, and learn what the spirit says without words.

I noticed an elderly man with long black hair squatting above the stream bank, where he could watch and seemingly give counsel from time to time. When the work was done and the women had gathered up the viscera in pots and baskets, strong hands helped the patriarchal man onto crutches. He was without legs below the knees. The deference shown to him made me wonder if he was Chief Seymour. I could neither ask nor greet him.

As the company began to disperse, I intended to go back to Zazy, ready to take her to a place where we would sleep as soon as she had finished her hay. However, my two guides, unnamed to me, returned, carrying the baby and extending an invitation to me to come to the house for supper. A vision of fresh steak flitted through my mind.

In the largest cabin, two women were stoking the fire under several pots on the stove. As the largest came to a boil, it evoked a strong bovine smell. I thought of sausage casings. People from the slaughter site were reassembling. More and more men and women came into the room. Some helped with supper. Children tumbled and played on the floor. An ancient wrinkled woman carried a baby tied in a shawl on her back, as she laid the board table. I had seen the girls with her at the stream. Unoccupied people like me backed against the wall to conserve space. Steam from the big pot filled the room and drew in puppies, cats, kittens, and a chicken or two. Someone pulled a folding gate across the doorway, and then the game was to bail the animals out over the top as fast as they wriggled in underneath.

The room was noisy with action, but I heard few words. The Native people seemed to speak to each other quietly and concisely, if they spoke at all. They were in touch in so many other ways, as they turned, smiled and occasionally laughed, helped, caught up a child or a puppy. Something beyond gestures seemed to link them, and without conversation, they were bringing me inside their circle.

Women were carrying supper items to the table: bread, salt, sugar, tall pots of tea, and one small opened tin of salmon. Then came steaming bowls of rice and potatoes, and a single huge bowl of chopped tripe and intestines. We all found places on the benches and sat down shoulder to shoulder, until only a chair at the head of the table remained empty. The bowls went round to every person and we filled our plates. Hardly anyone touched the salmon that I knew from childhood as a special treat. I took a small portion and passed on the tin.

The treat the crowd was waiting for was the last bowl to move, the tripe and guts. At first it was so heavy that men rose to lift and pass it. Before it was halfway round the table, it had to go back to the stove to be refilled. I suspected that the salmon was presented as a courtesy to me, an alternative to the stew. Though my taste was not tuned to the strongly flavoured food, I ate my share, helping it down with salt. Clear tea helped too, though it tasted bitter. Glancing around, I saw that my tablemates drank their tea loaded with sugar.

We all were eating when the man on crutches entered the room and took the empty seat. A lull fell on the table talk as the respected one bowed his head for several moments. Then he raised it, received the bowls, and joined in the banquet.

As soon as the meal ended, most people went away in the dark to their own cabins. The old matriarch told me through one of the girls that there would be room for me to sleep in this cabin with her. She would not hear of my camping outdoors, for fear of heavy rain. Zazy was already fed and watered, so I was content to accept the woman's offer. In fact, I was very glad to be able to relax from the uncertainty of what was expected of me.

Suddenly conscious of my very dirty feet, I asked where I could wash. A girl led me back to the bank of the stream. Bathing in the icy cold water, I admired the stamina of those women who had had their arms in it all afternoon.

Something changed Grandmother's plans while I was away. I was asked persuasively if I would rather sleep in the tent with the girls. Doubtfully, I agreed.

The tent was pitched beyond the porch and lighted by an oil lamp. A large bed occupied all the space, except for standing room in the doorway and a narrow passage along the far side of the bed due to the slope of the canvas. The two girls sat down on the bed, and made a place for me. They talked together in their own tongue, head to head with much giggling, and then they engaged me in English with trivia, as though to fill in time. I wanted simply to put my head down and go to sleep. What were they stalling for?

In walked George, the young man who had supervised the hanging of the beef and who now turned out to have a smattering of English. He joined us on the bed, and more hilarious conversation moved past me. It ended with the younger girl disappearing and the older one undressing, getting into bed with George, and inviting me to do the same.

I groped for a polite way to decline. Were they simply sharing a bed? Were they having a joke on me? I chose to stay on familiar ground, assured the couple that I would be comfortable on the floor, and lay down on the cardboard beside the bed. The girl dropped a quilt on me and put out the lamp.

Chaos crashed my sleep. A truck came rattling and banging its way down the canyon road and labouring onto the village trail, greeted by the guard dog chorus. The truck arrived at our camp, fell silent, and disgorged noisy, unhappy passengers. Heavy footfalls on the wooden steps of the cabin followed.

The silhouette of a woman appeared in the tent doorway. A thick voice mumbled: "I wanna sleep with George." The sleepers barely stirred. "I'm gonna sleep with George!" declared the voice. The intruder stepped inside the tent and stumbled over my feet.

"Who's there?" Hostility flared.

"I am," I replied foolishly.

"Who are you?" demanded the understandably annoyed woman.

"Just a traveller passing through." I think she wrote me off as an idiot at that point!

George grumbled at being disturbed, and growled the woman off when she tried to crawl in beside him. She stumbled away, snarling, and stomped into the cabin.

Sleep prevailed until I was roused by something scratching on the tent wall near my ear. I listened; the scratching stopped. Something was sliding under the canvas. Snake stories sprang to mind. A snake was coming in from the cold. Perhaps if I lay quite still, it would keep peace with me and simply share my body heat. It crawled down past my left ear, over my shoulder and under the quilt at waist level. Something bigger than a snake was in my bed. I reached down, and felt the warm caress of a puppy's tongue. We slept together until morning.

Early the camp was alive with activity. I went to the stream and washed the unfamiliar bad taste of the stew from my mouth and the lethargy from my head. In the cabin, I was able to help set the table for breakfast, and to clear the table afterwards. The stew bowl was empty.

I said goodbye to the wise old woman with a new generation in the shawl on her back. She said that her people hoped I would return. I believed her, for I knew that I had found soulmates among these first Canadians. Our cultural differences were good jokes; my natural affinity had led me into their home.

George and the two girls walked me to the corral. The stallion came pounding up to the rails, nickering to Zazy. I bridled her and George swung open the gate. Few words and the firm grip of weathered hands clinched our good wishes. Salt bag in hand, I sprang on the mare's strong back. Our friends watched us leave, quietly as we had come, in fellowship now. A new banner cloud was forming in my sky, a deep sense of belonging.

6

Forty miles of canyon road lay ahead of us: the rest of the Nicola River pass and the Thompson River canyon south to the Fraser River at Lytton. I had lost the illusion that we were practically on Peg and Charlie's doorstep. In its place, I had a sombre premonition that this last day's ride might be tougher than any before.

The mileage was long, the altitude was a challenge, lack of oats sapped Zazy's reserves, and we were tired of travelling. Fatigue goaded me toward my goal. Zazy could neither read the map nor envision my goal. She had to depend on my will to keep her going into terrain that she knew would not be generous to a horse.

Zazy carried me well enough over the first ten misty miles. Then her energy waned and I took on the tiresome burden of urging a dogging horse. Every stop we made for water or a bite of grass heartened her, but soon she would sink again to plodding. I was bound to be at Lytton before another night passed. I slipped over from riding her forward to pushing against her lassitude, and she pushed back. She flatly refused to step out.

Angrily, I got down to lead her. She refused to follow at my pace. I pulled off her bridle, railed at her bitterly, and strode on without her. She turned about and set off alone, retracing her steps, probably toward the last feed source she knew.

Now each step I took seemed heavier than the last. Pride told me to go on. A deeper, quieter voice told me to stop, look back. I turned, just in time to see Zazy stop and look back toward me. For a long moment, we stood considering each other. Then we met halfway, and went on together, she a little faster and I a little slower.

Zazy was far from spent. She was sleek, muscular, and possessed of energy kept secret until we came into Spences Bridge and stopped to buy oatmeal and buns. I tied her to what looked like a sturdy veranda post at the store on the main street. In my absence, a train came puffing into town. Zazy was not about to share the street with a train. I rushed out just in time to see her rearing back against her neck rope, about to pull down the creaking veranda. The proprietor followed me in consternation. The train passed and Zazy and I shamefacedly descended the steep riverbank to eat our lunch in exile.

The afternoon was hot, and Zazy was thirsty. She had not been able to reach the water at lunch. Now she spotted a water sprinkler in a tomato field, just out of town. The garden and the grower's stand were poised on a rich bench on top of the canyon wall.

The grower gladly gave Zazy what she came for, and would not let me leave without tasting his choicest tomatoes. Presenting them to me, one by one, he watched as I discovered each distinctive flavour. He laughed at my offer to pay him; the glow of pride in his products gift-wrapped the goods.

The canyon narrowed. Far below, we could see the brown water of the Thompson. Up and down, in and out, we followed the road as we had done for hundreds of miles that lay behind us, creeping on and on like the water, finding our way to the sea. From a promontory, I looked across a gap and saw our road ahead, built of planks laid across buttresses that were no more than timbers propped obliquely into niches in the rock face.

Soon we were well out on the 'bridge', looking down on a railway line threading the gorge near the water's edge. Even as we paused, noise broke upon natural sound, filling the air. A train was coming, labouring into view, billowing smoke in our direction. Zazy was gravely concerned. She neither pranced nor reared; she was fully with me as I rode her quietly off the overhang and in against the canyon wall.

The noise intensified. It seemed to envelope us. Another train was above us! Zazy was trembling, gathering herself, poised between trust in me and panic. I held her in trust. No car came to upset her fragile balance. She held firm, for all these terrifying minutes while the trains were passing. My very good friend, my Zazy!

We relaxed, slowed our breathing, continued climbing. As Zazy became steady, I began to realize what had happened, and what might have happened. I felt exhausted, emptied. Something was sucking substance out of the world, and we were in a vacuum, moving like sleepwalkers. Zazy knew where she was going, and she carried me forward.

Over the top of the grade, we came onto a gentler slope. Zazy stepped into a grassy recess and held her head for me to remove her bit. I did that, keeping the rein around her neck for safety. Her joy was real, and I shared it, and then I noticed a fern I hadn't met before, and then we discovered the tiny spring in the rock that watered the garden, and I washed in its trickling flow until I was whole again.

We persisted, Zazy and I, and we were moving toward Lytton, but when we would get there I had no idea. Distance was unreal, so was time. And the sun was saying that we had spent most of the afternoon getting this far—wherever we were.

— —

An oncoming station wagon pulled over and a man got out and walked up to me. He offered a weathered hand, as if he knew me, and his grip was honest. "I'm John Dunn from Kamloops. I'm the veterinarian for the Indian School. I've just come from there. Charlie asked me to tell you that he and Peg are expecting you in tonight."

He did not ask for an answer. I said, "I'm not sure if we can make it tonight," but he had already made time and distance, and Peg and Charlie, and Lytton, become real again to me. He had spoken as if the folks were just down the road.

"You can do it. Only eighteen miles to go! I know your mare, and you can make it. I'll phone from Spences Bridge and tell them you're on your way." And he got back in his car and was gone up the canyon.

I told myself, "He believes in us. I believe in him. Now he's gone. Miles of mountains are closing around us again. He came through them from Lytton to us. That's real now. And Peg and Charlie are as real as the mountains. We will keep going now." Zazy agreed.

— —

It's getting late. I can hardly see the far side of the canyon. There's no place to get off the road now, no place to rest.

"Why do you step out, Zazy? What do you see? You're right, here is a place, a loop of the old road bypassed by the new. It's been given back to nature. Time doesn't matter much, now that it's almost dark. Go ahead, old friend, turn in. We'll walk together and rest our nerves for the night."

How welcome I feel here, how safely off the road! Here's another tiny waterfall springing from the rock. Zazy's found the grass in the soil around the basin. Spring water feels good on my face, and all the way down my throat. Hands, arms, are all coming alive again. We'll have a picnic here; we have oats and buns left over from lunch, and berries on the brow of the spring. "Rest, Zazy, have your oats and let's share the last two buns for the road."

Wouldn't this be a nice place to sleep? Why must we get to Lytton tonight? Darkness walls us in; we're safe here. Friends are part of some other existence, and we are so tired!

But I phoned from Merritt and told them we might make it tonight. Doc said they expect us. Doc's cheering for us. Only eighteen miles. Sleep will steal away the night. We can do it; Doc said so. "Drink from the spring once more, my old friend, and I will let the spray fall on my face. Now we are ready to go."

"Easy, Zazy, another car. Crowd the wall; we can't see the edge. Let's hope the driver sees your white blaze in the headlights!" Those lights are blinding me. Hold, hold, there, they're gone behind us and around the bend."

It's darker now. No moon tonight. Just starlight, but wow, look at those stars! And there's a kind of glow behind the heights that calms me.

We're home here, among you enduring mountains. Do I really want to come to the end of you, the end of our special time together?

Can I ever leave you, you familiar forms creating perils and my protection, my solitude and the path beneath my feet? Austere when my eyes are blinded by too much light, you are steadfast for me, there in the starlight.

Now only swamping weariness is real. My horse and I must stop, yet we cannot, for we are committed to go on to the end.

Zazy at Lytton just after our arrival at the Indian Residential School. August 1950.

Zazy patiently carries me forward, down another grade, up and up another slope that curves as it climbs around a dark buttress. What's that, a low star? There, far ahead, below us. A point of light is twinkling, vanishing. Zazy has seen it too. She's stepping more quickly, even as we climb. It's there again, with another, and another. The lights of Lytton!

Song is rising inside me, orchestral, moving out to the edge of me. I hear it escape into an anthem, a familiar anthem of thanksgiving, and I am singing "The Gloria." It flows through me, stretching the limits of my vocal chords, and I let it happen to me, this glorious excess that I never knew could be mine. Now as we come over the top in the darkness, alone yet not alone, with almost all of Canada behind us, and our goal in view, I too can offer the whole song of thanks to its climax in the clear mountain air.

> For thou only art holy;
> Thou only art the Lord;
> Thou only, O Christ, with the Holy Ghost,
> Art most high in the glory of God the Father.
> Amen.

The lights of Lytton blur out through my tears. Zazy is finding our way down the mountain.

The streets of the little town are quiet. Zazy comes clip-clopping on the pavement. A man is on the sidewalk. "Could you tell us the way to the Indian School, please?"

"Yes. Go on down here and over the bridge and follow the road 'til you come to the school. It's quite a way."

I peer into the darkness where the bridge should be. A figure steps out of the shadows. Charlie is beside us, saying, "Barb! Thank God you're safe!" He's shaking and shaking my hand.

"Hey, watch out, here I come!" and I land beside my buddy from Mascouche days.

"Barb, you must be tired." He turns. "Zazy, good little Zazy," and he is hugging the mare as if he had been expecting never to see her again. I lift off her bridle and we three follow the canyon to Peg.

~ Epilogue ~

The lights of Lytton marked a wide turning in our trail, not an end. As the brown water of the tumbling Thompson River meets at Lytton the stronger, steadier Fraser, so Zazy's and my narrow, turbulent way was running inevitably into a wider, steadier course.

For a short time, our life on the farm remained discrete from our future, as the brown water at first remains aloof from the passing blue flood with which it must surely merge.

Caught in the romantic colour of this dry interior plateau, I was swept from the threats and promises of life on the road, into the drama of life on a thousand-acre farm. The farm was the food support system for St. George's Indian Residential School, and Charlie was hired to manage it.

I stayed for about ten days with Peg and Charlie and their baby, Helen Barbara. I learned to herd sheep, handle hay under irrigation, and partner with a Native boy who was like a son to my friends. Dairy cattle, pigs, turkeys and chickens, and sheep had to be tended, crops to be grown, cream to be shipped by train to Kamloops. Charlie was kept busy. Besides, he had to maintain the water supply on which the whole institution depended.

One evening, the flume that brought the water down from a mountain spring broke. Charlie got word from a traveller late at night, and at earliest light, he went up the mountain to the school's water gate and diverted the flow. By that time the flood had washed out the road and a sizeable chunk of mountain, and covered a field of mown hay with silt. The whole farm went dry until help came and the failed section of the flume was replaced.

Two days later, a railway strike stopped the train service to Kamloops, and we were flooded again, this time by cans of cream filling all the refrigerator space at the school. Peg turned some of it into butter, churning it in a retired diaper tub, but the pigs had to help clean up the surplus before the trains ran again.

Zazy spent happy days with her chestnut friend Tony in the wild

Zazy after four thousand miles, with Baby Helen, the author,
and a ranch hand. Lytton, BC. August 1950.

pasture above the barley fields. One day Charlie and I took the horses and rode high up the mountain to a meadow luxuriant with grasses, sedges, and flowers, watered by a spring. Charlie said that springs and snowfields watered meadows like that all through the mountains at high altitudes, and that was where cattle fed in summer. At last I was seeing inside the mystery of the summer ranges!

Another day, Charlie took me to meet Sampson Dan, an elderly Native man. We found him at the end of a steep, two hundred foot descent to the bank of the Fraser River, fishing salmon for his family. Sampson Dan could sweep the eddy so neatly and set the net so correctly that it would catch no sticks, only salmon. Annually he caught his legal limit, one thousand fish. He was taking a big spring salmon from the water when we arrived.

Sampson Dan encouraged me to try to set a net in another eddy near his. Though he guided me, and I tried my best, I snagged his net on sticks. He did not complain or make fun of me, but he gently forgave me and freed the net. I felt a deep kinship with this man, so grafted into his niche on our planet.

He led the way with the agility of a goat up the cliff face. Peg and Baby Helen were waiting halfway up, at the cobalt cave where the spring issues from the overhanging rock, curtains the cave mouth, and flows sparkling to fill the natural basin where Sampson Dan cleans his fish. The eagles know the place well. The fisherman gutted the salmon, closed the body, and with an eloquent smile folding his suntanned face

Cobalt cave and basin where salmon are washed. Lytton, Fraser Canyon, BC. September 1950.

into a story, handed the fish to Peg. Sampson Dan knew Peg and Charlie as family.

— —

A telephone call from the secretary of the Chilliwack Riding Club brought me to terms with my need to get on with the rest of the trip to the coast. Time was running out for me to complete the 150-mile journey, return Zazy to Lytton, and catch a midnight train to Ontario in time to be in Guelph by registration day at the veterinary college.

Chilliwack was halfway to Vancouver. The Riding Club was inviting me to be a guest in their town and to arrive in time for the opening of the Abbotsford Fair. Peg encouraged me to go. "You've achieved something, Babs. Go take your bows to society."

I had always chosen to be an anonymous tramp with Zazy. However, the chance to meet accomplished horsemen and attend a fair definitely attracted me. Even more strongly, the Pacific Ocean and the course of the river to the sea called me. I reached for the wider horizon, and preparations swung into motion.

Reluctantly, I set out from Lytton with an equally reluctant horse. Once again we were burdened with a saddle and gear. It was lent to me

Sampson Dan's fishing hole,
Fraser River, Lytton, BC. September 1950.

to save me from looking strange without tack. It hindered Zazy and killed my enthusiasm to arrive in time for the opening of the fair. I felt unmoored.

We followed the Fraser beyond sight of the plateau and the benchlands, past Jackass Mountain with a hole being blasted in its face for the sake of a wider road. We followed until the sun dropped below the canyon's edge and abruptly extinguished the day.

In another day we passed Boston Bar, where we were turned away from a roadside café lest we damage the grass. Again the mountains heartened me, bringing me to sit quietly as an eagle above Hell's Gate, watching the swift, turbid flow solemnly turning a log the size of a telephone pole like a toy into an eddy, spinning it, drawing it into a vortex, and slowly dragging it butt-first to drown below the oily surface. Rebalanced, I breathed deeply and rode away.

In afternoon sunshine, the road turned us to look down on a human artifact of sheer beauty. The silvery, delicate Alexandra Bridge hung like a dewy cobweb across a wider, calmer Fraser, now blue again and flecked with foam. At dusk we were close by the water's edge. Silence reigned, but for an eerie, ceaseless sifting, sifting of fine talus sliding on the steep bank towering beside us.

We were due to arrive in Chilliwack the following day. My road dirt began to make a private statement about my need for a wash. I ventured into Yale Auto Court with two questions: Would they allow a horse on the premises? Could I afford the cost of an overnight? The young couple that had recently opened for business gladly received us as their guests. They found a stable for Zazy and gave me a cabin beneath the arms of a Douglas fir tree. After my shower, I joined them in an evening of mutual discovery, for we all were travelling new roads and putting all we had into the journey.

At Hope, the road turned from south to west and we came into the fertile Fraser Valley. Here the moist air of the Pacific Ocean conspired with gentling slopes and alluvial soil to fill every niche with vegetation. I was fern-watching when we came to a pullout where a truck hooked to a horse trailer was parked. A tall, lean man with an easy smile and a western drawl greeted me. Ray Wells had come into our lives. He lowered the ramp, I loaded the horse, and Ray trundled us into our next adventure.

We unloaded Zazy at the Chilliwack Fairgrounds, where she was stabled in luxury next door to a pair of grey thoroughbreds. Their owner was on hand to take charge of her. Ray booked me into the Grand Hotel for five days as a guest of the owners. The gentle urban hospitality of Ellen and Jim, my hosts, melted my self-consciousness. I went shopping, forsook my dusty jeans and outworn shoes for a pair of jodhpurs and boots, and began to relax.

In company with members of the riding club, I was immersed for my waking hours during the next four days in an equestrian world. At the Abbotsford Fair on Sunday, I watched a horse show for the first time. Horses of every size, shape, and aptitude were being shown, in hand,

*Riding down the Fraser Canyon at the invitation of the Chilliwack Riding Club.
Discomfort of the unwanted saddle and gear delayed us, so we missed the honour-ride at the
opening of the Abbotsford Fair. September 1950.*

under saddle, or in harness. For me it was a wonderland, and I regretted that my hesitation had brought us there too late to take our place in the grand opening ride. I would remember that mistake for good.

The Palomino horses that I assumed were being shown as a breed surprised me in their diversity of both conformation and colour. Every horse had a blond mane and tail, but the body colour varied between pale gold and smoky brown. Heavy-bodied working ranch horses competed with fine pleasure horses. Ray and Ma Wells patiently answered my endless questions.

After the fair, club members took me into the countryside to meet horse breeders and see their horses at home. At one farm, I saw Arabians for the first time. Before my eyes were the attributes I had read about: strength, gentleness, and the depth of friendship that grows between creatures knowing each other well. Back in Chilliwack, I was invited to ride an Arabian gelding named Sinbad. I felt airborne, flying at his speed, sailing over jumps, living childhood dreams. Now I was determined that the foal I hoped for Zazy to bear someday must be sired by an Arabian horse.

Zazy surprised us all on the morning after we arrived. She hobbled out of her stall as if she were foundered. I was puzzled, for she had not been mismanaged. Horsemen came and examined her, and they too were puzzled. It was not classical laminitis, but Zazy was crippled. Within a few days, she was responding to cold water on her legs, light feed, and minimal exercise. Nevertheless, her lameness seemed to have snatched the plans for our trip out of my hands. For the present, I had to set the problem aside and hope for her recovery.

My one obligation, which was also a privilege, was to speak to the riding club at their Wednesday meeting. Preparing that talk was a war game between my common sense and my thieving inner custodian. While I was sweating out the struggle, Ellen kept in touch with me. She took me to the meeting on Wednesday night, where more good friends were gathered. A whisper had gone round about Zazy, so I soon knew that I was not alone in my concern for her.

The meeting was about to begin. I grew tense. Ray Wells turned out to be president of the club, as well as MC for the night. He rose, looked down from an altitude of six feet, removed the cigar from his mouth, and proceeded to introduce Rowena Moyer. She and her pony had ridden in from Vancouver and found a welcome with Ma and Ray Wells. She had come to speak about her ride, and she was to go first.

I enjoyed Rowena's casual style, and everyone entered into her story. When my turn came, I didn't need my notes. Afterward, people rallied to help me arrange to complete the ride to Vancouver. Ray offered to outfit me. Rowena invited me to travel with her. The owner of the grey thoroughbreds assured me

Ray Wells with Nell, the mare that took me on from Chilliwack to Vancouver and back. September 1950.

that Zazy could stay in his care. After all, I was set to go to the coast.

This wonderful evening continued with Ellen and Jim and a few friends in their suite at the hotel. We spun horse tales and people tales, and nibbled on spareribs delivered to the room at midnight. Another *first* for me! At 3 AM the party broke up and I went to sleep feeling like Cinderella.

Ellen drove me to Cultus Lake Stables in the morning. Ray went up the stony trail beside the barn and returned leading a grey mare. He seemed to be hardly looking as he tacked her up and tied on a sleeping bag. He glanced down at her feet, said he thought her shoes would do, told me her name was Nell, handed me the reins, and wished me a good trip as I mounted. Rowena and Spud were ready, and we rode away in joyful awe at the generosity showered on us.

Nell stood a hand taller than Spud, but they travelled well together. He single-footed at a great rate; she chose an easy trot that was smooth for me to ride. Rowena was fun to be with. During our three days on the trail, we were as compatible as our horses. I knew I'd always remember her when I ate dates and cheese, or heard a mouth organ.

We neared Vancouver on Saturday morning and became caught in the noon-hour traffic streaming over the mile-long Patullo Bridge into

New Westminster. We just had to get in the line, trust our mounts, and go across. Unpopular but safe, we came off the bridge and retreated into the first boarding stable we saw.

Rowena completed her ride to her home stable at Point Grey in the quiet of Sunday morning. Peg's parents took me driving. They showed me a view of the Pacific Ocean from Marine Drive. I spent a few minutes on a beach, wet my hands and feet in the sea, and glimpsed some ships as we crossed the Lion's Gate Bridge. We looked at the lacy cedar trees in the park at Capilano Canyon and walked across the swinging bridge. Then the day was over. I had seen the coast possessed by the city, and I wished not to stay. Zazy could not be there, and this was not our world.

Fulfillment would come gradually, over a lifetime. I knew that I would home to the western sea again and again, to wade in the waves on wild beaches, feel the soaking spray, wait quietly for tide pool creatures to come out of hiding, look to the mountaintops from sea level, and fall asleep to the song of the wind in tall trees. Zazy would not be with me, but it was because of her bringing me as far as she did, that I would be able to go the rest of the way, returning heart and soul to the sea.

— —

Two days remained for me to return Nell to Ray Wells, arrange for Zazy to be trucked back to Lytton, and catch the midnight train that would take me in three days to Toronto. I would just get to Guelph in time to register in veterinary school. I was at the stables by 7 AM on Monday morning, ready to tack up.

First I checked Nell's shoes. My prospect changed; her front shoes were ready to fall off. The farrier was expected at the stables that morning, about 9 AM, the stableman thought. By 10 AM, he said casually: "He comes when he gets around to us. Something must have held him up."

Nell and I left New Westminster with front shoes reset, at half past noon. Once we were across the bridge and past the stoplights, the mare tackled the seventy-five miles to her home with a reaching trot. She would not stop to eat or drink, all day. If I stopped her, she would wait politely for me, and then trot away again.

At evening, the snowy peak of Mount Baker was caught in a flood of sunset light and carried in golden splendor to float above a vague purple void. We were nine hours and forty-five miles on our way.

Around 1 AM, I needed to rest. I reined Nell into an open field at a bend in the road, unsaddled her, ground-tied her, leaving the bit behind her jaw to let her graze, rolled myself in the saddle blankets and dozed.

Something woke me; I peered around; my horse was gone. I saw a dim form mounting the shoulder of the highway, just before the

Ma's Inn, Cultus Lake, BC. A warm welcome and a hearty breakfast after a non-stop, seventy-five-mile ride on amazing Nell. September 1950.

headlights of a truck cut a swath in the darkness. The trucker slowed and passed the mare in a wide arc. I called her name, she slowed, I spoke again, and she turned and came back to me.

Nell proved her fidelity again toward morning. We came to flares marking a detour, but no arrows in view to show the way. I ignored the flares, thinking we could ride around the obstruction. A mile farther on, we came to a bridge under reconstruction, marked by more flares on heaps of fill.

The black water forbade our fording the river. The bridge looked partly intact. I walked out on loose planks. Nell hesitated, and then followed on slack reins. The cross planks gave way to wide timbers running lengthwise. Still Nell followed. My foot hit a standing spike, and I saw water below. Slowly I turned, took a rein in each hand, and ever so gently urged her to back, one step at a time. Without a hasty move, she cooperated until she stood again with four hooves on solid ground. By dawn light I saw the arrows I had missed. Gratefully I took the detour, miles around to the foot of a mountain, to cross a bridge and regain the highway.

We passed hop yards and came to the Cultus Lake turnoff too early to arrive at the ranch. I stopped where the grass looked irresistible, offered Nell oats, and got a flat refusal. I gave up trying! At the stables, Ray was unimpressed by my concern, especially about his mare's refusal to drink. He simply stripped off the tack and turned her back to pasture. I let my worries blow away and sat down to the wonderful breakfast that Ma made to set me up for the day.

— —

Zazy was safe, and sound again. Members of the riding club managed to find a trucker who would take her up to Lytton on half a day's notice. By evening we loaded the mare, and it was time to say goodbye to these friends who had feted us, cared for Zazy, and rescued my ride to the sea.

The truck took us out of the valley, into the canyon, and back toward the meeting place of the rivers. Day died, leaving the driver and me talking to keep each other awake. Now we were stopping for coffee at Boston Bar. Now we were watching for the bridge at Lytton. Now I was pointing out the School Road. Now Zazy was stabled beside Tony, and the driver was drinking coffee in Peg's kitchen while I settled the account. Then he was gone.

Peg, Charlie, and I reunited so briefly, knew we were about to let our lives flow apart again. We didn't talk about that. We had parted before and come together again. Had Zazy shown us the road to forever? We were sad but not afraid to say goodbye.

The hands of the clock went round to midnight, and Charlie said it was time to go. Peg stayed with Helen. Charlie took me to the station in the pickup. The train pulled in, and a dark hand drew me up the steps from the platform and into a darkened coach. Heavy curtains closed me into my dimly lit berth and sleep swept over me, while rolling wheels bore me away.

— —

Zazy stayed in the care of Peg and Charlie Dobson when I left Lytton to enter veterinary college in Guelph, Ontario. After three years, I was able to pay the fare for her to come by rail to Guelph. She arrived in the station in a boxcar, heard me speak on the platform, and called out her greeting. Zazy and I walked up the College Hill to the Large Animal Infirmary. There she was rested and examined by Dr. Frank Milne. After her train trip and her epic journey with me, Dr. Milne found her completely sound.

The little mare lived on an Arabian farm for two years, until I graduated and was married to Anthony Kingscote. Then she joined the family that was evolving at our Spirit Valley Farm: two baby girls named Phoebe and Robin, Azata the Arabian stallion, and other horses, besides the Muscovy ducks, cats, and dogs.

Phoebe began riding as soon as she could sit up, sitting in front of me on Zazy. By eighteen months, she was sitting safely on Azata, and within the next year Zazy became her riding teacher. By her third birthday, she rode alone, always bareback, and that summer she inveigled the mare to go far enough from the barnyard to be provoked to canter on the way back.

Zazy was the first riding teacher for many children. She considered them, stopping if she felt a child sliding off her back, waiting until the rider had returned into balance, standing still if a child did happen to fall

Phoebe Kingscote on Zazy's son, Valley Sandpiper, 1965.

off. Phoebe would stand in the barnyard beside the stonewall and tempt the mare to come up from the pasture. Phoebe would then climb onto the wall, cross over to Zazy's back, and ride away wherever Zazy took her.

Zazy bore a colt to Azata a year before Phoebe's birth. He was named Valley Sandpiper. When he was three years old, he became Phoebe's Sandy. Two years after Sandy joined the family, Zazy produced another Azata colt, Eagle Spirit. A year later, his future owner, Robin, was born.

The two brothers were black like their mother, marked like her with a blaze and socks. They stood fourteen-two hands tall, an inch shorter than Zazy, and were built like her except for the refinement that their sire conferred. Zazy had no more children, and neither did I.

Zazy lived out her twenty-eight years at Spirit Valley Farm. Her sons were rugged, adaptable companion horses on the trail as well as good pony club ponies. They were willing jumpers, especially outdoors. They and Azata swam eagerly in lakes and rivers on our ride-and-trailer trip to Saskatchewan when the girls were ten and twelve years old. In competitive and endurance riding, Zazy's children were as tough as their mother.

When my children were grown up and I moved to Alberta, their horses came with me. They lived long enough for my grandchildren to know them and ride them. So the Zazy horses spanned three generations, and they graced my life for forty years, heartening many a child who needed a special friend.

– Acknowledgements –

The ride, along with the writing of this story and its publication, are the achievements not only of Zazy and me, but also of many people of goodwill. I thank them all:

My parents, Ethel and Frank Bradbury, and my sister Joan, who built strength into my body and mind, let me go, and faithfully cheered me on, no matter how unusual might be the direction I chose.

Charlie and Peg Dobson, who loved me as a stumbling teenager and gave me a stalwart equine companion for my road into adulthood.

All the people who helped Zazy and me along our way, and told me from their hearts what Canada means.

Valerie Henderson, whose delightful company and literary expertise saw me through the revision of the first draft.

Terry Connellan and Ellen Tremblay, who never ceased to believe in the value of the story, and Kelly Quine, who prepared the draft they saw, as well as the final product.

Lorne Macpherson, who said in 1989, "Change your priorities now, Barb. Go full-time into writing. Go and meet Eunice Scarfe."

Eunice Scarfe, whose mentoring was vital to the effective telling of the story.

Lillian Macpherson, whose insight prompted me to contact Eva Radford.

Eva Radford, who took the whole project to heart and worked with me through version after version, until together we got the story told.

Halfway through the last century, I rode westward from Montreal on my mare, Zazy. My map suggested that the Pacific Ocean was 3000 miles away. In fact, Zazy and I travelled more than 4000 miles to reach it. My venture into personal freedom was fulfilled by our final 500 mile journey, freed of baggage and tack. In August 1950, we reached the Pacific Coast.

Immediately after the ride, I entered the five-year program at the Ontario Veterinary College. I graduated and was married in 1955.

Life as a veterinarian, wife, traveller, mother of two girls, horse breeder, researcher, and finally single mom repeatedly swamped my efforts to write. All the while friends, and especially children who came to the farm to ride Zazy, cheered on the telling of our story.

My prospect took a decisive turn in 1979. I moved within the federal service from Ontario to Alberta and fell in love with the western prairie. Free to make a new start, I enjoyed the land and its people to the full. There was no time for writing, but there were invitations to speak. Whether my topic was stars or careers, faith or reindeer herding in the Arctic with my second husband, the story of the ride always surfaced. It seemed to open a new prospect to youth, an adventure for the taking. This book is for them and for everyone with a taste for the celebration of life.

Barbara Kingscote, Elnora, Alberta, November 4, 2005